A Special Blend
of Traditional and Contemporary Recipes
from
The Junior League of Winston-Salem, Inc.

Stirring PERFORMANCES

Additional copies of *Stirring Performances* may be obtained from:

The Junior League of Winston-Salem, Inc.
909 S. Main Street
Winston-Salem, NC 27101
(919) 773-0675
For your convenience, order blanks are included in the back of this book.

Copyright © 1988
The Junior League of Winston-Salem, Inc.
First printing May 1988   10,000
Second printing November 1988   10,000
Third printing June 1990   15,000
ISBN Number: 0-9615429-2-6

Printed in the United States of America
by S. C. Toof & Company

Cover design and graphics by The Russell Agency

Introduction, photo captions, and back cover
by Barbara Payne Long
Introduction to Grilling section
by Cynthia Yeager Bouldin

Cover photo by Richard Haggerty Photography, Inc.

Stirring Performances cover menu clockwise from the top: Orange Blossom Pound Cake, Grilled Salmon with Garlic and Lime, Dixie Pasta, Cream of Lettuce Soup, Assorted Breads

Back cover photo by Smith/Weiler/Smith Photography
The Stevens Center of the North Carolina School of the Arts

table of contents

Appetizers   9

Breads and Beverages   33

Soups and Salads   61

Pasta, Eggs and Cheese   115

Grilling   131

Meats   155

Poultry   173

Fish and Shellfish   193

Vegetables   213
  (and Side Dishes)

Desserts   239

Index   302

Co-Chairmen
Susan Richardson Hauser
Jeannette Anderson Parker

Assistant Chairman
Clark Kitchen Larson

Proposal Committee
Chairman
Gigi Rolfes

Terrie Allen Davis
Leigh Wood Pate
Elizabeth Perkinson

Design and Layout Committee
Chairmen
Peggy Ward Gaddy
Kathy Linville Robinson

Susan Carson
Judy Shepherd Eddins
Nancy Edwards Fitzgerald
Barbara Payne Long
Meg Leckie Roberts
Ruth Delapp Sartin
Nancy Pulliam Sullivan

Steering Committee
Anne Phillips Copenhaver
Robbie Weathers Irvin
Leigh Emerson Koman
Nancy Richardson Noell
Anita Hauser Ogburn
Nancy Meacham Spaugh
Lawren Groce Thach

Typist
Ellen Hendricks Bumgarner
    Headquarters Secretary

Recipe Committee
Chairman
Deede Dunn Grainger

Jeanne Clement Booras
Cynthia Yeager Bouldin
Katherine Leinbach Drown
Cindy Corey Christopher
Sally Remick Colacicco
Elizabeth Combs
Ann Thompkins Faris
Margaret Leinbach Hawkins
Ann Waynick Hill
Sally Anne Irvin
Nancy Jobe Koehler
Julie Dalton Laughter
Melanie Indorf McCabe
Candy Ludwick Palmer
Martha Riggs
Sharon Rowe Spangler
Pollyann Elliott Weeks

Special Events and Marketing Committee
Chairmen
Anna Ballentine Steele
Sharon Amos Shealy

Betty Shull Butler
Carrie Wall Malloy
Gayle Gilbert Meredith
Deidra Broadwater Mulloy
Ann Hill Paschold
Nancy Meacham Spaugh
Marion Sternberger Wilhelm

Sustaining Advisors
Libby Wilson Britton
Jane Cottle Joyner

Winston-Salem is a city of contrasts. Futuristic high-rise buildings dazzle the downtown skyline only blocks from the spot where a determined group of Moravian settlers founded the village of Salem in the winter of 1766.

Members of one of the earliest Protestant denominations, the Moravians came to America from Germany to escape religious persecution. After establishing a thriving community in Bethlehem, Pennsylvania, they traveled south to the beautiful rolling hills of the North Carolina Piedmont where they first settled in Bethabara. Thirteen years later they founded the larger settlement of Salem, a name derived from the Hebrew word for peace.

Today the restored 18th Century community of Old Salem serves as a constant reminder of the strength and spirit upon which the city was founded. These Moravian forefathers instilled a respect for hard work, a belief in the importance of education, and a love for music, arts, and crafts.

By 1913, when Salem consolidated with the nearby town of Winston, workers were flocking to the city to take jobs in the tobacco and textile factories. As the industrial base grew, so did the need for educational and cultural opportunities. A diverse group of community members and representatives from local arts groups met in the summer of 1949 to discuss the development of a common organization that would raise money for and coordinate arts events in the community. They founded what was to become the first arts council in the nation.

The arts have remained a vital part of the fabric of Winston-Salem as it has grown from a provincial mill town to a thriving and sophisticated city with a reverence for tradition and an eye to the future. Corporate, community, and individual support for the arts has flourished throughout the years as shown by the fact that Winston-Salem has been called the cultural center of the Southeast.

Theaters, artists studios, shops, galleries, street fairs, and lunch time concerts have become an integral part of the revitalization of the downtown area. A glance at a monthly arts calendar reveals almost endless opportunities for exploring the arts – performances by internationally acclaimed dance and theater groups, community theater and repertory companies, several symphony orchestras, opera theater, arts and crafts organizations and exhibitions, cultural centers, museums, and art galleries.

The city also boasts four major institutions of higher education whose students, faculty, and visual and performing arts programs greatly enrich the community.

In this book we honor those artists and organizations who provide the "Stirring Performances" that enhance the quality of life of those who reside in this community. We are indeed fortunate to have such a wealth of talent to draw upon – so much, in fact, that we could only feature a few groups by name.

We hope that the more than 500 outstanding recipes we have collected will inspire further exploration into the fine art of cooking. You can create your own "Stirring Performances" with recipes and menus that are suitable for all the stages in your life and for a variety of lifestyles. Both the novice in the kitchen (more than two-thirds of the recipes are simple to prepare) and the accomplished cook can choose from an eclectic blend of recipes – from contemporary and cosmopolitan to down-home and traditional.

Of special note is the unique grilling section with fabulous recipes for everything from appetizers to entrées and desserts – all prepared completely on the grill. Also included are helpful tips for smoking a variety of foods.

Whether preparing an elegant after-theater dinner for friends or a relaxed Sunday evening picnic for your family, we guarantee "Stirring Performances," standing ovations, and rave reviews.

The Junior League of Winston-Salem, Inc. is an organization of women committed to promoting voluntarism and to improving the community through the effective action and leadership of trained volunteers. Its purpose is exclusively educational and charitable.

Founded in 1923, the Junior League of Winston-Salem, Inc. has contributed over three-quarters of a million dollars to the community and, more importantly, thousands of volunteer hours. It has been instrumental in founding many community agencies and programs such as The Arts Council, Horizons, Nature Science Center, Juvenile Justice Council, Child Guidance Clinic, and Cancer Patient Support Services. Other past project involvements include ChildSafe, Youth Opportunity Homes, The Voluntary Action Center, Ronald McDonald House, and The Nutcracker Ballet.

Training is an important aspect of Junior League membership. Ongoing opportunities include skill-building workshops, educational seminars, leadership roles, on-the-job training with community agencies, and participation in Junior League fundraising activities and projects.

Funds from the sale of this cookbook will help to ensure that the Junior League can continue to make a difference in the community.

Through the Association of Junior Leagues, Inc., the Junior League of Winston-Salem, Inc. is united with 269 other autonomous organizations in the United States, Canada, Mexico, and Great Britain which include 180,000 members.

Stirring Performances includes some of the best recipes from Heritage of Hospitality, a cookbook published in 1975 by the Junior League of Winston-Salem, Inc., now no longer in print.

acknowledgements

Special Thanks

Village Tavern
Ryan's Restaurant
Last Catch
Newmarket Grille
Don McMillan
Beth Tartan
Carswell Distributing
Fran Creighton
Typography Studio
Linda Darnell
Sara Lee Corporation
Davidson & Co.—Marietta, Ga.
Long, Haymes & Carr, Inc.

For Photography Assistance

The Center Shop – SECCA
Jack Paul
La Cache
The Craft Shop of Piedmont Craftsmen, Inc.
Fine Lines
Janet Grennes
Donna Richardson
Schiffman's

Photo Models

*North Carolina School of the Arts –
    School of Dance*

Vickie Adams
Melinda DeChiazza
Amy Freed
Amanda Henzter
Stewart Lee
Cari Martin
Perry Mauzy
Deanna Seay
Claire Turman

The Nature Science Center

Lauren Millsaps
Lily de Grazia
Lee Hemphill
Ebony Hicks
Wesley Hsu

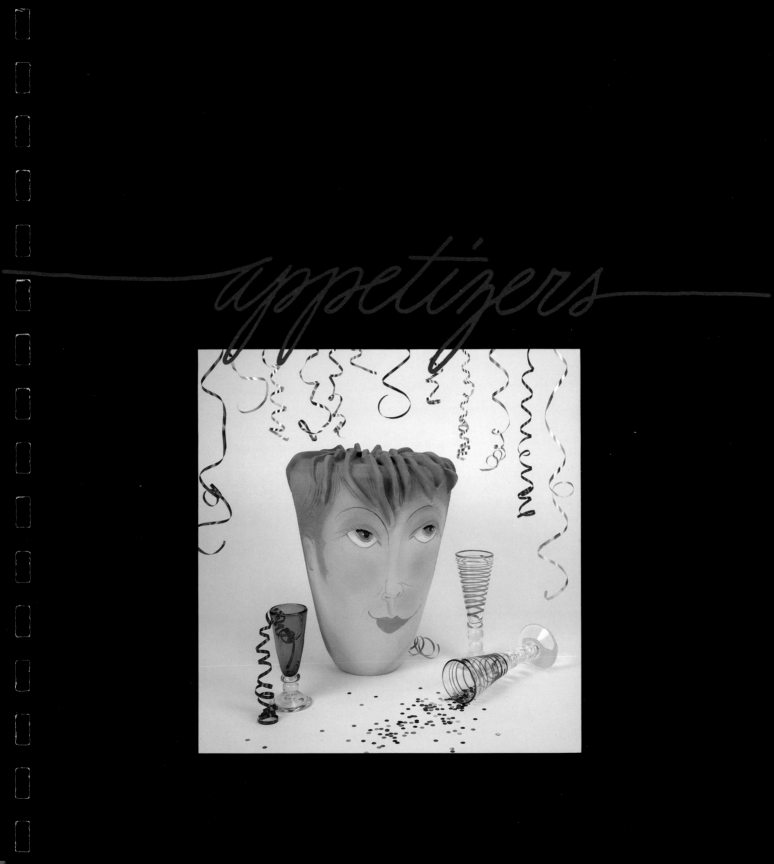

appetizers

Opening Reception

California Salsa
Marinated Broccoli and Cauliflower
Chutney Cheesecake
Mushroom Puffs
Scallops Seviche
Chocolate Truffles

"A-Head-Pot" by Peg Morar and "Swirl Goblets" by glassblower William Bernstein, shown at The Craft Shop of Piedmont Craftsmen, Inc.

Hailed as a "showcase for southern crafts," Piedmont Craftsmen, Inc. presents and promotes examples of the finest crafts in the southeast.

Exhibiting members, who are chosen by jury selection, display work in fiber, glass, wood, clay and other media at The Craft Shop of Piedmont Craftsmen located in downtown Winston-Salem. Each fall, the organization sponsors a nationally recognized crafts fair which features a dazzling array of innovative, high quality crafts.

Photo by Smith/Weiler/Smith

Cognac Mushrooms

40 medium-sized fresh mushrooms, washed, dried, stems removed
½ cup butter, melted
8 ounces cream cheese, softened
¾ cup Parmesan cheese
1 tablespoon cognac
4 tablespoons milk
½ teaspoon garlic powder
2 tablespoons chives, finely chopped
Parsley
Paprika

- Preheat oven to 350°.
- Prepare mushrooms and dip in melted butter, coating all sides and cavities of each mushroom. Place on cooking sheet or in large round baking dish with 2 inch sides. Set aside.
- In bowl or food processor, mix cream cheese, Parmesan cheese, cognac, milk, garlic powder, and chives.
- Place a generous teaspoonful of cream cheese mixture in each mushroom cap, mounding gently.
- Bake until lightly browned. Serve at once, garnished with parsley and paprika.
- These can be prepared up to one day ahead, and are best when prepared 6-8 hours before baking.

An old wine bottle cork that plugs the center of the food processor bowl makes soaking or washing the food processor bowl much easier.

Pita Cheese Crisps

⅔ cup Romano or Parmesan cheese, grated
4 cups Cheddar cheese, grated
¾ cup unsalted butter, softened
1 clove garlic, minced
¾ teaspoon Worcestershire sauce
1 teaspoon paprika
¼ teaspoon cayenne pepper
6 large pita loaves

- Preheat oven to 350°.
- In a large mixing bowl or food processor, combine cheeses, butter, garlic, Worcestershire sauce, paprika, and cayenne pepper.
- Split the pita loaves. Spread with cheese mixture and cut into small wedges using a serrated knife.
- Place wedges on an ungreased cookie sheet, ½ inch apart. Bake for 10-12 minutes and serve warm.
- May be made ahead and frozen before baking.

Cheese Straws

Easy
4 Dozen

2 cups flour
1 teaspoon red pepper
½ teaspoon salt
2 (8-ounce) packages New York
  extra sharp Cheddar cheese,
  grated
1 stick butter

- Preheat oven to 350°.
- Mix all ingredients in food processor until blended.
- Place dough in a cookie gun fitted with a cheese straw disc. Press out 3-inch straws onto an ungreased cookie sheet. (Dough may be flattened, chilled 30 minutes, and rolled by hand on a floured surface. Cut into rectangles 1-inch x 3-inches.) Bake 8-10 minutes until lightly browned. Cool on a wire rack before storing in airtight tins.
- Cheese straws may be frozen or stored in tins for 4-5 days.

Oyster Cracker Snacks

Easy

1 cup corn oil
1 (0.4-ounce) package buttermilk
  salad dressing mix
1 teaspoon salt
1 teaspoon lemon pepper
1 teaspoon dill weed
4 (5-ounce) boxes oyster crackers

- In a small saucepan, mix first five ingredients. Heat over low heat, being careful not to boil.
- Place oyster crackers in a large mixing bowl. Pour mixture over crackers. Toss to coat evenly with mixture. Stir periodically for one hour. Store in an airtight tin.
- These are best made one day in advance and stored in an airtight tin.

Artichoke Appetizers

Easy
48 Appetizers

1 (13-ounce) can artichoke hearts,
  drained
1 (4-ounce) can chopped, green
  chilies
1 cup Parmesan cheese
1 cup mayonnaise
¼ cup Dijon mustard (optional)
6 English muffins

- Chop artichoke hearts and green chilies.
- In mixing bowl, combine artichokes, chilies, cheese, mayonnaise, and mustard. (Mixture may be prepared to this point up to several days, refrigerated.)
- When ready to serve, preheat oven to 350°.
- Split English muffins and spread mixture on each half.
- Bake for 30 minutes until browned. Cut each half into quarters to serve as bite-sized pieces.
- Muffin halves may be served whole as a luncheon entrée.

Cherry Tomatoes Stuffed with Pesto

Average
30-40 Servings

30-40 cherry tomatoes
  2 cloves garlic, minced
  4 tablespoons parsley, minced.
  3 tablespoons pine nuts, minced
  1 tablespoon basil
  ¼ cup fresh Parmesan cheese, grated
  1 cup fresh, fine white bread crumbs
  ¼ cup olive oil
    Salt and pepper to taste
    Whole pine nuts for garnish

- Preheat oven to 350°.
- Cut off stem end of each tomato and remove pulp with small melon ball cutter.
- Sprinkle inside each tomato lightly with salt. Invert on paper towels to drain.
- Combine remaining ingredients in food processor or blender and process until well blended.
- Stuff each tomato with stuffing mixture and top with a pine nut. Place tomatoes on a lightly greased baking dish. Bake for 10 minutes.
- Serve hot or at room temperature.

Using a pastry bag makes stuffing tomato shells a breeze!

Fresh Vegetable Mold

Easy
4-5 Cup Mold

  1 cup celery
  1 small green pepper
  1 cucumber
  1 onion
  2 tomatoes
    Salt and pepper to taste
  1 envelope plain gelatin
  1 cup mayonnaise
  1 (8-ounce) carton sour cream

- Finely chop all vegetables and drain on paper towels.
- Add salt and pepper to taste.
- Dissolve gelatin in ¼ cup hot water, then mix with ¼ cup cold water and stir well.
- Combine gelatin mixture with mayonnaise and sour cream in large bowl.
- Stir in vegetables.
- Pour mixture into a 4-5 cup mold that has been rinsed with cold water.
- Chill several hours or overnight.
- Unmold and serve as an hors d'oeuvre with crackers or as a sandwich spread.

Mushroom Appetizers

Easy
32 Appetizers

1 (4-ounce) can mushroom
   pieces, drained
1 (8-ounce) package cream
   cheese, at room temperature
  Salt and pepper to taste
1 (8-ounce) can refrigerated
   crescent rolls
1 egg, lightly beaten
  Poppy seeds

- Preheat oven to 350°.
- Stir together the mushrooms, cream cheese, salt, and pepper.
- Cut each crescent triangle in half and then in half again, so that you have four triangles from each original one.
- Fill each triangle with one teaspoon of the cream cheese mixture. Bring three points of the triangle together and pinch.
- Brush each appetizer with egg and sprinkle with poppy seeds.
- Bake on a greased cookie sheet for 10 minutes or until browned. Serve.
- Appetizers may be made ahead and frozen before baking. They may be baked ahead and reheated in a microwave to serve, if desired.

Marinated Broccoli and Cauliflower

Easy
18-24 Servings

2 bunches broccoli
1 head cauliflower
1 cup cider vinegar
1 tablespoon sugar
1 tablespoon dill weed
1 tablespoon salt
1 teaspoon pepper
1 clove garlic, minced
1½ cups vegetable oil

- Cut broccoli and cauliflower into small florets.
- Mix remaining ingredients well and pour over broccoli and cauliflower. Cover and refrigerate 24 hours. Baste occasionally with marinade.
- Drain before serving. Garnish with cherry tomatoes if desired.

Mushroom Puffs

Pastry:
- 3 ounces cream cheese, softened
- ½ cup butter, softened
- 1½ cups flour

• In a bowl, mix cream cheese and butter. Stir in flour and blend well. Chill 30 minutes before rolling.

Filling:
- 1 small onion, minced
- 3 tablespoons butter
- ½ pound mushrooms, minced
- ¼ teaspoon thyme
- ½ teaspoon salt
- Pepper to taste
- 2 tablespoons flour
- ¼ cup sour cream

• In a medium-sized skillet, sauté onion in butter. Add mushrooms and cook 3 minutes. Add thyme, salt, and pepper and blend.
• Sprinkle flour over mixture. Add sour cream and cook until thickened. Do not boil.

To Assemble:
• Preheat oven to 450°.
• On a floured board, roll out chilled dough until very thin.
• Cut 3-inch rounds and place a little less than 1 teaspoon filling on each. Fold edges over and press together with tines of fork. Prick with fork.
• Bake on ungreased cookie sheet for 15 minutes.

These freeze beautifully before baking. If frozen, allow extra time for baking.

Roasted Herbed Walnuts

Easy

- 2 tablespoons butter
- 2 tablespoons olive oil
- 1 pound walnut halves
- 1½ tablespoons crushed dried rosemary
  - or
- 5 tablespoons finely chopped fresh rosemary
- 1 teaspoon paprika
- 2 teaspoons salt

• Preheat oven to 325°.
• Place butter and oil in a jelly roll pan. Place in oven to melt.
• Remove pan from oven and scatter nuts over pan. Stir to coat with butter and oil mixture.
• Scatter rosemary, paprika, and salt over nuts and bake 20-25 minutes until golden brown. Drain on paper towels and serve warm or at room temperature.

Sweet and Sour Chicken Drummettes

Easy
4-6 Servings

1   (12-ounce) jar apricot jam
1   (8-ounce) bottle Russian
    dressing
1   package onion soup mix
4-6 chicken breast halves
    or
2-3 pounds chicken drummettes

A great addition to any picnic!

• Preheat oven to 325°.
• Mix jam, dressing, and soup to form sauce.
• Place chicken in baking dish and cover with sauce.
• Cover and bake for 1 hour; turn. Continue to bake for 30 minutes or until glazed and brown.

Sesame Chicken Rolls

Easy
25-35 Servings

1½ cups chicken, cooked and
    finely chopped
½   cup ginger marmalade
2   shallots, finely minced
2   teaspoons curry powder
    Salt and pepper to taste
2   teaspoons fresh lemon juice
8   ounces cream cheese, softened
4   tablespoons unsalted butter,
    softened
¾   cup sesame seeds, toasted

• Put all ingredients except sesame seeds in a food processor. Turn on briefly to combine.
• Remove from processor and shape chicken mixture into two rolls about 2-inches by 10-inches.
• Sprinkle toasted sesame seeds evenly onto two pieces of waxed paper. Roll chicken until coated with sesame seeds.
• Chill well.
• Serve with thinly sliced French bread or your favorite crackers.

14

Spinach Wrapped Chicken with Sesame Dip

Average
6-8 Servings

2   whole chicken breasts
1¾ cups chicken broth
¼   cup soy sauce
1   tablespoon Worcestershire sauce
1-2 pounds fresh spinach leaves,
      uniform in size

- In a 3-quart saucepan, simmer the chicken breasts in broth, soy sauce, and Worcestershire sauce until tender, about 15-20 minutes. Remove the chicken and let it cool.
- Discard the chicken bones and skin. Cut meat into 1-inch cubes. Set aside.
- Thoroughly wash spinach leaves and place in a colander. Pour 2-3 quarts of boiling water over the leaves. Drain completely and set aside to cool.
- Place a chicken cube at the inside seam of a spinach leaf. Roll over once, fold leaf in on both sides, and continue rolling. Secure end of leaf with a toothpick. May be prepared several hours ahead and refrigerated until ready to serve.
- To serve, cover a platter with leafy lettuce. Place sesame dip in center and surround with chicken pieces.

Sesame Dip:

2   teaspoons sesame seeds,
      toasted
1   cup sour cream
½   teaspoon ground ginger
4   teaspoons soy sauce
2   teaspoons Worcestershire sauce

- Combine all ingredients, stirring gently.
- Chill at least 4 hours before serving.

Buffalo Hot Wings
Village Tavern

Easy
20 Drummettes

20 chicken drummettes
1   (3-ounce) bottle Texas Pete
      hot sauce
7   tablespoons butter, melted
½   cup bleu cheese dressing
      Celery sticks

- Deep fry drummettes until golden. Drain.
- Combine Texas Pete hot sauce and melted butter in a mixing bowl.
- Dip drummettes into hot sauce. Shake off excess and place on serving platter.
- Serve with bleu cheese dressing for dipping and celery sticks.

15

Black-Eyed Susans

8 tablespoons butter, softened
1 pound sharp Cheddar cheese, grated
2 cups flour, sifted
Pinch of cayenne pepper
2 (8-ounce) boxes dates, pitted
¾ pound walnuts
Sugar

- Preheat oven to 325°.
- In a large bowl, mix together butter, cheese, flour, and cayenne pepper. Refrigerate.
- Cut dates in half lengthwise. Cut walnuts in half lengthwise and put inside date half.
- Use half of the cheese mixture and roll it out to ¼-inch thickness on a lightly floured board. Cut out circles that are 1 to 1¼-inches in diameter. Fold circles around dates and pinch in the middle with your thumb.
- Bake on greased cookie sheets for 10-15 minutes or until lightly browned. Do not overcook. Cool slightly and roll in sugar.
- These may be made ahead and stored in an airtight tin for up to 4 days or frozen.

Avocado Pinwheel

1 envelope unflavored gelatin
¼ cup cold water
3 avocados, mashed (1 cup mashed)
1 tablespoon lemon juice
1 (0.6-ounce) package dry Italian salad dressing mix
2 cups sour cream
3 tablespoons parsley, chopped
Dash of hot pepper sauce
3-4 drops green food coloring (optional)

Garnishes:
Green onions, chopped
Tomatoes, chopped
Ripe olives, chopped
Cooked shrimp, chopped
Green pepper, chopped

- Brush an 8-inch springform pan or flan tin with indented bottom with oil. Line with plastic wrap and brush wrap lightly with oil.
- In a small saucepan, combine gelatin and cold water. Set aside to soften.
- In the bowl of a food processor, combine avocados, lemon juice, dressing mix, sour cream, parsley, hot pepper sauce, and food coloring. Blend thoroughly.
- Melt gelatin over low heat and blend into avocado mixture. Pour into prepared tin and chill until set.
- When ready to serve, unmold onto a platter. Arrange four to five selected garnishes in concentric circles on top of mold. Serve with cocktail bread rounds, crackers, or tortilla chips.
- Other suggested garnishes: chopped cucumber, smoked salmon, red or black caviar.
- Mold may be prepared one day in advance and refrigerated until ready to garnish.

Cheese Roll-Ups with Mustard Sauce

Average
55 Roll-ups

1 pound Monterey Jack jalapeño
   cheese, grated
1 egg, beaten
   Salt to taste
1 pound phyllo pastry sheets,
   thawed
1 pound butter, melted

- Combine cheese, egg, and salt; mix well.
- Unroll phyllo dough and place one sheet on work surface. Keep the remainder of the dough covered with wax paper and a damp towel to prevent drying. Brush phyllo sheet with melted butter and top with a second sheet; brush with butter.
- Cut phyllo lengthwise into five strips. Place one and a half teaspoons of the cheese mixture at the end of each strip. Fold a corner of the sheet over the filling into a triangle. Continue folding to the end of the strip, and you will have a triangular-shaped pastry. Brush the pastry with butter.
- Repeat with remaining phyllo and cheese.
- Preheat oven to 400°.
- Bake roll-ups on ungreased baking sheets until crisp and golden, about 12-15 minutes.
- Serve warm.
- Roll-ups may be made ahead and frozen. Thaw 15 minutes in refrigerator before baking.

Mustard Sauce

Easy
1½ Cups

2 eggs
½ cup brown sugar
½ cup canned consommé soup
½ cup white wine vinegar
¼ cup dry mustard
1½ teaspoons flour
   Dash hot pepper sauce

- In a saucepan, beat eggs lightly. Add remaining ingredients.
- Cook over medium heat until thickened, about 15-20 minutes.
- This can be doubled easily and lasts for weeks.

Feta Tarts

Filling:

⅔ cup half and half
10 ounces Feta cheese, crumbled
2 eggs
¾ teaspoon cornstarch
¼ teaspoon thyme
1 small clove garlic, crushed
   Pepper to taste

- Combine all filling ingredients in a blender or food processor. Blend.

Dough:

3 ounces cream cheese, softened
1 stick butter, softened
1 cup flour, sifted
12-18 Greek olives, pitted

- Blend cream cheese and butter together with a fork.
- Cut flour into cheese and butter. Knead gently and form into a ball. Chill, covered, 1 hour.

To assemble:

- Preheat oven to 350°.
- Press 2 teaspoons of chilled dough into 1½-inch tart pans. Prick sides and bottoms with a fork. Bake for 8 minutes.
- Remove shells from oven and fill each with 1-2 tablespoons of cheese filling. Top each tart with three thin slices of Greek olive.
- Bake 30-35 minutes or until browned. Serve hot.
- Tarts may be baked ahead and reheated to serve.

Cheese and Herbs Appetizer

1 loaf French bread, thinly sliced
¼ cup extra virgin olive oil
   Freshly ground pepper to taste
4 tablespoons one, or more, fresh herbs (parsley, basil, thyme, dill, oregano)
8 ounces of one, or more, mild cheeses (Chèvre, mozzarella, Provolone, Havarti)

- Brush one side of bread with olive oil. Sprinkle with pepper.
- Finely chop herbs. Sprinkle on bread and top with a thin slice of cheese.
- Possible combinations: Chèvre/thyme; Chèvre/basil; Chèvre/parsley; mozzarella/basil; mozzarella/oregano; Provolone/basil; Provolone/thyme; Provolone/oregano; Havarti/dill; Havarti/thyme.
- Garnish with sprigs of fresh herbs.

Cheese Tart With Apples

Easy
2 8-Inch Molds

24 ounces cream cheese, softened
2   tablespoons sour cream
4   ounces Camembert
4   ounces bleu cheese
4   ounces Gruyère
5   ounces pecans, chopped

- In food processor or mixer, blend together 16 ounces cream cheese and sour cream.
- In a separate bowl, combine remaining cream cheese with camembert, bleu cheese, and gruyère.
- Line two 8-inch pie pans with foil.
- Layer the sour cream mixture, pecans, and cheese mixture in each pan.
- Refrigerate for at least two days or up to three weeks.
- Serve surrounded by fresh apple slices.
- Garnish with apples and parsley in a ring to look like a Christmas wreath.
- May be frozen up to six months.

When cooking with fresh herbs, use three times as much as with dried, and vice versa. Bruise or crush leaves gently before using to release flavorful oils.

Mushroom Bleu Cheese Spread

Average
8-12 Servings

2   ounces butter
1   pound mushrooms, sliced
1   clove garlic, crushed
    Nutmeg to taste
    Pepper to taste
1   tablespoon Dijon mustard
⅓   cup dry white wine
8   ounces cream cheese
3   ounces cream cheese
      with chives
2   ounces bleu cheese
    Parsley

- Melt butter over low heat and sauté mushrooms and garlic.
- Add nutmeg, pepper, mustard, and white wine.
- Add both cream cheeses, stirring until blended over low heat.
- Crumble in bleu cheese, a little at a time.
- Garnish with parsley and serve hot with melba rounds.

Chutney Cheesecake

2 (8-ounce) packages cream
   cheese, softened
2 cups Cheddar cheese, shredded
⅓ cup dry sherry
2 tablespoons Worcestershire
   sauce
1½ teaspoons curry
1 (8-ounce) jar good quality
   chutney
¼-½ cup dry roasted peanuts,
   chopped
½ cup shredded coconut

- Mix cream cheese, Cheddar cheese, sherry, Worcestershire sauce, and curry in food processor.
- Process until combined.
- Press in springform pan and chill. (At this point, may be left in refrigerator several days.)
- To serve, unmold onto serving dish and top with chutney.
- Garnish with chopped peanuts and coconut, alternating to form a decorative pattern.
- Serve with melba rounds.

Use clothespins to close potato chip bags.

Herbed Cheese Spread

1 (8-ounce) tub whipped sweet
   butter
2 (8-ounce) packages cream
   cheese, softened
½ teaspoon marjoram
½ teaspoon oregano
½ teaspoon garlic powder
½ teaspoon basil
½ teaspoon dill weed
½ teaspoon pepper
½ teaspoon thyme

- Blend butter and cream cheese together with a wooden spoon.
- Blend in marjoram, oregano, garlic powder, basil, dill weed, pepper, and thyme. Refrigerate.
- Serve with crackers or on endive leaves.

Tomato Cheese Spread

Easy
12 Servings

8   ounces Cheddar cheese, grated
1   cup tomatoes, peeled and
      chopped
8   ounces cream cheese, softened
4   ounces margarine, softened
1   small onion, grated
1   teaspoon salt
½   teaspoon cayenne pepper
      Garlic powder to taste
1½ cups pecans or walnuts, chopped

- Combine all ingredients, except nuts, in mixing bowl or food processor.
- Process until combined.
- May at this point shape into a log or ball and roll in nuts.
- Or, stir in nuts and serve as spread for crackers.
- Best if prepared a day ahead.
- May be frozen up to two months.

To seed a tomato, slice in half horizontally and squeeze each half gently. Seeds should fall out.

Paté Hater's Delight

Average
20 Servings

3   tablespoons butter
2   tablespoons onion, minced
8   ounces fresh chicken livers
½   teaspoon curry powder
¼   teaspoon paprika
½   teaspoon salt
½   teaspoon pepper
¼   cup chicken broth
16 ounces cream cheese, softened
1   cup walnuts, toasted and
      chopped

- In a large skillet, melt the butter over moderate heat and sauté onion and livers for 5 minutes. Stir in curry, paprika, salt, pepper, and broth. Remove mixture from heat and let cool.
- Pureé mixture in a food processor until smooth, about 30-45 seconds. Add cream cheese and blend again.
- Chill 6-8 hours in the refrigerator.
- To serve, mound the paté on a platter or spoon into a crock. Press walnuts to cover surface. Serve with party rye bread.

Herb Pizza

Dough:
    1   16-ounce box hot roll mix
    6   8-inch aluminum pie tins
        Olive oil

- Mix dough according to package directions for pizza crust. Let rise. Punch down and divide into six pieces.
- Brush pie tins lightly with olive oil. Spread dough in bottom of each. Pinch edges to form a border.

Sauce:
    1   tablespoon olive oil
    1½   cups onion, chopped
    1   clove garlic, minced
    1   (8-ounce) can tomato sauce
    1   (6-ounce) can tomato paste
    1   teaspoon salt
    ¼   teaspoon oregano
    ⅛   teaspoon pepper
    1   pound mozzarella cheese, grated
    1   (3½-ounce) package sliced
         pepperoni
    6   tablespoons Parmesan cheese,
         grated
    1   tablespoon dried parsley flakes

- Heat olive oil in a sauté pan. Add onion and garlic. Sauté until transparent.
- Add tomato sauce, tomato paste, salt, oregano, and pepper. Stir to combine ingredients. Cook 2-3 minutes.
- Divide sauce evenly among pizzas and spread to cover each. Top each with eight slices of pepperoni and sprinkle with remaining mozzarella cheese. Add Parmesan cheese and parsley flakes to each.
- Pizzas may be frozen at this point and baked as needed. Bake in a preheated 450° oven for 15-20 minutes or until bubbly and golden. Cut into serving wedges with kitchen scissors.

A great appetizer pizza for football or basketball crowds

Taco Dip

    1   pound hamburger
    1   package taco seasoning
    1   (16-ounce) can refried beans
    ½   (8-ounce) bottle green taco
         sauce
    12   ounces sour cream
    2   cups Cheddar cheese, grated
         Taco chips

- Preheat oven to 350°.
- In a large skillet, brown hamburger; drain excess grease. Add taco seasoning and prepare according to package directions.
- Spread hamburger mixture in bottom of a 13x9-inch baking dish. Spread refried beans over hamburger. Sprinkle taco sauce over beans, sour cream over taco sauce, and Cheddar cheese over sour cream.
- Bake for 15 minutes. Serve with taco chips.

Tavern Nachos
Village Tavern

1 pound ground beef
1 (1¼-ounce) envelope taco seasoning mix
1 (11-ounce) bag Tortilla chips, traditional flavor
1 (7½-ounce) container nacho cheese sauce, heated
1 cup bottled taco sauce, mild or hot
2 cups lettuce, shredded
½ cup green onions, chopped
½ cup fresh tomatoes, chopped
½ cup ripe olives, chopped
2 heaping tablespoons sour cream

- Brown beef in a skillet. Drain and return to pan.
- Add taco seasoning mix and cook according to package directions. Keep warm.
- Spread Tortilla chips on a baking sheet and warm in a 300° oven for 5 minutes.
- Arrange chips on a serving platter and top with warm nacho cheese sauce. Add seasoned beef and top with taco sauce. Place shredded lettuce on top of beef and sauce. Garnish with green onions, tomatoes, black olives, and sour cream. Serve.

Tex-Mex Dip

3 ripe medium-sized avocados, peeled and pitted
2 tablespoons lemon juice
½ teaspoon salt
¼ teaspoon pepper
1 cup sour cream
½ cup mayonnaise
1 envelope taco seasoning mix
2 (10½-ounce) cans bean dip
1 bunch green onions, diced with some green tops
2 cups tomatoes, cubed
2 (3½-ounce) cans pitted ripe olives, sliced
8 ounces sharp Cheddar cheese, grated

- Mash avocado with fork and blend with lemon juice, salt, and pepper.
- In another bowl, combine sour cream, mayonnaise, and taco seasoning mix.
- In a 9x12 inch shallow dish or a large decorative platter, arrange in layers as follows: bean dip (bottom layer), avocado mixture, sour cream mixture, onions, tomatoes, olives, and cheese.
- Chill overnight. Serve with tortilla chips.
- Can be prepared 1-2 days ahead.

A real crowd pleaser.

Avocado and Tomato Dip

½ pint sour cream
1 (0.4-ounce) package Italian
    salad dressing mix
1 tablespoon mayonnaise
    Juice of ½ lemon
½ avocado, chopped finely
½ tomato, chopped
    Dash of hot pepper sauce

- Mix all ingredients thoroughly. Serve immediately with chips or fresh vegetables.

Great on a hot summer day.

Oysters Orleans
The Last Catch Cafe and Bar

18 slices bacon
36 oysters, out of shell
    Peanut oil for frying
¼ cup Dijon mustard
2 cups heavy cream
½ tomato, diced
¼ cup flour
2 eggs
½ cup fine bread crumbs
    Lemon slices and fresh parsley
     for garnish

- Preheat oven to 350°.
- Cook bacon in oven until opaque, not crisp.
- Drain bacon and wrap each oyster with ½ slice bacon. Secure with a toothpick.
- Heat oil to 350°.
- In a pan, combine mustard, cream, and tomatoes and cook until reduced by half.
- Dip oysters in flour, then in egg mixture, then in bread crumbs. Fry in batches. Keep warm in oven.
- To serve, line bottom of a plate with mustard sauce and place oysters on top. Garnish with lemon and parsley.

Smoked Oyster Spread

8 ounces cream cheese, softened
1 tablespoon mayonnaise
1 tin smoked oysters, drained
    and chopped
½ cup olives, minced
    Dash each of salt, garlic powder,
     and lemon juice

- Cream together the cheese and mayonnaise.
- Add the olives and smoked oysters.
- Blend in salt, garlic powder, and lemon juice.
- Serve on buttered toast points.

Charleston Marinated Shrimp

Easy
8-12 Servings

2   pounds shrimp, boiled and peeled
2   onions, sliced
4   ounces mushrooms, sliced
8   bay leaves
1¼ cup vegetable oil
¾   cup vinegar
1½ teaspoons salt
2½ teaspoons celery seed
2½ tablespoons capers
    Hot pepper sauce to taste

- Combine all ingredients in large bowl, stirring well.
- Refrigerate at least 2 hours or overnight, turning occasionally.
- To serve, partially drain marinade. Place shrimp in serving bowl and serve with toothpicks.

Marinated Shrimp

Easy
8-12 Servings

1½-2 pounds large shrimp, cooked, shelled, and deveined
1⅓ cups olive oil
⅔   cup tarragon vinegar
1   large onion, coarsely chopped
1   clove garlic, mashed
3   tablespoons Dijon mustard
1   tablespoon German style mustard
2   tablespoons horseradish
1   tablespoon thyme
½   teaspoon salt
¼   teaspoon pepper
¼   teaspoon paprika

- Put shrimp in a large bowl or glass jar.
- In a food processor or blender, add all ingredients, except shrimp. Blend until onion is finely minced.
- Pour marinade over shrimp and chill until icy cold.
- To serve, drain off marinade.
- Shrimp may marinate up to two days in the refrigerator.

Tea Smoked Shrimp

Grated rind and juice from 2 oranges
1 teaspoon salt
2 tablespoons rice wine vinegar
30 large shrimp, unpeeled
½ cup strong loose tea (preferably Chinese)
½ cup sugar
1 teaspoon cayenne

- Combine orange rind, orange juice, salt, and vinegar in a mixing bowl.
- Pour over shrimp and marinate in refrigerator overnight.
- Line a wok with aluminum foil. Sprinkle tea, sugar, and cayenne on the foil. Set a rack on top. Cover tightly and turn burner on high. Pot will start smoking as sugar melts. Turn off burner. Place shrimp on rack, re-cover, and turn heat back on high. Smoke for 5 minutes. Do not overcook.
- Will keep 3-4 days in the refrigerator.

Shrimp Dip

1 (8-ounce) package cream cheese, at room temperature
½ cup mayonnaise
½ pound shrimp, cooked and chopped
   or
1 (4½-ounce) can shrimp
½ cup mayonnaise
1 bunch green onions, chopped
½ cup celery, chopped
4 tablespoons parsley, chopped
2 tablespoons fresh lemon juice
Cayenne pepper to taste
Salt to taste

- In a large mixing bowl, mix cream cheese with ½ cup mayonnaise.
- Combine next six ingredients and blend well. Add to cream cheese mixture and mix until well blended.
- Season with cayenne pepper and salt. Chill.
- Serve with crackers.

Better if prepared several hours ahead.

Scallops Seviche
Heritage of Hospitality

½   pound fresh scallops (preferably tiny bay scallops)
1   large tomato, peeled and chopped
2   small green chilies, seeded and chopped
1   onion, chopped
    Juice of 5 limes
¼   cup olive oil

- If tiny bay scallops are not available, cut large scallops in half.
- Combine all ingredients and let stand, covered, in refrigerator at least 12 hours. The lime juice "cooks" the scallops.

This is great as an appetizer served with toothpicks, or as a first course or main course served on lettuce. Other white fish may be used.

Hot Crab Canapés

8   slices white bread
½   cup flaked crabmeat
½   cup shredded Cheddar cheese
¼   cup plus 2 tablespoons mayonnaise
1   tablespoon onion, grated
¼-½   teaspoon curry powder (optional)
¼   teaspoon salt
    Parsley

- Preheat oven to 425°.
- Cut each slice of bread into four decorative shapes using 1½ inch cutters.
- Place cutouts on ungreased baking sheet and broil for 1 minute until lightly browned. Cool.
- Combine crabmeat, cheese, mayonnaise, onion, curry, and salt, mixing well.
- Spread crabmeat mixture on bread.
- Bake for 5-7 minutes. Garnish with parsley.

Special Crabmeat Appetizer

Easy
4-6 Servings

2 tablespoons butter
1 teaspoon flour
½ cup milk
1 pound fresh backfin crabmeat
2 heaping tablespoons
  mayonnaise
1 teaspoon prepared mustard
1 teaspoon Worcestershire sauce
1 tablespoon hot pepper sauce
  Dash garlic salt
1 teaspoon lemon juice
¼ cup fresh buttered bread crumbs

- Melt butter in a saucepan. Add flour and whisk until smooth. Add milk and heat, stirring, until sauce thickens.
- Add crabmeat and remaining ingredients, except bread crumbs.
- Spoon crabmeat mixture into individual ovenproof ramekins or scallop shells. Top each with buttered bread crumbs and bake in a preheated 350° oven for 15-20 minutes. Serve.

Collect large seashells at the beach and use for serving!

Crabmeat Spread

Easy
4 Servings as First Course
8 Servings as Appetizer

1 pound fresh crabmeat
1 tablespoon lemon juice
2 teaspoons Dijon mustard
2 tablespoons fresh parsley,
  chopped
¼ teaspoon pepper, freshly ground
1 tablespoon capers
2 tablespoons mayonnaise
  (or more if desired)

- Gently remove any shell remaining in crabmeat.
- Place cleaned crabmeat in medium mixing bowl. Add lemon juice, mustard, parsley, pepper, capers, and mayonnaise. Mix gently.
- Refrigerate until ready to serve.

This is great served on homemade melba toast as an appetizer, on lettuce as a first course, or in pita bread as a sandwich.

Crunchy Crab Puffs

Easy
30

1	#10 can refrigerator buttermilk biscuits
1	(6½-ounce) can crabmeat, drained
8	ounces Swiss cheese, grated
1-2	stalks celery, chopped or
½	(7-ounce) can water chestnuts, chopped
1	small onion, grated
½	teaspoon curry powder
1-1½	cups mayonnaise

- Preheat oven to 375°.
- Divide each biscuit into thirds. Place on a cookie sheet.
- Blend remaining ingredients and spoon onto each biscuit section.
- Bake 10 minutes or until puffy and browned.

Artichoke Clam Puffs

Easy
30-40 Appetizers

2	(15-ounce) cans artichoke hearts
8	ounces cream cheese, softened
2½	tablespoons sherry
¼	teaspoon hot pepper sauce
1	(7-ounce) can minced clams, drained
	Paprika

- Halve or quarter artichoke hearts. Drain on a paper towel.
- Combine cream cheese, sherry, hot pepper sauce, and clams in a mixing bowl or food processor and blend until smooth.
- Spread cheese mixture on top of each artichoke piece and place on a cookie sheet.
- Sprinkle with paprika. Broil until puffed and lightly browned. Serve hot.
- Appetizers may be made one day in advance and refrigerated, covered, until ready to broil.

Salmon Mousse

Easy
4-cup Mold

1   envelope plain gelatin
2   tablespoons lemon juice
1   small onion, sliced
½   cup boiling water
½   cup mayonnaise
¼   teaspoon paprika
1   teaspoon dill weed
1   (15½-ounce) can salmon, drained
1   cup sour cream

- In a blender, add gelatin, lemon juice, onion, and boiling water and blend for 40 seconds.
- Add mayonnaise, paprika, dill weed, and salmon. Blend briefly at high speed.
- Add sour cream, ⅓ cup at a time, blending in between. Blend 30 seconds.
- Pour into a 4-cup mold and chill until set.

Rosa's Cheese Souffle Sandwiches

Average
6 bite-sized pieces make 75-80
4 bite-sized pieces make 50

1   pound butter, softened
4   (5-ounce) jars Old English cheese
1   teaspoon hot pepper sauce
1   teaspoon onion powder
1½   teaspoons Worcestershire sauce
1   teaspoon seasoned salt
1½   teaspoons dill weed
2½   loaves very thin white bread, crust removed

- Combine butter and cheese in a large mixing bowl; beat with mixer until fluffy. Add hot pepper sauce, onion powder, Worcestershire sauce, seasoned salt, and dill weed. Mix well.
- Spread three slices of bread with cheese mixture and stack. Cut into four or six bite-sized sandwiches. Spread sides or "ice" with cheese mixture. Repeat using rest of bread and cheese mixture.
- Place little sandwiches on cookie sheet and bake in a preheated 325° oven for approximately 15 minutes until edges brown.
- Sandwiches may be made ahead and placed on cookie sheets to freeze. Store in baggies after frozen.

California Salsa

2 tomatoes, diced
1 onion, diced
1 (8-ounce) can tomato sauce
1 small can chilies
   Salt and pepper to taste
4 dashes hot pepper sauce
   Chili powder to taste
1 tablespoon parsley, chopped
1 tablespoon cilantro, chopped
   (optional)

• Combine all ingredients in a mixing bowl.
• Serve as a dip with tortilla chips or use as a topping for rice, beans, or ground beef.

Sakowitz Remoulade Sauce

1 pound fresh spinach
   or
1 (10-ounce) package frozen
   spinach
2 hard-boiled eggs
4 green onions, chopped
3 cloves garlic
3 cups mayonnaise
2 teaspoons Worcestershire sauce
2 teaspoons creole mustard
2 teaspoons lemon juice
2 teaspoons anchovy paste
   Hot sauce to taste

• Cook spinach and drain well. Remove all water or sauce will be thin.
• Place all ingredients in blender or food processor and mix until smooth. Chill.
• Serve as a dip with fresh vegetables, shrimp, or French bread.

Scioto Dip

1 (8-ounce) package frozen chopped spinach, thawed and drained
1 cup mayonnaise
1½ cups sour cream
1 (1.4-ounce) package dry vegetable soup mix
1 (8-ounce) can water chestnuts, chopped
Garlic powder to taste
1 round rye bread

- Blend all ingredients in a mixing bowl or the bowl of a food processor. Refrigerate until ready to serve.
- Cut the center out of the bread round and cut into cubes. Fill the cavity with dip. Arrange the bread in the center of a serving platter surrounded with cubes for dipping.
- Dip may also be served in a bowl with homemade rye melba or fresh vegetables for dipping.

Dill Dip

⅔ cup mayonnaise
⅔ cup sour cream
1 tablespoon shallots, minced
1 tablespoon fresh parsley, minced
1 tablespoon dill weed
1 teaspoon seasoned salt
1 loaf German rye bread

- Mix first six ingredients thoroughly. Chill at least 1 hour.
- Remove center from rye bread and use as a container for dip. Serve with assorted fresh vegetables. (Bread from center may be cubed and served with dip if desired.)

Unflavored yogurt may be substituted for sour cream.

Curry Dip

1 cup mayonnaise
2 teaspoons tarragon vinegar
1 teaspoon black pepper
½ teaspoon salt
⅛ teaspoon thyme
¼ teaspoon curry
2 tablespoons ketchup
1 tablespoon onion, finely chopped

- Mix all ingredients well. Chill.
- Serve with fresh vegetables.

breads & beverages

Formal Dinner

Smoked Salmon Timbales with Coulis de Tomatoes
Roast Lamb with Herbed Mustard
Broccoli Stuffed Tomatoes
Rosemary Potatoes
Watercress, Mushroom, and Endive Salad
French Bread
Pecan Roll with Caramel Nut Sauce

The Winkler Bakery, Old Salem

Built in 1800, the Winkler Bakery is one of the most popular and memorable stops on the Old Salem tour. Each day bakers hand-knead dough and cut cookies with hammered-tin cutters. The delectable breads, love feast buns, sugar cakes, and cookies are then baked to a golden brown in an authentic wood-fired oven.

Photo by Robert Madden

Rich Tea Scones

2½ cups self-rising flour
1 tablespoon sugar
½ teaspoon salt
3 tablespoons lard or butter (cut into small pieces), chilled
1 egg
½ cup milk

- Preheat oven to 400°.
- In a mixing bowl, combine flour with sugar and salt. Add the lard or butter and mix until it resembles coarse meal.
- Beat egg, reserving 1 tablespoon. Combine remaining egg with milk. Add to flour mixture and shape into a ball quickly. Knead briefly. Roll out to a ¼-inch thickness and cut into 2-inch rounds. Place on a buttered baking sheet, brush tops with reserved egg, and bake approximately 15 minutes.
- Serve with jam and whipped cream.

Pancake Winx
Heritage of Hospitality

½ cup flour
½ cup milk
2 eggs, lightly beaten
Pinch of nutmeg
4 tablespoons butter
2 tablespoons powdered sugar
Juice of ½ lemon
Jelly, jam, marmalade, or syrup for topping

- Preheat oven to 425°.
- Mix together in a mixing bowl flour, milk, eggs, and nutmeg. The batter should be lumpy.
- Melt butter in a 12-inch skillet with heat-proof handle. When very hot and foam subsides, pour in batter.
- Bake at 425° for 15-20 minutes, or until golden brown.
- Sprinkle with sugar and return briefly to oven.
- Sprinkle with lemon juice and serve with a favorite topping.

A variation of the Swedish pancake. This may also be served as a dessert in the summer with sliced fresh berries, a sprinkling of brown sugar, and dollops of sour cream.

33

Blackberry Pancakes

Easy
12 Pancakes

2 tablespoons margarine or butter, melted
1 egg, beaten
1 cup milk
½ cup unbleached flour
½ cup whole wheat flour
½ teaspoon salt
1 tablespoon baking powder
1 cup fresh blackberries, lightly mashed (blueberries may be substituted)

- Combine margarine or butter, egg, and milk.
- Mix together the flours, salt, and baking powder. Quickly whisk the dry ingredients into the milk mixture.
- Stir in blackberries.
- Cook over medium high heat on a lightly greased skillet.

To freeze pancakes: Freeze separately on a piece of foil. After they are frozen, wrap in a package of 3 or 4, Reheat in toaster.

Wheat Germ Pancakes

Easy
16 Large Pancakes

1 cup whole wheat flour
1 cup unbleached flour
⅔ cup wheat germ
¼ cup sugar (optional)
4 teaspoons baking powder
1 teaspoon salt
2½ cups milk
½ cup vegetable oil
2 eggs

- Place flours, wheat germ, sugar, baking powder, and salt in large mixing bowl. Stir to blend.
- In a separate bowl beat together milk, oil, and eggs. Pour into dry ingredients and stir until moistened. (Batter should be lumpy.)
- Pour batter, ⅓ cup at a time, onto hot, lightly oiled griddle or skillet. Cook until edges are dry and bubbles appear near center. Turn and cook other side.

This batter is best if prepared a day ahead.

Whole Wheat Oatmeal Hot Cakes

Easy
15-20 Medium Pancakes

Whole Grain Pancake Mix:

      4   cups whole wheat flour
      4   cups unbleached white flour
      3   cups quick-cooking oats
      3   tablespoons baking powder
      1   tablespoon salt
      3   tablespoons sugar

- Combine all ingredients for whole grain pancake mix. Store covered in refrigerator and use as needed.

Hot Cake Batter:

      2   eggs
      2   cups milk
      1   tablespoon vegetable oil
    2½   cups whole grain pancake mix

- Beat eggs. Add milk and oil. Beat until frothy.
- Stir in pancake mix.
- Ladle onto hot skillet and cook until bubbles form in pancakes. Turn and cook until brown.

Waffles: Cook waffles for 30 seconds before closing the waffle iron top. Results will be fluffier waffles and no leakage.

Dot's Waffles

Easy
4 Large Waffles

      2   cups flour
      3   teaspoons baking powder
     ½   teaspoon salt (heaping)
      2   teaspoons sugar
    1¼   cups milk
      2   egg yolks, beaten
      6   tablespoons melted butter or
            vegetable oil
      2   egg whites, beaten stiff

- In a large bowl sift together the flour, baking powder, salt, and sugar.
- Add milk, egg yolks, and butter or oil. Blend well, using whisk.
- Carefully fold in egg whites.
- Ladle onto hot waffle iron and cook until done.
- Leftover waffles can be frozen and reheated.

Jalapeño Corn Bread

3   cups self-rising corn bread mix
2½ cups milk
½   cup vegetable oil
3   eggs, beaten
1   large onion, grated
1½ cups Cheddar cheese, grated
¼   pound bacon, fried and crumbled
¼   cup pimentos, chopped
2   tablespoons sugar
1   cup creamed corn
    Chopped jalapeño peppers, with
       juice as desired

- Preheat oven to 400°.
- Mix all ingredients together and blend well.
- Pour batter into 3 greased 8x8-inch pans.
- Bake 35 minutes or until done. Can be frozen after baking.

Monterey Jack cheese may be used for a different flavor.

Spinach Corn Bread

4   eggs
½   teaspoon salt
1   (1-pound, 3-ounce) box corn
       bread mix
6   ounces cottage cheese
½   cup margarine, softened
½   cup chopped onion
1   (10-ounce) package frozen
       chopped spinach, cooked and
       drained well

- Preheat oven to 400°.
- In a mixing bowl, beat eggs.
- Add remaining ingredients and mix well.
- Pour batter into a generously greased 10x6x1¾-inch baking dish.
- Bake for 30 minutes or until brown on top.
- Can be frozen after baking.

Children love this! Easy and great for any "casual meal" side dish.

Hatteras Corn Bread

⅓ cup vegetable oil
2 cups white corn meal
¾ cup flour
2 teaspoons salt
¾ cup sugar
5 cups boiling water
1 (13-ounce) can evaporated milk
2 teaspoons baking powder
3 eggs

- Prepare a 2½-quart rectangular baking dish by filming with oil. Place in oven and preheat to 400°.
- In a large bowl, place corn meal, flour, salt, and sugar. Mix to combine.
- Pour in boiling water and mix well.
- Add evaporated milk, baking powder, and eggs, one at a time, mixing well with a wire whisk. (Batter should be free of lumps and mushy.)
- Remove baking pan from oven. Pour in corn meal batter. It should sizzle as it hits the hot oil. Oil should come up over the batter.
- Bake 50-60 minutes. Bread should be slightly crunchy on the exterior and soft on the interior.
- Cool 5 minutes. Slice and serve.

Applesauce Muffins

1 cup margarine, softened
2 cups sugar
2 eggs
3 teaspoons vanilla
4 cups flour
1 teaspoon cloves
2 teaspoons allspice
1 tablespoon cinnamon
1 (16-ounce) can applesauce
2 teaspoons baking soda

- Preheat oven to 400°.
- Cream margarine and sugar in a mixer until light. Add eggs one at a time. Blend in 1 teaspoon vanilla.
- Sift flour and spices together; add to creamed mixture.
- Blend 2 teaspoons vanilla into applesauce; then add baking soda. Combine with flour mixture. Batter will be stiff.
- Spoon into greased muffin tins, one-half full.
- Bake 12 minutes.
- Can be frozen after baking.

Batter will keep for several weeks in the refrigerator.

Bran Muffins

Heritage of Hospitality

Easy
2 Dozen Large Muffins
6-8 Dozen Mini-Muffins

3	cups all bran
1	cup boiling water
½	cup shortening, melted
1½	cups sugar
2	eggs, beaten
1	pint buttermilk
2½	cups flour
2½	teaspoons soda
1	teaspoon salt

- Put 1 cup bran in boiling water and set aside.
- Mix shortening, remaining bran, sugar, eggs, and buttermilk.
- Sift together flour, salt, and soda.
- Combine all ingredients.
- Pour batter into greased muffin tins and bake at 400° for 15-20 minutes.

This mix keeps in refrigerator for six to eight weeks.

Buttermilk Corn-Cheese Muffins

Easy
16 Muffins

½	cup unbleached flour
1	tablespoon baking powder
2	tablespoons sugar
¾	teaspoon salt
1	cup corn meal
1	egg, lightly beaten
3	tablespoons butter, melted
¾	cup buttermilk
1¼	cups sharp Cheddar cheese, grated

- Preheat oven to 425°.
- Combine dry ingredients.
- Stir together egg, butter, and buttermilk. Blend into dry ingredients quickly. Stir in 1 cup of the cheese. Do not overmix.
- Spoon into greased and floured muffin tins. Sprinkle remaining ¼ cup of cheese on top.
- Bake 25 minutes.
- Can be frozen after baked.

Apple Muffins

1½   cups packed brown sugar
⅔   cup vegetable oil
1   egg
1   cup buttermilk
1   teaspoon baking soda
1   teaspoon vanilla
1   teaspoon salt
2½   cups sifted flour
1½   cups apples, peeled and diced
½   cup nuts, chopped

Topping:
⅓   cup sugar
1   tablespoon butter, chilled

- Preheat oven to 325°.
- In a large mixing bowl combine brown sugar, oil, and egg.
- In a second bowl mix buttermilk, baking soda, vanilla, and salt.
- Blend flour into brown sugar mixture alternating with buttermilk mixture. Do not overmix. Fold in apples and nuts.
- Spoon batter into greased muffin tins.
- Mix sugar and butter together until crumbly. Sprinkle on top of each muffin.
- Bake 30 minutes.
- Can be frozen after baking.

Squash Muffins

2   pounds squash, sliced
2   eggs, lightly beaten
1   cup margarine, melted
1   cup sugar
3   cups flour
1   tablespoon plus 1 teaspoon
     baking powder
1   teaspoon salt

- Preheat oven to 375°.
- Cook squash in a small amount of water until tender. Drain and mash thoroughly. Measure 2 cups of squash.
- Combine squash, eggs, and margarine, stirring well. Set aside.
- Combine sugar, flour, baking powder, and salt in a mixing bowl. Make a well in the center and stir in the squash mixture until moistened.
- Spoon into greased muffin tins, three-fourths full.
- Bake for 20 minutes.
- Can be frozen after baking.

This versatile recipe can be made using yellow squash, zucchini, or even butternut squash.

Zucchini Raisin Muffins

Average
16 Muffins

2 cups unbleached flour
   or
1 cup unbleached flour and 1 cup whole wheat flour
1 tablespoon baking powder
1 teaspoon cinnamon
¾ teaspoon salt
2 eggs
¾ cup milk
⅓ cup vegetable oil
¼ cup honey
1 cup unpeeled zucchini, coarsely grated
⅔ cup raisins

- Preheat oven to 375°.
- Sift together dry ingredients in a large mixing bowl.
- In another bowl beat eggs and then beat in milk, oil, and honey. Combine with dry ingredients, stirring just until moist.
- Quickly stir in zucchini and raisins. Do not overmix.
- Spoon batter into greased and floured muffin tins.
- Bake for 25 minutes until golden brown.
- Can be frozen after baking.

Blueberry Muffins

Average
12 Muffins

2 cups flour
½ cup sugar
2 teaspoons baking powder
½ teaspoon salt
2 cups fresh blueberries or frozen, thawed
1 cup milk
⅓ cup vegetable oil
1 egg, lightly beaten
1 teaspoon vanilla
   Sugar

- Preheat oven to 400°.
- In a large bowl combine flour, sugar, baking powder, and salt. Stir in blueberries.
- In another bowl whisk together milk, oil, egg, and vanilla.
- Make a well in the flour mixture and pour in milk mixture all at once. Stir quickly until ingredients are moistened. Do not overmix. Batter will be lumpy.
- Spoon batter into greased muffin tins and lightly sprinkle sugar on top.
- Bake 20-25 minutes. Let cool slightly before removing from muffin tin.
- Can be frozen after baking.

Morning Glorious Muffins

    2   cups flour
 1¼   cups sugar
    2   teaspoons baking soda
    2   teaspoons cinnamon
  ½   teaspoon salt
 1½   cups carrots, grated
 1½   cups apples, peeled and grated
  ¾   cup coconut, grated
  ½   cup dates, chopped
  ½   cup pecans, chopped
    3   eggs, lightly beaten
    1   cup vegetable oil
  ½   teaspoon vanilla

- Preheat oven to 375°.
- Combine flour, sugar, soda, cinnamon, and salt in a mixing bowl.
- In a second bowl combine carrots, apples, coconut, dates, and pecans. Stir in eggs, oil, and vanilla. Add to dry ingredients stirring until moistened.
- Spoon batter into paper-lined muffin tins.
- Bake 18-20 minutes.
- Can be frozen after baking.

Orange Raisin Muffins

  ½   cup unsalted butter, softened
    1   cup sugar
    2   eggs
    1   teaspoon baking soda
    1   cup buttermilk
    2   cups flour
  ½   teaspoon salt
    1   cup raisins
        Peel of one orange

Topping:
        Juice of 1 orange
  ¼   cup sugar

- Preheat oven to 400°.
- In a large bowl of an electric mixer, cream butter and sugar until smooth. Add eggs, one at a time, and beat until light and fluffy.
- In another bowl, add baking soda to buttermilk and set aside.
- Sift flour and salt together and add to the creamed mixture alternately with the buttermilk mixture. Stir just until mixed.
- In a food processor or blender, grind raisins and orange peel. Stir into batter.
- Spoon into greased muffin tins.
- Bake 12 minutes or until golden brown.
- Remove from oven and brush tops with orange juice and sprinkle with sugar.

Cranberry Muffins

Average
24 Medium Muffins

2 cups unbleached flour
1 cup whole wheat flour
4 teaspoons baking powder
1 teaspoon salt
½ teaspoon baking soda
⅔ cup butter, softened
1 cup sugar
2 eggs
1-1¼ cups milk
2 cups cranberries, coarsely
    chopped and tossed with ¼
    cup flour
    Grated peel of 2 medium lemons
4 tablespoons sugar

• Preheat oven to 375°.
• Grease and flour muffin tins.
• Sift first five ingredients together.
• Cream butter and sugar together in an electric mixer. Beat in eggs one at a time.
• By hand blend milk into batter alternately with dry ingredients. Stir in berries.
• Toss lemon peel with sugar.
• Pour batter into tins. Sprinkle with sugared lemon peel.
• Bake 25 minutes or until tops are golden.
• Can be frozen after baking.

Nice holiday hostess gift.

French Breakfast Muffins

Easy
12 Muffins

⅓ cup butter, softened
1 cup sugar
1 egg
1½ cups sifted flour
1½ teaspoons baking powder
¼ teaspoon salt
¼ teaspoon nutmeg
½ cup milk
1 teaspoon cinnamon
6 tablespoons butter, melted

• Preheat oven to 350°.
• Cream butter. Gradually add ½ cup of the sugar, beating until light and fluffy. Add egg and mix well.
• In a separate bowl, sift flour, baking powder, salt, and nutmeg. Add to creamed mixture alternately with ½ cup milk, beginning and ending with dry ingredients.
• Spoon into a greased muffin pan, filling two-thirds full. Bake at 350° for 25 minutes until lightly browned.
• Combine remaining ½ cup sugar and cinnamon.
• Remove muffins while still warm. Roll in melted butter, then in sugar mixture.
• Can be frozen after baking.

Angel Biscuits
Heritage of Hospitality

5	cups flour
1	teaspoon salt
3	teaspoons baking powder
1	teaspoon soda
¼	cup non-fat dry milk powder
¼	cup sugar
1	cup shortening
2	cups buttermilk
1	(1-ounce) package dry yeast
2	tablespoons warm water

- Preheat oven to 400°.
- Sift together dry ingredients. Cut in shortening with a pastry blender. Blend in buttermilk.
- Soften yeast in warm water. Add to flour mixture. Blend thoroughly.
- Turn out onto a lightly floured board. Roll out to ⅛-inch thickness. Cut with a small biscuit cutter.
- Place on greased baking sheet. Bake for 8-10 minutes or until done.
- Dough can be stored, covered, in refrigerator for up to a week. Bake until completely risen, but not browned, and freeze. Reheat and brown.

Bunker Hill Brown Bread

1½	cups flour
1½	teaspoons salt
2	teaspoons baking soda
1	cup wheat germ
1	cup graham cracker crumbs
2	eggs
½	cup vegetable oil
1	cup molasses
2	cups buttermilk

- Preheat oven to 350°.
- Sift flour, salt, and soda into a mixing bowl. Add wheat germ and graham cracker crumbs. Stir to combine.
- In a second bowl combine eggs, vegetable oil, molasses, and buttermilk. Blend.
- Add liquid ingredients to dry ingredients. Stir until well blended.
- Pour batter into 2 well-greased and floured tall one-pound coffee cans (or prepared Bundt pan).
- Bake for 50-55 minutes or until bread tests done.

An easy bread with a delicious flavor. Spread with cream cheese or serve plain.

43

Pita Bread

Average
20 Standard Sized Pitas
40 Cocktail Sized Pitas

2   (1-ounce) packages yeast
¼   teaspoon sugar
2   cups water, 105-110°
6   cups flour, unbleached
1   teaspoon salt
¼   cup olive oil
    Corn meal

- Place yeast and sugar in ½ cup of the warm water. Stir to dissolve. Let stand in a warm area for 5 minutes to proof.
- Place 2 cups of the flour in a large mixing bowl. Stir in salt. Add the proofed yeast. Stir in remaining warm water. Add olive oil and stir to mix.
- Add remaining flour, 1 cup at a time, until dough is smooth and elastic, but not dry.
- Shape into a ball, cover, and let rise until doubled in bulk (about 1½ hours). When doubled, punch down and let rest for 10 minutes.
- Divide into balls 2½ ounces each for standard sized pitas or 1-ounce balls for cocktail sized pitas. Cover and let rest for 20-30 minutes.
- Flatten each ball with rolling pin and roll to ⅛-inch thickness. Dust baking sheets with corn meal and place circles on the corn meal.
- Cover and let rest again for 30 minutes.
- To bake, place in a 500° preheated oven on the lowest rack of the oven for about 3½ minutes or until puffed. Transfer sheet to top rack and continue baking for 2½ to 3 minutes or until lightly browned.
- Remove pitas from baking sheets immediately to prevent a crisp crust from forming. The pitas will deflate upon cooling.
- Can be frozen when cool.

Pita bread recipe to be used when making Party Lamb Pitas, page 142.

Zucchini Bread

3   eggs
2   cups sugar
1   cup vegetable oil
½   teaspoon salt
1   teaspoon baking powder
1   teaspoon soda
1   teaspoon cinnamon
1   teaspoon vanilla
1   teaspoon nutmeg
⅛   teaspoon ground cloves
3   cups flour, sifted
2   cups zucchini, unpared and shredded
1   cup walnuts, chopped
    Zest of one orange, grated
¼   cup milk

- Preheat oven to 350°.
- In a large mixing bowl, mix first 10 ingredients at medium speed for 1-2 minutes.
- Gradually blend in flour.
- Add zucchini, walnuts, grated zest of orange, and milk. Mix until just incorporated.
- Pour mixture into 2 greased and floured 9x3½x2-inch pans or 1 greased and floured 10-inch Bundt pan.
- Bake at 350° for 45 minutes if loaf pans, and for 1 hour, 15 minutes if Bundt pan.

Apricot Nut Bread

1   cup dried apricots, chopped
1½   cups sugar
2   tablespoons margarine
1   egg, beaten
½   cup fresh orange juice
2   cups flour
2   teaspoons baking powder
½   teaspoon soda
½   teaspoon salt
1   cup pecans, chopped

- Soak apricots in warm water for 20 minutes.
- Cream 1 cup sugar and margarine.
- Add egg and mix well.
- Stir in ½ cup sugar and orange juice.
- Sift flour, baking powder, soda, and salt.
- Add dry ingredients to sugar mixture; blend well.
- Drain apricots.
- Stir apricots and nuts into batter.
- Bake in greased and floured 5x9-inch loaf pan at 350° for 60-65 minutes, or bake 25 minutes at 350° in three 5x3-inch greased, floured, small loaf pans.

While still warm, you can glaze with icing of powdered sugar and orange juice. Wrapped in clear cellophane and tied with ribbons, the small loaves make special individual gifts.

Poppy Seed Bread

Average
2 Loaves

2 eggs
¾ cup vegetable oil
1½ cups sugar
1 tablespoon poppy seeds
1 tablespoon vanilla
1 tablespoon butter flavoring
1 teaspoon almond extract
1 cup milk
2 cups flour
1 teaspoon baking powder

Glaze:
¼ cup orange juice
¾ cup sugar
½ teaspoon vanilla extract
½ teaspoon butter flavoring
½ teaspoon almond extract

- Preheat oven to 350°.
- Combine all ingredients in the bowl of an electric mixer. Blend 2 minutes.
- Pour batter into 2 loaf pans.
- Bake one hour or until bread tests done.
- Combine glaze ingredients in a mixing bowl. Stir to dissolve sugar.
- Pour over warm loaves while in pans and let stand at least 20 minutes.

Strawberry Nut Bread
Casey Sinkledam, Master Pastry Chef

Easy
2 Loaves

4 eggs
1 cup oil
2 cups sugar
2 (10-ounce) packages frozen sliced strawberries, thawed
3 cups flour
1 tablespoon cinnamon
1 teaspoon baking soda
1 teaspoon salt
1¼ cups nuts, chopped

- Preheat oven to 350°.
- In a bowl, beat eggs until fluffy. Add oil, sugar, and strawberries and blend.
- In a separate large bowl, sift together flour, cinnamon, soda, and salt. Add strawberry mixture and mix until well blended. Stir in nuts.
- Pour into two greased and floured 9½x5x3-inch or 8½x4½x2½-inch loaf pans.
- Bake for 1 hour and 10 minutes or until done. Cover loosely with foil if bread begins to brown too much.
- Cool in pans for 10 minutes, then turn out of pans and cool on racks.

Bread slices best when chilled. Serve with whipped cream cheese or use to make tea sandwiches.

Whole Wheat Bread

4 cups whole wheat flour
½ cup light brown sugar, packed
2 (1-ounce) packages yeast
3 tablespoons white sugar
1 tablespoon salt
1½ cups water
¾ cup milk
¼ cup shortening
2-2½ cups flour, unsifted

- Preheat oven to 350°.
- Mix first five ingredients in the bowl of an electric mixer.
- In a small saucepan, heat water, milk, and shortening until warm and shortening is melted.
- Add liquid to dry ingredients and mix on low speed until moistened.
- Beat on medium speed for 2 minutes.
- Stir in 1½ cups white flour, knead 10 minutes adding remaining 1 cup of flour as needed. (Use dough hook on mixer or knead white flour in by hand.)
- Place dough in greased bowl and cover with a towel.
- Place bowl in oven with a pan of hot water. Let rise for 1-1½ hours.
- Beat down dough, divide in half, and place in 2 greased loaf pans. Dough should touch the ends of pans. Let rise for 40 minutes.
- Bake 35-40 minutes until bread tests done.
- Bread may be frozen after baking.

Dilly Bread

1 package dry yeast
¼ cup warm water
2 tablespoons sugar
1 cup cottage cheese
1 tablespoon instant minced onion
1 tablespoon butter, melted
2 teaspoons dill seed
1 teaspoon salt
¼ teaspoon baking soda
1 egg, beaten
2½ cups flour
Butter (optional)

- Preheat oven to 350°.
- Soften yeast in water and sugar.
- Warm cottage cheese to lukewarm. Combine with onion, butter, dill, salt, baking soda, egg, and softened yeast in the bowl of an electric mixer. Blend to combine ingredients. Add flour to form a stiff dough.
- Place dough in a greased bowl. Cover and let rise until double in bulk (50-60 minutes).
- Stir down dough. Turn into a well-greased loaf pan. Let rise until double (35-40 minutes).
- Bake 40-50 minutes. Cool slightly, turn loaf out, and brush top with butter if desired.

Whole Wheat Seed Bread

Average
2 Loaves

2 cups warm water
2 packages dry yeast
2 tablespoons honey
2½ cups unbleached flour
3½ cups whole wheat flour
½ cup yellow corn meal
2 teaspoons salt
½ cup hot water, 115°
½ cup molasses
2 tablespoons corn oil
1¼ cups sunflower seeds, raw, shelled
¼ cup poppy seeds
¼ cup sesame seeds

- Grease 2 loaf pans.
- In large bowl combine warm water, yeast, and honey.
- Stir until yeast is dissolved.
- Stir 1 cup unbleached flour and 1 cup whole wheat flour into yeast mixture. Set aside until light and bubbly, about 20 minutes.
- Add 2½ cups whole wheat flour, corn meal, salt, hot water, molasses, and corn oil. Mix well.
- Stir in sunflower, poppy, and sesame seeds.
- Mix in 1½ cups unbleached flour.
- Turn dough out onto lightly floured surface; knead until elastic, about 10 minutes.
- Transfer dough to greased bowl. Turn to grease top. Cover with plastic wrap; let rise until double, approximately 1 hour.
- Punch down and let rise until double again, approximately 1 hour.
- Punch down again. Transfer dough to a lightly floured surface. Divide in half. Shape into 2 loaves. Arrange seam side down in loaf pans. Let rise until almost double.
- Bake 40-45 minutes or until loaves sound hollow when tapped. Remove from pans and cool on a wire rack.
- This bread freezes well for up to 3 months.

If you are into bread making, this is a wonderful recipe!

Spray plastic wrap with vegetable shortening spray to cover already shaped yeast bread and rolls for the final rising. This will prevent sticking.

Fresh Loaf Bread

Average
2 Medium Loaves

½   stick margarine
½   cup sugar
2   teaspoons salt
2   cups scalded milk
1   egg, beaten
1   (1-ounce) package yeast
1   teaspoon sugar
¼   cup warm water
6-7   cups flour

- In a large dough bowl (or electric mixer), combine margarine, sugar, and salt. Add scalded milk. Stir until shortening is melted and mixture is cooled to lukewarm. Stir in egg.
- Dissolve yeast and sugar in warm water. Add to cooled milk mixture.
- Gradually stir in enough flour to make a stiff dough. Beat or knead until smooth.
- Place dough in a lightly greased bowl. Grease top, cover, and let rise until double (approximately 1 hour). Knead lightly and shape dough into two loaves. Cover and let rise once again until double (approximately 1 hour).
- Bake loaves in a preheated 350° oven for 45 minutes.

This bread may be made with all-purpose flour or half all-purpose and half whole wheat. It makes delicious toast!

Egg washes for bread:
—whole egg beaten with 1 teaspoon milk gives a shiny medium-brown glaze.
—Egg yolk beaten with 1 teaspoon milk gives the shiniest, brownest glaze.
—Egg white beaten with 1 teaspoon water gives shine without browness.

49

Date Twists

1   (13¾-ounce) package hot roll mix
1½ cups dates, chopped
⅓   cup water
½   cup brown sugar
¾   cup nuts, chopped

Topping:
1½ cups powdered sugar, sifted
2   tablespoons milk
1   teaspoon vanilla

- Prepare hot roll dough according to directions; let rise as directed.
- Combine dates, water, brown sugar. Cook over low heat for 10 minutes, stirring.
- Remove from heat and stir in nuts.
- Roll out dough on floured surface to 18 inches x 12 inches.
- Spread dough with date filling.
- Fold dough over in thirds, lengthwise.
- Cut in 16 strips. Twist each strip twice.
- Place on greased cookie sheet.
- Let rise 1 hour.
- Bake at 375° for 15-20 minutes.
- Combine powdered sugar, milk, vanilla, and drizzle over warm twists.

Fennel Breadsticks

2   packages dry yeast
1   tablespoon sugar
1½ cups warm water
2   teaspoons salt
¼   cup olive oil
1   tablespoon fennel seed
3-4 cups flour
    Cornmeal
1   egg yolk, beaten with 1 tablespoon water

- In a large mixing bowl, combine yeast with sugar and warm water to proof. Beat in salt, olive oil, and fennel seed. Add flour, 1 cup at a time, until a soft dough is formed. Remove to a floured surface and knead until smooth, 5-10 minutes.
- Preheat oven to 300°.
- Let dough rest, covered with a damp towel, for 5 minutes. Shape into a long roll, 20-22 inches in length. Cut into 20-24 pieces. Rest, covering again, 3-4 minutes. Roll out each piece, using hands, into sticks about 8 inches long. Arrange on greased baking sheets sprinkled with corn meal and let rise, covered, 20 minutes. Brush with egg yolk mixture and bake 30 minutes until medium brown.

Carolina Cheese Bread

Difficult
1 Loaf

2 pounds Havarti or Tilister cheese, grated
3 tablespoons butter, melted
2 eggs
½ teaspoon white pepper
Pirozhki Yeast Dough (recipe follows)
Cornmeal
2 tablespoons heavy cream
1 egg

- Combine cheese, butter, eggs, and pepper.
- On a lightly floured surface, punch the dough down and roll out into a 20-inch circle. Fold the circle lightly into quarters and put the center of the folded circle in the center of a 9-inch pie plate that has been buttered and sprinkled with corn meal.
- Unfold the dough over the plate, letting excess dough hang over the edge. Press the dough lightly into the plate.
- Spread the cheese filling over the dough, mounding it slightly in the center. Lift sides of dough into loose, even folds. Gather the ends of dough in center and twist them into small knot.
- Let dough rise, covered, in warm place 20 minutes.
- Preheat oven to 350°.
- Beat cream and egg together. Brush over dough and bake 1 hour 10 minutes, or until golden.
- Let the bread cool in pan for 10 minutes. Transfer to a bread board and serve hot, cut into wedges.

Pirozhki Yeast Dough

1 envelope active dry yeast
¼ cup lukewarm water
1 teaspoon sugar
¾ cup milk, scalded
1 stick butter, cut into pieces
2 tablespoons sugar
1½ teaspoons salt
4 cups flour
2 eggs
1 egg yolk
Melted butter

- In a small bowl, combine yeast, water, and sugar. Stir to dissolve and let stand 10 minutes.
- In large bowl, combine milk, butter, sugar, and salt. Stir until butter melts. Cool until lukewarm.
- Stir in 2 cups flour and beat until smooth.
- Add yeast mixture, eggs, and egg yolk and lightly beat for 2 minutes.
- Turn dough out onto a lightly floured surface. Knead in 2 cups flour (or enough to make a soft dough) and continue to knead for 10 minutes, or until smooth and satiny.
- Form dough into a ball and place in a buttered bowl. Brush the top with melted butter. Cover bowl with plastic wrap. Chill dough for at least 4 hours or overnight.

Served hot, the cheese is melted like Welsh Rarebit. Add a salad to make a complete meal. The baked bread freezes perfectly.

51

French Bread

½ cup milk
1½ cups water
1 tablespoon sugar or honey
1 tablespoon butter
1½ teaspoons salt
5 cups flour
1 package yeast
Cornmeal
1 teaspoon cornstarch
½ cup water

- In a saucepan, combine milk, water, sugar or honey, butter, and salt. Heat until just warm enough to melt butter.
- In a mixer, combine 2 cups of the flour with yeast. Blend.
- Pour warm milk/water mixture into flour and blend at medium high speed for 2 minutes. Add enough of remaining flour to make a sticky dough.
- Sprinkle work surface with flour. Turn out dough and knead in enough flour to make a smooth, springy ball.
- Place dough in a lightly greased bowl. Cover with a damp cloth and let rise until double in bulk (45-60 minutes).
- When bread has doubled, punch down and knead lightly. Divide into three pieces. Roll each section into an oval approximately 15x4-inches. Roll up each jelly roll fashion into a baguette. Pinch seams to seal.
- Lightly grease baguette pans and sprinkle with cornmeal. Place loaves in the pan. Slash each diagonally four to six times with a serrated knife. Cover with a linen towel and let rise until double (45-60 minutes).
- When bread is ready to bake, dissolve cornstarch in cold water. Heat mixture until milky and slightly thickened. Paint each loaf with mixture. Bake in a preheated 375° oven for 30 minutes or until golden.

Bragg Bread

Reynolda House, Museum of American Art

White Bread:

- 3 tablespoons yeast
- ⅓ cup sugar
- 3 cups warm water
- 2 eggs
- ⅓ cup corn oil
- 2 tablespoons salt
- 1 teaspoon ginger
- 3 cups flour (plus)

Herb Bread:

Same ingredients as white bread plus:

- ½ cup onion, finely chopped
- ½ cup parsley, finely chopped
- 6 cloves garlic
- 1 tablespoon rosemary, ground with mortar and pestle
- 1 teaspoon dill weed

Raisin Bread:

Same ingredients as white bread except use whole wheat flour or ½ whole wheat and ½ white

- 1 box raisins
- 1 tablespoon cinnamon

White Bread:

- In a large bowl, mix yeast and sugar with the warm water. Stir until sugar is dissolved (honey or molasses may be substituted).
- In a separate bowl, mix eggs, oil, salt, and ginger.
- When yeast produces a foam, add flour until mixture is fairly dry. More flour may be added to reach this stage.
- Add contents of second bowl (eggs, oil, salt, and ginger) to yeast mixture and work by hand adding flour until a dough ball is produced. (May add up to as much as 2 additional cups of flour.)
- Transfer dough ball to a larger bowl which has been greased with corn oil, for rising. Cover with plastic wrap and place in a warm spot or on top of the stove which has been turned on to warm.
- When the dough has doubled in size, place it on a floured work table and knead 100 times.
- Divide the dough into three loaf pans which have been sprayed with a no-stick cooking spray. Cover with plastic wrap for second rising.
- Preheat oven to 350°.
- When loaves double in size, place in oven and bake until brown.

Herb Bread and Raisin Bread:

- Bake in preheated 325° oven until bread is brown.

When making the Herb or Raisin Bread, mix in the herbs and/or raisins in the second bowl with the eggs and oil, and then follow the same procedure.

Julia Ross' Moravian Sugar Cake
Heritage of Hospitality

2   envelopes dry yeast
⅓   cup plus ½ teaspoon sugar
1   cup warm water (110°)
2   tablespoons dry skim milk
     powder
2   tablespoons dehydrated potato
¾   teaspoon salt
2¾ cups flour, unsifted
2   eggs
⅓   cup butter or margarine, melted
     and cooled

Topping:
⅔   cup brown sugar (packed)
1   teaspoon cinnamon
½   cup butter or margarine, melted
     and cooled

- In a mixing bowl, sprinkle yeast and ½ teaspoon sugar into warm water; stir to dissolve.
- When yeast begins to foam, add skim milk powder, potato, ⅓ cup sugar, salt, and ¾ cup flour. Beat 2 minutes on medium speed.
- Add eggs, butter, and 1 cup flour. Beat 2 minutes on high speed.
- Add 1 cup flour. Mix by hand with a wooden spoon. This will make a very soft dough.
- Cover and put in a warm place to rise until doubled in bulk, about 1 hour. Beat down and let rise again for 30 minutes.
- Stir down the dough and spread in a greased, shallow pan, about 17x12x1-inch deep. Let rise until doubled.
- Mix together brown sugar and cinnamon. Spread evenly over the top of the dough.
- Make indentations in the dough with the fingertips and dribble butter.
- Bake at 375° for 15 minutes or until done.

Fruit Punch

Easy
2¼ gallons

6   cups water
4   cups sugar
1   (46-ounce) can pineapple juice
4   cups orange juice
    Juice of 2 lemons
6   bananas, mashed
3   quarts 7-Up

• Combine water and sugar in a saucepan. Boil 3 minutes. Remove from heat.
• Add fruit juices and banana. Freeze.
• When ready to serve, thaw slightly and mash to a slushy consistency.
• Add 7-Up and serve.

The addition of rum gives this delicious drink extra punch!

Mint Tulips

Easy
2 Gallons

1½   cups water
     Handful of mint leaves
1½   cups sugar
2½   cups lemon juice
8   (28-ounce) bottles of ginger ale
     Sprigs of fresh mint

• Heat water and pour over mint leaves.
• Dissolve sugar in hot water.
• Steep 30 minutes to 2 hours. Strain out leaves.
• Add lemon juice and ginger ale when ready to serve.
• Pour over ice and serve with sprig of mint in each glass as garnish.

A refreshing beverage served at the historic Chatwood Inn in Hillsboro, North Carolina.

Children's Punch

Easy
1 Gallon

1   quart pineapple juice
1   quart orange juice
1   quart lemonade
1   (33.8-ounce) bottle ginger ale, chilled

• Combine first 3 ingredients.
• Gently stir in ginger ale just before serving. Serve over crushed ice.

Selfridge's Tea Room Tomato Juice

Easy
1¾ Quarts

1 (48-ounce) can tomato juice
¼-⅓ cup A-1 sauce
2 tablespoons mustard
1 teaspoon salt
⅓ cup vinegar
2 teaspoons Worcestershire sauce
5 tablespoons powdered sugar
⅓ cup chili sauce
¾ cup water
1 clove garlic

• Combine all ingredients and mix well.
• Chill, preferably overnight.
• Remove clove of garlic before serving.

Mulled Cider

Easy
1 Gallon

6-8 whole cloves
1 teaspoon dried orange peel
2-3 sticks cinnamon
Orange slices
Lemon slices
1 gallon apple cider
½ cup brown sugar
⅓ cup lemon juice concentrate

• Tie cloves, orange peel, cinnamon, orange and lemon slices in bag.
• Heat all ingredients together and allow to simmer at least 30 minutes (the longer the better).

Optional: Add 2 cups apple brandy just before serving.

Hot Percolator Punch

Easy
16 Servings

1 quart apple juice
1 pint cranberry juice cocktail
1 pint orange juice
¼ cup sugar
1 teaspoon whole allspice
1 teaspoon whole cloves
3 cinnamon sticks

• Combine juices in percolator.
• Place everything else in basket; perk and serve.

Pappa's Punch

2	cups bourbon
2	cups water
1¼	cups sugar
1	cup fresh lemon juice
	Rinds of 3 lemons

- Combine first four ingredients. Stir until sugar dissolves.
- Add lemon rinds.
- Store overnight in an airtight container. (Do not refrigerate.)
- Remove lemon rinds.
- Serve over finely crushed ice.

Sangria

1	large orange, peeled in a spiral, juiced
2	small limes or lemons, thinly sliced
	Juice of 1 lime or lemon
2	bottles chilled red wine (4/5 quart each)
¼	cup sugar, optional
1	quart bottle sparkling soda or water, chilled
½	cup triple sec
½	cup brandy

- In large glass bowl, add first five ingredients.
- Chill 4 hours.
- Just before serving add soda, triple sec, and brandy.

Mary's Dubonnet Fizz

32	ounces cranberry juice cocktail
2	quarts Dubonnet
1½	quarts ginger ale

- Chill all ingredients for several hours.
- Mix together in large punch bowl or glass pitcher.
- Serve immediately.

For a special effect freeze some of the cranberry cocktail in a ring or in cubes and let float in punch. A great holiday punch!

Strawberry Margarita Sorbet

Average
4 Cups

1	cup water
1	cup sugar
2	pints fresh strawberries, washed and capped
4-8	tablespoons fresh lime juice
3-6	tablespoons tequila
2-4	tablespoons triple sec
	Mint leaves

- In a saucepan bring the water and sugar to a boil.
- Remove from heat; chill.
- Purée berries in food processor.
- Add lime juice, tequila, triple sec, and chill.
- Combine sugar syrup and berry mixture; freeze until firm.
- Remove from freezer and purée in food processor.
- Refreeze until firm.
- Serve as sorbet or soft as a margarita, garnished with mint leaves.

Peach Margarita

Easy
2 Servings

1	large fresh ripe peach
2	ounces tequila
1	ounce triple sec
1	ounce fresh lime juice
2	peach slices for garnish

- Place all ingredients in blender with ice.
- Blend until smooth.
- Garnish with peach slices.

Frozen Toasted Almond

Easy
1 Serving

1	ounce amaretto
½	ounce kahlua
¾-1	cup vanilla ice cream

- Place all ingredients in blender and blend until thick.

Great after dinner drink or cool summer drink.

Lovefeast Coffee
Heritage of Hospitality

1   pound coffee, tied in a bag
3   gallons boiling water
2   pounds sugar
1   quart milk

- Drop the bag of coffee into the boiling water. Reduce heat and let stand without boiling about 15 minutes, stirring bag through the water with a wooden spoon now and then.
- Remove the coffee bag when the liquid is strong enough. Stir in sugar until dissolved.
- Add milk and keep hot until ready to serve.

Coffee was made by the open-kettle method before the coffee urn was used. In each Moravian congregation, the man who made the coffee held a status like that of a master craftsman, for it was his taste alone which determined the strength of the coffee.

Southern Plantation Eggnog

24   eggs
1½   cups sugar
2¼   cups Captain Apple Jack Brandy (100 proof)
1   cup Myers's rum
1   pint heavy cream
   Nutmeg for garnish

- In a large pot, beat egg yolks, reserving egg whites, until light and cream-colored.
- Add sugar gradually, beating until completely dissolved.
- Add brandy, constantly, slowly beating.
- Add rum and blend.
- Beat egg whites until very stiff. Fold into mixture until well blended.
- Chill eggnog to mellow from 4-6 hours. Do not stir.
- Just before serving, whip cream to a custard consistency, not stiff, and fold gently into eggnog.
- Serve with sprinkled nutmeg on each cup.

The secret to good eggnog is the chilling 4-6 hours and the addition to rum which mellows it. Cheers!

Minted Ice Tea

Easy
8 Servings

1   cup fresh mint leaves and stems,
     tightly packed
4   tea bags, regular size
4   cups boiling water
     Ice cubes
     Fresh mint sprigs and lemon
      slices for garnish

- Wash mint leaves/stems and put in large pitcher.
- Crush gently with back of a spoon.
- Add the tea bags.
- Pour the boiling water over mint and tea bags. Let steep 15-20 minutes.
- Remove mint and tea bags.
- Add enough ice cubes to yield 8 cups of liquid.
- Serve with fresh mint sprigs and lemon slices.

Making an ice ring: Use boiled water so the ice will be clear.

Salem College Iced Tea

Salem College

Easy
1 Gallon

4   sprigs fresh mint
8-12 whole cloves
3   quarts water
1   ounce tea
     Juice of 8 lemons
     Juice of 6 oranges
1   (46-ounce) can pineapple juice
1   cup sugar
     Thin lemon slices or sprigs of
      mint

- Add mint and cloves to water and bring to a boil.
- Simmer for 10-15 minutes.
- Add tea and allow to steep for 10-15 minutes.
- Strain, while hot; add fruit juices and sugar. This step is important.
- Stir to dissolve sugar.
- Serve chilled, garnished with lemon slices or sprigs of mint.

Champagne Party Punch

Easy
26 (6-ounce) Servings

     Prepared ice ring
2   quarts champagne
8   ounces brandy
1   quart sauterne wine
2   quarts ginger ale

- Make ice ring by freezing seasonal fruits and water in a circular mold.
- Just before serving, add all liquids to a punch bowl and mix. Add ice ring and serve.

soups & salads

The Best of SECCA Santa Luncheons

Gazpacho with Fennel Breadsticks
Spanakopeta
Citrus Fruit with Honey-Celery Seed Dressing
Individual Chocolate Soufflés

"Dimensional Display" by Deb Fanelli, a site specific installation of wood and graphite exhibited at the Southeastern Center for Contemporary Art.

The visually stimulating contrast of an English-style manor house and a modern glass-enclosed exhibition wing welcomes visitors to the Southeastern Center for Contemporary Art (SECCA). Founded in 1956, SECCA features the work of nationally recognized painters, sculptors, printmakers, and other artists from 11 southern states.

Located in the home of former textile industrialist James G. Hanes, the organization sponsors approximately 50 exhibitions each year. SECCA is also well known for a comprehensive and diverse schedule of public education programs.

Photo by Smith/Weiler/Smith

Mexican Meatball Soup

Average
12 Servings

1½ pounds ground chuck
1 cup fresh bread crumbs
1 egg, beaten
3 tablespoons fresh parsley, chopped
6 cloves garlic, minced
3 tablespoons fresh mint, minced (optional)
3 teaspoons salt
½ cup flour
6 tablespoons olive oil
1 green pepper, seeded and chopped
3 medium onions, finely chopped
4 cups hot water
1½ cups dry red wine
2 (28-ounce) cans whole tomatoes
1 tablespoon vinegar
2 teaspoons sugar
1 teaspoon dried oregano

- In a large bowl, combine meat, bread crumbs, eggs, parsley, three of the cloves garlic, mint, and 1½ teaspoons of the salt. Mix with fork or by hand. Form into 2-inch diameter balls.
- Roll meatballs in flour and brown in olive oil in large Dutch oven over moderate heat for 7 minutes. Remove from pan and set aside.
- Sauté pepper, onion, and remaining 3 cloves garlic in drippings for 7-10 minutes.
- Add remaining 1½ teaspoons salt and 6 remaining ingredients. Simmer, covered, for 30 minutes.
- Add meatballs, cover, and simmer for 1½ hours.

First serving is great for soup, and leftovers make a tasty meal over buttered vermicelli.

Mexichili

Easy
6 Servings

1½ pounds ground beef
1 (16-ounce) can kidney beans, drained
1 (15-ounce) jar mild enchilada sauce
1 (8-ounce) can tomato sauce
1 tablespoon minced onion
1 (6-ounce) package corn chips
8 ounces Cheddar cheese, shredded
1½ cups sour cream

- Preheat oven to 375°.
- In a skillet, brown the beef and drain well.
- In a large mixing bowl, combine beans, enchilada sauce, tomato sauce, and onion. Reserve 1 cup of corn chips and ½ cup of cheese, and add remaining chips and cheese to mixture along with the beef. Stir lightly to blend.
- Pour mixture into 2-quart casserole and bake, uncovered, for 30 minutes. Spread top of casserole with sour cream, sprinkle with reserved cheese, and ring remaining corn chips around edge. Return to oven 5 minutes.

Eggplant Supper Soup

Average
12 Servings

2   tablespoons olive oil
2   tablespoons butter
1   medium onion, chopped
1   pound ground chuck
1   medium eggplant, peeled and
      cubed
1   clove garlic, crushed
1   cup carrots, finely sliced
1   cup celery, chopped
2   (16-ounce) cans whole
      tomatoes
3½ cups beef broth
½   teaspoon nutmeg
1   teaspoon sugar
1   teaspoon salt
½   teaspoon pepper
½   cup barley or macaroni
2   tablespoons fresh parsley,
      minced
    Parmesan cheese for garnish

- Heat oil and butter in 6-8 quart Dutch oven. Add onion and sauté until light brown (about 8 minutes).
- Add meat and brown, draining fat.
- Add eggplant, garlic, carrots, celery, tomatoes (break up whole pieces), broth, nutmeg, sugar, salt, and pepper. Bring to a boil, reduce heat, cover, and simmer 2½ hours.
- 10-15 minutes before serving, add barley or macaroni and parsley. Simmer until barley or macaroni is cooked.
- Serve hot with Parmesan cheese sprinkled on top.

"Eggplant is mystery ingredient. No one would know!"

Sweet and Sour Beef Stew

1½   pounds beef stew meat (cut in bite-size pieces)
2   tablespoons vegetable oil
1   cup carrots, chopped
1   cup onion, chopped
1   (8-ounce) can tomato sauce
¼   cup brown sugar
¼   cup vinegar
1   tablespoon Worcestershire sauce
½   cup water
1   teaspoon salt
4   teaspoons cornstarch
¼   cup cold water
    Fresh chopped parsley

- Brown beef in hot oil.
- Add next 8 ingredients. Cover and cook over low heat until meat is tender, about 2 hours.
- Combine cornstarch and ¼ cup cold water. Add to beef mixture.
- Cook and stir until thick and bubbly.
- Serve over noodles or rice. Garnish with fresh chopped parsley.

Children love this hearty family dish.

To peel and chop an onion — Peel and leave root end in. Cut onion in half. Lay flat edge on work surface and slice horizontally several times, vertically several times, and then crosswise.

Italian Sausage Soup

24 ounces spicy Italian sausage,
    sliced ¼ inch thick
2 cloves garlic, minced
2 onions, chopped
1 (28-ounce) can whole tomatoes
1½ cups dry red wine
4 cups beef broth
¾ teaspoon basil
¾ teaspoon oregano
¾ teaspoon fennel
3 tablespoons fresh parsley,
    chopped
1 medium green pepper, seeded
    and chopped
2 medium zucchini, sliced ¼-inch
    thick
2 cups bow tie noodles
    Salt and pepper to taste
    Parmesan cheese for garnish

- In a large Dutch oven, cook sausage over medium heat until lightly browned (10 minutes). Remove from pan and drain all but 3 tablespoons fat from pan.
- Sauté garlic and onion in sausage fat until transparent.
- Add sausage and cook 2-3 minutes, stirring constantly.
- Add tomatoes, breaking apart, wine, beef broth, basil, oregano, and fennel. Simmer, uncovered, for 45 minutes. Skim excess fat from top.
- Soup may be held at this point until ready to serve.
- Before serving, add parsley, green pepper, zucchini, and noodles. Simmer for 20 minutes, until noodles are tender.
- Add salt and pepper as desired.
- Serve in large soup bowls with Parmesan cheese sprinkled on top.

Quick sautéed onions: Chop onions in food processor. Leave onions in work bowl, cover with plastic wrap, and transfer to microwave. Cook on high 30-90 seconds.

Peasant Soup

Average
10-12 Servings

1 veal shank with 2 pounds meat
2 quarts cold water
1 teaspoon salt
¼ teaspoon pepper
¼ cup vegetable oil
2 cloves garlic, minced
½ cup onion, chopped
½ cup green pepper, chopped
½ cup celery, chopped
1 cup fresh spinach, chopped
½ pound pepperoni, peeled and
     thinly sliced
2 cups potatoes, cubed
2 cups turnips, cubed
2 cups carrots, chopped
1 (10-ounce) package frozen peas
1 (28-ounce) can whole tomatoes,
     coarsely chopped, undrained
4 cups beef broth
2 cups macaroni shells
2 teaspoons salt
1 teaspoon basil
½ teaspoon pepper
   Parmesan cheese, grated

- Place veal shank in a stock pot with 2 quarts cold water. Add salt and pepper. Cover and bring to a boil. Reduce heat and simmer, covered, 2 hours.
- Cool meat in broth and remove from shank. Reserve meat; chill broth and discard shank. Skim fat from broth when chilled.
- Heat oil in a sauté pan. Add garlic, onion, and green pepper. Sauté until onion is golden. Add celery and chopped spinach. Cook until spinach is wilted.
- Reheat broth to a simmer. Add sautéed vegetables, pepperoni, potatoes, turnips, and carrots. Simmer, uncovered, 15-20 minutes.
- Add reserved veal, peas, tomatoes, beef broth, and macaroni. Season with salt, basil, and pepper. Continue to cook, uncovered, 20-30 minutes.
- Serve in large bowls topped generously with fresh grated Parmesan cheese.

Sprinkle chopping board with salt before chopping garlic. This helps to keep garlic flavor from being absorbed by the wood.

Sopa De Guadalajara

3 pounds boneless pork, trimmed and cut into one-inch cubes
1 tablespoon vegetable oil
1 cup onion, finely chopped
2 cloves garlic, minced
2-3 teaspoons chili powder
1 teaspoon oregano
1 teaspoon ground cumin
5 cups water
5½ cups beef broth
1 cup dried pinto or small red beans
4 cups carrots, thinly sliced
2 (4-ounce) jars baby corn on the cob, drained
Salt and pepper to taste

- In 5-quart kettle, brown meat in oil. When browned, push meat aside and add onion and garlic. Sauté until tender.
- Stir in chili powder, oregano, cumin, water, broth, and beans.
- Cover and simmer 1½ hours or until meat and beans are tender. (May be done ahead to this point. Cover and refrigerate.)
- Skim fat from broth and heat to boiling. Add carrots; cover and simmer 30 minutes or until tender.
- Stir in corn, salt and pepper to taste.
- Serve hot with condiments.

Condiments:
Cherry tomato halves
Sliced green onions
Fresh cilantro, chopped
Sour cream
Lime wedges
Parmesan cheese, grated

Warm, buttered corn tortillas are a nice accompaniment to this hearty soup.

Broccoli and Ham Soup

¼　cup onion, chopped
¼　cup celery, chopped
1　clove garlic, chopped (optional)
1　bunch fresh broccoli, cut into stems and pieces and florets
2　teaspoons lemon juice
4　cups chicken broth
3　tablespoons flour
1　cup milk
1　cup cooked ham, cubed
1　medium carrot, thinly sliced
2　tablespoons sour cream (optional)

- Place onion, celery, and garlic in a large soup pot. Add broccoli stems and pieces and lemon juice. Reserve florets. Cover with chicken broth and cook, uncovered, 15-20 minutes or until broccoli is tender.
- Purée and strain mixture. Return to pot.
- Dissolve flour into a small amount of the milk. Add to the soup with remaining milk. Bring to a boil. Stir until slightly thickened.
- Reduce heat. Add broccoli florets, ham, and carrots. Simmer for 5-7 minutes.
- For added richness, stir in sour cream just before serving.

New England Clam Chowder

4　slices bacon, diced
1½　cups onion, chopped
¼　cup flour
¼　cup carrots, grated
¼　cup celery, chopped
3　cups potatoes, peeled and diced
1　teaspoon salt
⅛　teaspoon pepper
　　Water
3　(6½-ounce) cans chopped clams
1　cup evaporated milk

- Cook bacon in large saucepan until slightly brown. Drain, reserving one tablespoon drippings and set aside bacon.
- Sauté onion in drippings until translucent. Stir in flour. Add bacon, carrots, celery, potatoes, salt, and pepper.
- Drain clams, reserving liquid. Add enough water to the clam juice to make 4½ cups.
- Stir liquid into the vegetable mixture and bring to a boil. Reduce heat and cook until vegetables are tender (about 20 minutes), stirring occasionally.
- Add clams and cook 5 minutes more.
- Add evaporated milk and reheat. Garnish with fresh chopped parsley.

Takes awhile, but everyone who eats it says it's the best. If preparing a day ahead, wait until ready to serve before adding clams and milk. A thick and rich chowder.

Crab and Mushroom Bisque

Easy
4 Servings

6	tablespoons butter
4	tablespoons onion, finely chopped
4	tablespoons green pepper, finely chopped
1	scallion, including top, coarsely chopped
2	tablespoons parsley, chopped
1	cup fresh mushrooms, sliced
2	tablespoons flour
1½	cups milk
1	teaspoon salt
⅛	teaspoon pepper
¼	teaspoon mace
	Dash hot sauce
1	cup half and half
1½	cups crabmeat, cooked
3	tablespoons dry sherry

- In medium skillet, heat 4 tablespoons of the butter. Add onion, green pepper, scallion, parsley, and mushrooms. Sauté until soft. Set aside.
- In large saucepan, heat remaining 2 tablespoons of butter; remove from heat. Stir in flour and gradually add milk. Cook, stirring constantly, over low heat until thickened and smooth.
- Stir in salt, pepper, mace, and hot sauce. Add sautéed vegetables and cream. Bring to a boil, stirring frequently.
- Reduce heat and add crabmeat. Simmer, uncovered, for 5 minutes.
- Just before serving, add sherry.

Chilled Shrimp and Cucumber Soup
Ryan's Restaurant

Average
6-8 Servings

3	cucumbers, peeled and seeded
1	small onion, coarsely chopped
½	bunch celery, trimmed, peeled, and coarsely chopped
½	pound frozen popcorn shrimp, thawed
2	tablespoons butter
½	teaspoon cajun spice mix or to taste
½	teaspoon dill weed
2	tablespoons butter, melted
2	tablespoons flour
4	cups half and half

- Purée cucumbers, onion, and celery individually in the bowl of a food processor. Combine all in a mixing bowl and set aside.
- Melt butter in a stock pot. Add shrimp and stir to coat. Season with cajun spice mix and dill weed.
- Whisk melted butter and flour together. Stir mixture into shrimp and cook over low heat for 1 minute.
- Slowly add half and half, stirring constantly. Add puréed mixture and simmer over low heat for 20 minutes, stirring occasionally. Remove from heat and chill completely before serving.

Shrimp-Okra Soup

¼   cup butter
½   pound cooked ham, diced
2   cups chicken breast, uncooked, diced
1   pound fresh okra, sliced
    or
2   (9-ounce) packages frozen okra, thawed
1½ cups onion, chopped
1   large green pepper, diced
1   clove garlic, minced
1   (2-pound, 3-ounce) can Italian tomatoes, chopped
3½ cups chicken broth
½   teaspoon salt
¼   teaspoon crushed red pepper
1   pound shrimp, uncooked, peeled, deveined

- Melt butter in 6-quart heavy saucepan.
- Add ham and chicken and cook over medium heat for 5 minutes, stirring frequently.
- Add okra, onion, and green pepper. Cook for 6 minutes more, stirring frequently.
- Add garlic, tomatoes, chicken broth, salt, and pepper. Bring to a boil. Reduce heat to low and cook for 45 minutes.
- Add shrimp and cook for 5-7 minutes (until shrimp is cooked).

Clam Bisque

4-6 slices of bacon
1   onion, chopped
1   large bell pepper, chopped
1   (10¾-ounce) can cream of potato soup, undiluted
1   (10-ounce) can chopped clams, drained
2   cups half and half
½   teaspoon salt
    Pepper to taste

- Fry bacon in heavy saucepan or Dutch oven. Remove bacon.
- Sauté onion and pepper in drippings until onion is translucent.
- Return crumbled bacon to pan. Add soup, clams, and half and half. Season with salt and pepper.
- Heat thoroughly, but do not boil.

Chicken Vegetable Soup

1   pound chicken breasts, skinned
     and boned
2   tablespoons butter
1   cup onion, chopped
2   cups potatoes, cut into ¼-inch
     cubes
2   cups turnips, cut into ¼-inch
     cubes
2   cups parsnips, cut into ¼-inch
     cubes
1½ cups carrots, diced
1   large leek, split, diced
5   cups chicken broth
     Salt and pepper to taste

- Cut chicken breasts into one-inch cubes. Set aside.
- Melt butter in a stock pot. Add onion and cook until wilted.
- Add chicken and all vegetables. Stir to blend and cook 2-3 minutes.
- Add broth and season with salt and pepper. Bring to a boil. Reduce heat and simmer, uncovered, 30-45 minutes.

After cooking a chicken, save the leftover broth for soup stock. Place stock with its fat in freezer. The fat will rise to the surface and once frozen, can be easily scraped off with a knife.

Mom's Chicken Soup

1   tablespoon vegetable oil
1   cup celery, diced
1   cup carrots, diced
1   cup onions, diced
1   clove garlic, minced (optional)
2   quarts chicken stock
4   cups diced, cooked chicken
½   cup noodles or rice

- Heat oil in a stock pot.
- Add celery, carrots, onions, and garlic if desired. Cover and cook over low heat for 10 minutes.
- Add stock. Bring to a boil and simmer, uncovered, for 10 minutes.
- Add chicken and noodles or rice. Simmer until noodles or rice are tender.

This has such a good flavor and will cure any cold.

Chicken-Apple Curry Soup

1 tablespoon butter
3 tart green apples, peeled and
   sliced
1 large onion, sliced
1 teaspoon curry powder
   Salt and pepper to taste
3 drops hot sauce
3 cups chicken broth
1 cup dry white wine
½ cup chopped, cooked chicken
1 cup half and half

• Melt butter in a saucepan. Add apples and onions and cook until soft. Stir often.
• Stir in curry powder and cook 3 minutes.
• Add salt, pepper, hot sauce, broth, and wine. Simmer, covered, for 10 minutes, stirring frequently. Cool.
• Add chicken.
• Place mixture in a blender and purée. Blend in half and half.
• Serve hot or chilled. Garnish with a sprig of watercress or a thin slice of green apple in each serving.

A delicious soup that may be doubled or tripled easily.

Turkey Vegetable Soup

¼ cup butter
2 medium onions, chopped
2 tablespoons flour
2 teaspoons curry powder
3 cups chicken broth
1 cup potatoes, cubed
½ cup carrots, thinly sliced
½ cup celery, chopped
2 tablespoons fresh parsley,
   chopped
½ teaspoon sage
2 cups turkey, cooked and cubed
1½ cups half and half
1 (10-ounce) package frozen
   chopped spinach, thawed
   Salt and pepper to taste

• Melt butter in large saucepan over medium high heat. Add onions and sauté until translucent (about 10 minutes).
• Stir in flour and curry and cook 2-3 minutes.
• Add broth, potatoes, carrots, celery, parsley, and sage and bring to a boil. Reduce heat to low, cover, and simmer for 10 minutes.
• Add turkey, half and half, and spinach. Cover and simmer until heated through (about 7 minutes).
• Season to taste with salt and pepper.

Great change for leftover turkey.

Brunswick Stew

2 (28-ounce) cans tomatoes, undrained
1 teaspoon baking soda
12 cups chicken broth
1 (5-pound) hen
3 pounds stew beef or round steak cut in 1-inch cubes
½ cup vinegar
¼ cup sugar
1 (14-ounce) bottle ketchup
½ cup Worcestershire sauce
Hot pepper sauce to taste
3 large baking potatoes, peeled and cubed
Salt to taste
½ cup butter
2 medium onions, sliced thinly
2 (16-ounce) cans butter beans, drained
2 (12-ounce) cans white shoepeg corn, drained
1-2 lemons, sliced very thinly
Fresh ground pepper to taste
½ cup fresh parsley, chopped

- Combine tomatoes and baking soda in a mixing bowl. Set aside.
- Place chicken broth, hen, and stew beef in a large stock pot. Add water to cover. Bring to a boil. Reduce heat, cover, and simmer slowly for 2 hours or until hen is very tender.
- Remove hen and beef from broth and cool. Degrease cooking liquid. Shred meats and return to cooking liquid.
- In a large saucepan combine tomatoes, vinegar, sugar, ketchup, Worcestershire sauce, hot pepper sauce, and potatoes. Season with salt to taste. Simmer on low, covered, 1 hour. Stir occasionally. Add to stew in broth.
- Melt butter in a sauté pan. Add onion and sauté until transparent. Add to the stew.
- Add remaining ingredients and simmer slowly, covered, 1-2 hours.
- Before serving remove cooked lemon slices. Serve in bowls.
- Stew may be made up to 2 days ahead and freezes well.

Sliced okra may be added.

To open jars with lids, use pointed end of "church key" to pop up the lid. This relieves pressure and makes jars easy to open.

72

Vichysquash

2 medium onions, chopped
3 tablespoons butter
12 medium yellow squash, sliced
1 cup chicken broth
  Salt and freshly ground pepper
    to taste
2 cups half and half
  Fresh chopped chives

- Sauté onion in butter in a large pan until wilted. Add squash and broth. Cover and cook briskly until squash is tender, about 15 minutes.
- Purée mixture in small batches in a food processor or blender. Season with salt and pepper. Chill thoroughly.
- Add half and half.
- Serve soup in chilled bowls. Garnish with fresh chopped chives. May be served hot. Do not boil after adding half and half.

Acorn Squash Bisque

3 tablespoons butter
¼ cup carrots, chopped
1 cup onion, chopped
2 medium potatoes, cubed
2 acorn squash, peeled, chopped
4 cups chicken broth
1 cup heavy cream
  Salt and white pepper to taste
  Dash cayenne

- Melt butter in saucepan. Add carrots and onions. Cover and cook for 10 minutes or until tender.
- Add potatoes, acorn squash, and chicken broth. Simmer, covered, for 25 minutes or until tender.
- Purée in food processor and return to saucepan.
- Add cream, salt, and white pepper. Cook until heated through. Sprinkle with cayenne.

Zucchini or yellow squash may be substituted to make a delicious summer soup!

Curried Zucchini Soup

1 pound zucchini, sliced, unpared
½ medium onion, sliced
1 tablespoon butter
2½ cups chicken broth
¼ teaspoon curry powder
½ teaspoon lemon juice
  Salt to taste

- Cook zucchini and onion with butter and ½ cup chicken broth in a covered saucepan until tender (about 10 minutes).
- Place mixture in a blender with remaining 2 cups chicken broth. Blend until smooth.
- Season with curry powder, lemon juice, and salt.
- Serve hot or cold.

Avocado Zucchini Soup

Easy
4 Servings

    1   cup zucchini, peeled and diced
    1   cup chicken broth
    1   medium ripe avocado, peeled,
          pitted, and cut into chunks
    ¼   cup onion, minced
    1½ cups plain yogurt
    ¼   cup fresh lime juice
        Salt to taste
    ½   teaspoon white pepper
    ¹⁄₁₆ teaspoon cayenne pepper
        Thin avocado slices and diced
          pimiento for garnish

- Purée first 4 ingredients in blender or food processor.
- Stir in the yogurt, lime juice, salt to taste, white pepper, and cayenne pepper.
- Refrigerate, covered, until very cold.
- Serve chilled. Garnish with avocado slices and pimiento.

Great summertime luncheon accompaniment with shrimp salad.

Zucchini Soup

Easy
6 Servings

    4   strips bacon, diced
    6   cups zucchini, unpared, chopped
    ½   teaspoon salt
    ¼   teaspoon pepper
    2   cloves garlic, minced
    ¼   teaspoon Italian seasonings
    1½ cups water
    1   (10½-ounce) can beef
          consommé

- Brown bacon in a saucepan. Remove all but one tablespoon of fat. Add zucchini and seasonings to bacon and cook until zucchini is tender.
- Purée in a blender or food processor.
- Return to saucepan. Add water and beef consommé. Simmer 15-20 minutes. Serve.

Very low in calories and freezes well.

Chilled Cucumber Soup with Fresh Dill

Easy
6-8 Servings

2 tablespoons butter
½ onion, diced
6 stalks celery, diced
½ leek, diced
4 medium cucumbers, peeled, seeded, and diced
2 cups white wine
1 cup chicken broth
2 cups heavy cream
1 cup sour cream
2 tablespoons fresh dill weed
Salt and pepper to taste

• Melt butter in a sauté pan. Add onion, celery, and leek. Cook until the onions are transparent.
• Combine sautéed vegetables with remaining ingredients in a blender. Purée soup and chill for several hours before serving.
• Garnish with a dollop of sour cream and a twig of dill on top.

Great in the summer on hot days.

Cheddar Chowder

Easy
8 Servings

2 tablespoons margarine
2 stalks celery, chopped
1 medium onion, chopped
6 medium potatoes, cubed
2 carrots, sliced
3 cups water
5 chicken-flavored bouillon cubes
¾ teaspoon seasoned salt
½ teaspoon thyme leaves
½ teaspoon rosemary, crushed
Dash pepper
Dash garlic powder
2 cups milk
2 cups Cheddar cheese, shredded

• Heat margarine in a Dutch oven. Add celery and onion and sauté until translucent. Add potatoes, carrots, water, bouillon, seasoned salt, thyme, rosemary, pepper, and garlic powder. Cover and simmer about 20 minutes or until vegetables are tender.
• Remove from heat and mash vegetables with a potato masher (or transfer vegetables with slotted spoon to food processor; process vegetables in several batches).
• Return puréed vegetables to liquid in Dutch oven. Add milk and cheese. Cook, stirring constantly, until cheese is melted. Soup may be thickened with instant potato flakes or thinned with milk. Do not bring to a boil after addition of milk and cheese.

Herbs make this a special potato soup!

75

Irena Kirshman's Minestrone
Heritage of Hospitality

2 cups beef broth
2 cups water
3 slices bacon, cut in small pieces
¼ small green cabbage, shredded
1 onion, chopped
1 clove garlic, crushed
2 carrots, chopped
2 stalks celery, chopped
Salt and pepper to taste
½ (10-ounce) package frozen chopped spinach, thawed and drained
or
½ pound fresh spinach
½ (10-ounce) package frozen green peas, thawed
1 (10-ounce) can navy beans
⅓ cup thin pasta (macaroni)
¼ teaspoon each of marjoram, thyme, and basil
1 cup fresh Parmesan cheese, grated

• In large heavy saucepan, bring broth and water to a boil. Add bacon, cabbage, onion, garlic, carrots, and celery. Salt and pepper to taste. Simmer, covered, about 15 minutes or until vegetables are almost tender.

• Add spinach, peas, beans, macaroni, and herbs. Simmer 8 minutes, covered, or until macaroni is tender.

• Serve hot with Parmesan cheese sprinkled on top.

Buttermilk substitute = ½ cup
¼ cup evaporated milk
¼ cup water
1½ teaspoons white vinegar
or
½ cup whole milk
½ teaspoon white vinegar

Green Split Pea Soup

1 ham bone
1 large onion, chopped
1 carrot, grated
8 cups water
1 pound green split peas, rinsed
1 pound bulk sausage, browned
   and drained
  Salt and pepper to taste

- Place ham bone, onion, and carrot in 8 cups water in 6-quart saucepan. Bring to a boil.
- Add peas and simmer 2-2½ hours. (If needed, add more water.) Stir often to prevent sticking.
- Remove bone and add sausage. Heat thoroughly.
- Season to taste.

Cream of Lettuce Soup

2 pounds Romaine lettuce
¼ cup green peas, fresh or frozen
6 tablespoons butter
½ cup green onions, minced
  Salt and pepper to taste
4 tablespoons flour
4 cups chicken broth, heated
  Generous pinch chervil
½-¾ cup heavy cream

- Wash, trim, and chop lettuce. Blanche in a large amount of salted boiling water, about 10 minutes. Add peas during the last 2 minutes. Drain.
- Melt butter in a stock pot. Add green onions and sauté until softened. Add lettuce mixture, salt and pepper. Cook stirring 2-3 minutes. Add flour and cook 2 minutes. Add chicken broth. Bring just to a simmer.
- Coarsely blend mixture in a blender or food processor.
- Return soup to pot. Season with chervil. Add cream.
- Soup may be served hot or cold garnished with shredded, blanched lettuce.

A wonderful soup and no one will ever guess it's lettuce!

Pumpkin Soup
Old Salem Tavern

Easy
4 Servings

4	tablespoons butter
1	clove garlic, minced
½	cup onion, finely chopped
1½	cups pumpkin purée
1½	cups chicken stock
½	teaspoon white pepper
2	tablespoons sherry
	Dash of hot sauce
½	tablespoon sugar
¼	teaspoon cloves
	Fresh grated nutmeg, to taste
1½	cups half and half
2	slices bacon, cooked until crisp

- In a Dutch oven, melt butter. Add garlic and onion and sauté until soft.
- Add remaining ingredients, except for bacon, and heat through.
- Serve hot, with bacon crumbled over top of soup.

Sour Cream and Mushroom Soup

Easy
6 Servings

3	tablespoons butter
¼	teaspoon nutmeg
½	teaspoon tarragon leaves
1	large onion, chopped
½	pound fresh mushrooms, sliced
¼	cup flour
3½	cups beef broth
1	cup sour cream
½	cup half and half
½	cup heavy cream
	Salt, pepper, dash hot sauce to taste
1	teaspoon lemon juice
	Paprika

- Melt butter in saucepan over medium heat. Add nutmeg and tarragon and cook 1 minute.
- Add onion and cook until tender. Add mushrooms and cook until tender, but still firm.
- Add flour and cook 3 minutes, stirring gently. Add beef broth and heat just to boiling.
- Reduce heat and stir in sour cream. Cook and stir until lumps dissolve.
- Add half and half and heavy cream. Stir in seasonings and lemon juice.
- Garnish with paprika.

Three-Potato Soup

3   medium potatoes, peeled and
    cubed
2   green onions, chopped
1   stalk celery, chopped
1   cup water
¼   teaspoon salt
1   (12-ounce) can evaporated milk
¼   cup butter
1   teaspoon dried parsley flakes
    Freshly ground pepper to taste
    Chopped green onions (optional
    garnish)

- Combine first 5 ingredients in a saucepan. Cover and cook 10 minutes or until potatoes are tender. (Do not drain).
- Mash vegetables slightly.
- Stir in evaporated milk, butter, parsley, and pepper to taste. Heat.
- Garnish with green onions, if desired.

Note: 2 cups of sharp Cheddar cheese may be added, if desired.

Puréed and chilled, this winter warmer can become a tasty vichyssoise. Garnish with snipped chives.

SECCA Santa Gazpacho

1   (28-ounce) can tomatoes,
    drained, liquid reserved
6   very ripe tomatoes, peeled,
    seeded, and chopped
3   tablespoons olive oil
3   tablespoons fresh parsley,
    chopped
1   clove garlic, chopped
1   medium-sized onion, chopped
2   tablespoons red wine vinegar
1   cup beef consommé
1   teaspoon salt
¼   teaspoon pepper

- Purée first seven ingredients. Pour purée in mixing bowl. Add consommé, salt, pepper, and reserved liquid. Chill well. Serve.
- Serve with Fennel breadsticks.

Easy Gazpacho

Easy
6-8 Servings

1   (10½-ounce) can beef broth
2½ cups tomato juice
3   tablespoons lemon juice
2   tablespoons onion, chopped
1   clove garlic, sliced
¼   teaspoon hot sauce
½   teaspoon salt
    Dash pepper
1   cup green pepper, chopped
1   cup tomatoes, chopped
1   cup cucumber, chopped
    Seasoned croutons
    Sour cream

- In a large jar or pitcher, combine broth, tomato juice, lemon juice, onion, garlic, hot sauce, salt, and pepper. Cover and shake (or stir) well.
- Chill for 4 hours. Remove garlic. Pour soup over chilled vegetables in bowls or mugs. Garnish with croutons and sour cream.

Good meal starter or quick light supper with sandwich.

Health Soup

Easy
8 Servings

1½ cups carrots, coarsely grated
1½ cups tomatoes, chopped
1½ cups cucumber, chopped
1½ cups green pepper, chopped
1   cup zucchini, grated
1   cup red onion, chopped
1   teaspoon hot sauce
2   cloves garlic, minced
3   cups V-8 juice
⅓   cup vegetable oil
2   tablespoons red wine vinegar
1   tablespoon lemon juice
1   teaspoon salt
    Croutons

- Combine all ingredients in a large plastic bowl with lid. Stir well. Chill at least 2 hours before serving. Garnish with croutons.

Lots of vitamins and fiber—virtually no calories.

Easy Onion Soup For Two

1 tablespoon butter or margarine
1 medium onion, chopped
2 cups beef broth
¼ cup water
 Salt and pepper to taste
¼ cup Madeira (optional)
 Parmesan croutons (see recipe)
¼-½ cup Swiss cheese, shredded

• Melt butter in a saucepan. Add onion; cover and cook 5 minutes.
• Uncover and continue cooking until onion is golden. Stir occasionally.
• Add broth and water; simmer 30 minutes. Season with salt and pepper. Stir in Madeira.
• Ladle soup into individual oven-proof dishes. Place a Parmesan crouton in each. Sprinkle with cheese. Bake at 400° for 15 minutes or until cheese is melted and bubbly.

Parmesan Croutons:

2 one-inch slices French bread
2 tablespoons butter, melted
2 tablespoons Parmesan cheese, grated
¼-½ cup Swiss cheese, grated

• Cut French bread slices in half.
• Brush both sides of bread with butter and sprinkle with Parmesan cheese.
• Place on a cookie sheet and bake 20 minutes at 350° until crisp and browned.

Super appetizer on a cold day. Just double or triple the recipe for more people.

Cabbage Soup

½ pound bacon, diced
2 cups onion, chopped
4 medium carrots, pared and cut in julienne strips
6 cups white cabbage, shredded
2 (10½-ounce) cans of beef consommé
3 cups water
1 teaspoon salt
 Pepper to taste

• Cook bacon in a large saucepan until crisp. Remove from pan and drain on paper towel. Reserve 2 tablespoons of bacon drippings.
• Sauté onion and carrots in reserved bacon drippings for 5 minutes.
• Add cabbage, consommé, water, salt, and pepper. Bring to a boil and simmer for 30 minutes or until cabbage is tender.
• Garnish with crisp bacon.
• Best served immediately.

Fresh Corn Chowder

4 medium potatoes, peeled, cubed
1 cup water
¼ teaspoon salt
6 strips bacon, diced
1 medium onion, chopped
1 medium green pepper, chopped
6 ears corn, cooked and cut from
   cob
3 cups milk
1 cup half and half
   Salt and pepper to taste

- Combine potatoes, water, and salt in a saucepan. Cover and cook 10-15 minutes or until tender. Drain.
- Cook bacon until crisp. Drain on paper towel. Remove all but 2 tablespoons of drippings from pan.
- Sauté onion in drippings. Add green pepper and continue to cook 1 minute. Add potatoes, corn, bacon, milk, and half and half. Season with salt and pepper. Heat, stirring, for about 5 minutes.

Chowder may be served as an appetizer in small cups. Serve a separate bowl of freshly popped, unsalted popcorn for guests to garnish their own cups of chowder.

Fresh Strawberry Soup

1 pint fresh strawberries, hulled
1 cup white wine
3 tablespoons honey
1 cup fresh orange juice
1 tablespoon fresh lemon juice
½ cup heavy cream
   Sliced strawberries and fresh
     mint for garnish

- Place first five ingredients in a blender. Blend at high speed for 1 minute.
- Add cream and blend to combine. Chill.
- Garnish with fresh sliced strawberries and a sprig of mint.

Fruit soups are served as a dessert in Scandinavia. In Germany and the United States they are often served as a summertime, chilled prelude to the entrée.

Cream of Spinach Soup
Zevely House Restaurant
Heritage of Hospitality

2 pounds fresh spinach, washed and ribbed
6 cups salted water
3 teaspoons granulated chicken or beef bouillon
3 cups milk
½ cup butter
1 teaspoon salt
1 teaspoon nutmeg
2 thick slices onion
3 tablespoons flour
Hard-boiled eggs, grated
Paprika

- Place spinach in salted water. Bring to a boil, simmer 5 minutes. Drain; reserve 3 cups of cooking liquid. Set aside.
- Blend spinach in food processor or blender to make a coarse paste (approximately 2 cups).
- Add bouillon to hot spinach stock. When bouillon is dissolved, add milk.
- In heavy saucepan, melt butter. Add salt and nutmeg. Sauté onion in butter 3 minutes. Remove onion.
- Add flour to butter while stirring. Gradually add milk, stock mixture, stirring vigorously. Continue to stir over medium heat until well blended.
- Add spinach paste. Beat well.
- Serve hot with grated hard-boiled eggs and paprika on top for garnish.

Wild Turkey Sandwich with Tarragon Dressing
Spring Garden Bar and Grill

Dressing:

1½	cups cream cheese, softened
1	cup mayonnaise
½	cup sour cream
⅛	cup lemon juice
¼	teaspoon salt
1½	tablespoons tarragon
1½	cucumbers, peeled, seeded, and chopped

- In a mixing bowl, combine first six ingredients and whip. Add cucumbers and mix.
- To make sandwich, spread dressing on both slices of bread; add turkey and cucumbers.

Sandwich:

	Oat or wheat bread, toasted
4	ounces turkey, cooked and sliced
3	cucumbers, peeled and sliced

Ham 'n Cheese Croissants

2	sticks margarine, softened
1	tablespoon Dijon mustard
3	tablespoons poppy seeds
1	tablespoon Worcestershire sauce
1	medium onion, finely chopped
8-10	croissants
8-10	slices ham
8-10	slices Swiss cheese

- Preheat oven to 325°.
- Blend margarine, mustard, poppy seeds, Worcestershire sauce, and onion in a medium bowl.
- Split croissants and spread margarine mixture on bottom half of each croissant. Place a slice of ham and slice of cheese on top of this.
- Bake on cookie sheet for 5 minutes and remove from oven.
- Spread margarine mixture on top half of each croissant and place top on sandwich.
- Bake an additional 5 minutes. Serve hot.

Good, quick sandwich that looks fancy and tastes great.

Baked Goat Cheese Salad

Easy
4 Servings

½ cup olive oil
4 sprigs fresh thyme
8 rounds goat cheese, cut ¾" thick
    from Montrachet log
¾ cup fine white bread crumbs
2 teaspoons fresh thyme, chopped
¼ teaspoon salt
    Pepper to taste
3 tablespoons balsamic vinegar
4 cups watercress (or available leaf
    lettuces, endive, spinach, or
    raddichio)

- Combine oil and sprigs of thyme. Pour over cheese rounds and marinate overnight.
- Preheat oven to 350°.
- Combine bread crumbs, chopped thyme, salt, and pepper in a bowl.
- Remove cheese from marinade, reserving marinade.
- Roll cheese rounds in bread crumb mixture. Place in baking dish and bake 15 minutes until crumbs are golden.
- Combine oil from marinade with vinegar and salt and pepper as desired.
- Toss oil and vinegar with salad greens.
- Serve four individual salad servings with two rounds of goat cheese on the side of each.

Do not wash mushrooms to clean. Brush away any dirt with paper towel moistened with lemon juice.

Watercress, Mushroom, and Endive Salad

Easy
4-6 Servings

Dressing:

1 tablespoon Dijon mustard
1 egg yolk
½ teaspoon garlic, minced
1 tablespoon red wine vinegar
2 tablespoons dry white vermouth
⅓ cup peanut oil
    Freshly ground pepper and salt
       to taste

- Combine mustard, egg yolk, and garlic in mixing bowl.
- Beat mixture with a wire whisk, while slowly adding the vinegar and vermouth.
- Gradually add oil, beating vigorously. Add salt and pepper. (Yield ¾ cup).

Salad:

½ pound mushrooms, sliced
1 bunch watercress, trimmed
2 cups endive, thinly sliced

- Combine mushrooms, watercress, and endive in salad bowl.
- Toss with salad dressing and serve.

Roasted Bell Pepper Salad or Sandwich
With Prosciutto and Provolone

Average
8 Servings

2   medium red bell peppers
8   croissants
8   pieces Boston lettuce
2   raddichio, broken into pieces
6   ounces prosciutto, thinly sliced
6   ounces provolone cheese,
      shredded

- Turn oven broiler on and char bell peppers four inches from heat, turning slowly until skin blackens on all sides (about 10 minutes). Place peppers in paper bag and close tightly for 10 minutes. Remove from bag, peel skin off peppers, and cut into strips.
- Slice croissants almost through and drizzle insides with Basil Vinaigrette.
- Fill croissants with Boston lettuce, raddichio, roasted bell pepper strips, prosciutto, and provolone cheese.
- Serve at room temperature or wrap in foil and heat.

Basil Vinaigrette:
½   cup basil leaves, chopped
6   tablespoons olive oil
2   tablespoons red wine vinegar
1   small clove garlic, minced

- Mix together all ingredients to make vinaigrette.

This makes a great salad if peppers, prosciutto, and provolone are placed on lettuce and raddichio with Basil Vinaigrette poured over.

Watercress Salad
Stocked Pot and Company

Easy
4 Servings

1   bunch watercress
2   medium tomatoes, sliced

Dressing:
Pinch salt
2   medium Vidalia onions, thinly
      sliced
¼   cup salad oil
⅓   cup wine vinegar
Milled pepper, 2 twists

- Wash watercress well. Dry and break watercress by hand. Arrange on glass plate.
- Arrange tomatoes over watercress.
- In a bowl, salt onions for 5 minutes.
- In a separate bowl, combine oil and vinegar. Add onions and mix. Add pepper and mix.
- Pour desired amount of dressing over salad.

Belgian Endive Salad with "Petite Marmite" Dressing

Easy
6 Servings

6 Belgian endive
1 pint cherry tomatoes
2 eggs
1 tablespoon mustard
3 parsley sprigs, tops only
½ tablespoon oregano
1 clove garlic, halved
½ teaspoon salt
½ teaspoon pepper
½ cup wine vinegar
1 cup olive oil
1 cup vegetable oil

- Wash and separate the endive. Rinse the tomatoes. Set these aside.
- In a food processor fitted with a steel blade, combine eggs, mustard, parsley, oregano, garlic, salt, pepper, and vinegar. Process on/off three times to chop ingredients.
- With machine running, pour in olive and vegetable oils in a steady stream. Refrigerate until serving time.
- To serve, arrange endive and tomatoes on a platter or in a serving bowl. Pour salad dressing over and serve.

Marinated Tijuana Tomatoes

Average
10-12 Servings

1½ cups vegetable oil
1 cup white wine vinegar
¼ cup sugar
1 clove garlic, minced
1 (9-ounce) can green chili salsa
6 green onions, chopped with tops
6 medium tomatoes, peeled, seeded, and chopped
½ teaspoon oregano
Dash celery seed
Salt and pepper to taste
6-8 tomatoes, peeled and cut into wedges
Butter lettuce
1 can flat anchovy filets, separated
Fresh chopped parsley

- Combine first ten ingredients and refrigerate.
- Four to six hours before serving, add tomato wedges. Toss gently and chill.
- To serve, arrange cups of lettuce on salad plates. With a slotted spoon, place tomato wedges in each lettuce cup. Allow most of the marinade to drain. Top each salad with a criss-cross of anchovy filets and fresh chopped parsley. Serve.

Wonderful during prime tomato season. The salsa marinade will keep 3-4 days and fresh tomatoes may be added daily.

Herbed Tomatoes

8   ripe tomatoes, peeled and cut
       into stars
1¼ teaspoons salt
¼   teaspoon pepper
¾   teaspoon leaf thyme
⅓   cup fresh parsley, minced
⅓   cup chives, minced
¾   cup vegetable oil
⅓   cup tarragon vinegar
¼   cup green onion, sliced

- Place tomatoes in a bowl; sprinkle with seasonings and herbs.
- Combine oil and vinegar; pour over tomatoes.
- Cover and chill for 2 hours; spoon dressing over tomatoes from time to time.
- At serving time, drain tomatoes and reserve dressing.
- Sprinkle more parsley over tomatoes and serve the dressing on the side.

Vegetable Seafood Salad

2   (10-ounce) packages frozen
       small green peas
1   cup celery, chopped
1   (16-ounce) can bean sprouts,
       drained
1   (7-ounce) can shrimp, drained
1   (7-ounce) can crabmeat, drained

Dressing:
½   cup mayonnaise
½   teaspoon curry powder
1   teaspoon soy sauce
1   teaspoon salt
½   teaspoon pepper
2   teaspoons lemon juice
1   tablespoon lime juice

- Cook peas according to package directions. Drain.
- Combine peas, celery, bean sprouts, shrimp, and crabmeat. Refrigerate 2 hours.
- To make dressing, blend mayonnaise, curry, soy sauce, salt, pepper, lemon juice, and lime juice. Pour over salad.
- Chill salad until ready to serve. Just before serving, toss well.

Salad may also be prepared with fresh shrimp and crabmeat.

Shrimp Salad New Orleans

Easy
4 Servings

¾ pound shrimp, cooked, shelled, deveined, and chopped (1½ cups cooked and chopped)
1 cup cold rice, cooked
¾ teaspoon salt
1 tablespoon lemon juice
¼ cup green pepper, slivered (optional)
1 tablespoon onion, minced
2 tablespoons Italian dressing
1 tablespoon olives, chopped
¾ cup raw cauliflower, diced
⅓ cup mayonnaise
Dash pepper

- Combine all ingredients and chill well before serving.
- May be made one day ahead.

San Francisco Crab Louis

Easy
4-6 Servings

Sauce:

½ cup mayonnaise
1 cup ketchup
10 ripe olives, chopped
¼ cup sweet pickle relish
2 tablespoons parsley, chopped
½ teaspoon Worcestershire sauce

1 small head of lettuce, shredded
2-3 avocados, halved
        or
4-6 large tomatoes, peeled and cut into stars
1 pound crabmeat

- In a bowl, mix together the mayonnaise, ketchup, olives, pickle relish, parsley, and Worcestershire. Chill.
- Place shredded lettuce in avocado half or tomato star. Spoon crabmeat on top of lettuce.
- Spoon sauce on top of crabmeat. Garnish with parsley.

Salad Niçoise

Easy
4 Servings

Dressing:

    1   clove garlic, crushed
    1   teaspoon salt
    ½   teaspoon dry mustard
    ½   teaspoon basil
    ⅛   teaspoon pepper
    2   tablespoons lemon juice
    2   tablespoons red wine vinegar
    6   tablespoons vegetable oil
    6   tablespoons olive oil

• In a small bowl, combine first five ingredients.
• Add lemon juice and vinegar; stir until smooth.
• With wire whisk, gradually beat in oils; set aside.

Salad:

  3-4   medium potatoes, peeled,
            cooked, and thinly sliced
    2   tablespoons green onion,
            minced
    ½   pound fresh green beans,
            trimmed and blanched
    1   large head Boston lettuce
    1   cup cherry tomatoes, halved
  2-3   eggs, hard-boiled
    5   anchovy filets
    1   (9¼-ounce) can tuna

• In a medium bowl, toss warm potatoes, onions, and ¼ cup dressing. Refrigerate both potatoes and remainder of dressing until chilled.
• Just before serving, arrange lettuce on a large platter; place tuna in the middle; and arrange potato salad, tomatoes, and green beans around the tuna. Garnish with the eggs and anchovies.
• Pour remaining dressing over all ingredients. Serve immediately.

Crab Pasta Salad

Easy
6-8 Servings

    8   ounces spiral noodles, cooked
            and drained
    ½   pound fresh crab meat
    2   (6-ounce) jars marinated
            artichoke hearts and liquid
    1   (3¼-ounce) can black olives,
            halved
    1   (16-ounce) box frozen peas,
            thawed and drained
    2   tablespoons olive oil
        Black pepper to taste

• Combine all ingredients; mix thoroughly.
• Serve chilled.

Shrimp and Pasta Salad with Basil-Lemon Dressing
Sea Products Seafood Market

Average
8-10 Servings

Basil-Lemon Dressing:
- 2 cups Hellmann's mayonnaise or homemade
- ¼ cup fresh lemon juice
- ½ cup fresh basil leaves, minced
- 2 cloves garlic, minced

Salad:
- 1 (1-pound) box medium pasta shells, cooked, drained, and cooled
- 2 pounds medium shrimp, cooked, shelled, and cut in half
- 1 cup frozen peas, thawed
- 1 cup black olives, sliced
- 1 sweet red pepper, diced
- ⅓ cup scallion, sliced
- Salt and pepper to taste
- 2 cups Basil-Lemon Dressing
- Whole black olives for garnish
- Sweet red peppers, cut into strips for garnish

- To prepare dressing, combine all ingredients and mix thoroughly.
- To prepare salad, combine all ingredients in a large bowl and refrigerate.
- To serve, arrange lettuce on a platter and top with pasta salad. Garnish with whole black olives and strips of sweet red peppers.

To peel a hard-boiled egg, shake hard in cold water first. Transfer to cold water after cooking to prevent "greening" from too much heat.

91

Seafood Pasta Primavera Salad
with Creamy Basil Dressing

1 pound pasta, fettucini or other
   shape
1/3 cup virgin olive oil
1/3 cup white wine vinegar
1 clove garlic, minced
24 asparagus spears, trimmed
2 cups fresh peas
3 cups broccoli florets
2 pounds shrimp, shelled
2 pounds scallops
1/4 cup virgin olive oil
3 tablespoons white wine vinegar
24 cherry tomatoes for garnish
   Bibb lettuce or spinach

Creamy Basil Dressing:
1/2 cup fresh basil, chopped
   or
3 tablespoons dried basil
1/4 cup white wine vinegar
2 tablespoons Dijon mustard
1 clove garlic, minced
1/4 cup virgin olive oil
1 cup sour cream
3 tablespoons fresh parsley,
   chopped
1/2 cup heavy cream

• Cook pasta according to package directions. Drain. Combine with next three ingredients. Refrigerate overnight.
• Steam or blanch in boiling water the asparagus, peas, and broccoli until crisp tender. Rinse with cold water and chill.
• Cook the shrimp in boiling, salted water until pink and firm. Drain.
• Poach the scallops in boiling, salted water for 2 minutes. Drain.
• Add the next two ingredients to the cooked seafood and chill.
• Prepare Creamy Basil Dressing: Combine the first four ingredients in a food processor and process briefly.
• With food processor running, drizzle the oil into the work bowl. Process until well combined.
• Fold in the remaining ingredients. Refrigerate.
• To serve, place bibb lettuce or spinach on a large serving platter. Layer the pasta, prepared vegetables, and top with prepared seafood. Garnish with cherry tomatoes. Sauce lightly with Creamy Basil Dressing.
• Place Basil Dressing on table for guests to serve themselves.

Recipe may be made completely the day before and then arranged prior to serving.

Seafood Pasta Salad

1 pound fresh shrimp, shelled
1 pound bay scallops
Fresh lobster chunks (optional)
8 ounces corkscrew pasta
1 cup tiny peas, fresh or thawed
½ cup sweet red pepper, chopped
¼ cup red onion, minced
1 cup black olives, sliced

Basil Dressing:

4 cups fresh basil leaves
½ cup plus 1 tablespoon olive oil
4 tablespoons fresh lemon juice
Salt and pepper to taste

- Quickly cook shrimp, scallops, and lobster, if used, in salted, boiling water. Drain.
- Cook pasta al dente in salted, boiling water. Drain pasta and run cold water over it until cooled.
- Combine seafood and pasta. Add vegetables and olives and gently toss.
- Make Basil Dressing. Purée fresh basil leaves with a tablespoon of olive oil. Whisk in ½ cup olive oil and lemon juice. Season with salt and pepper.
- Stir Basil Dressing into pasta salad. Serve at room temperature.

Tasty Pasta Salad

Dressing:

1 cup oil
1 cup vinegar
1 cup sugar
1 tablespoon salt
½ tablespoon pepper
1 tablespoon Accent (optional)
1 tablespoon garlic powder
4 tablespoons parsley flakes
4 teaspoons dry mustard

- Mix together all dressing ingredients.
- Cook rotini as directed on package.
- Combine onion, cucumber, pimiento, and green pepper with noodles.
- Pour dressing over salad and stir well.
- Refrigerate overnight before serving.

Salad:

1 (16-ounce) box rotini noodles
1 medium onion, chopped
1 cucumber, peeled and chopped
1 (6-ounce) jar pimiento, chopped
1 green pepper, chopped

A perfect summer side dish to accompany boiled shrimp.

Pasta Salad with Broccoli and Pesto

Easy
4 Servings

½   bunch broccoli, cut into florets and stems
1½   tablespoons olive oil
½   clove garlic, minced
½   pound rigatoni or other tubular pasta
1   tomato, juiced, seeded, and cut into strips
4   tablespoons fresh pesto sauce

- Steam broccoli 5 minutes. Cool and dry it.
- Heat oil in wok. Add garlic and broccoli. Stir fry 3 minutes and set aside.
- Cook pasta al dente. Drain and transfer to a large bowl while still warm.
- Add broccoli, tomato, and pesto sauce. Toss well.
- Serve chilled or at room temperature.

Garnishes: Use flower-shaped cookie cutter to cut out flowers from turnips, carrots, squash, etc. Top with radish roses. Use with any vegetable dish, pasta salad, potato salad, tomato aspic, etc.

Pesto Sauce

Easy
1 Cup

2   cups fresh basil leaves
½   cup olive oil
2   tablespoons pine nuts
2   cloves garlic, finely chopped
    Salt to taste
½   cup freshly grated Parmesan cheese
2   tablespoons freshly grated Romano cheese
3   tablespoons butter, softened

- Process basil, olive oil, pine nuts, garlic, and salt in a food processor or blender until smooth.
- Transfer to a bowl and beat in cheeses and butter by hand.
- Will keep 1 month in refrigerator.
- To freeze, leave out cheeses and butter. Add when mixture is thawed to serve.

Pat's Pasta Salad

2 cups fresh snow peas
2 cups broccoli florets
2 cups cherry tomatoes, halved
2 cups fresh mushrooms, quartered
1 (7¾-ounce) can whole, pitted, ripe black olives
1 (8-ounce) package spinach-cheese stuffed tortellini
4 ounces fettuccini
6 ounces Parmesan cheese, grated

- In a saucepan, blanch snow peas for 1 minute. Remove from heat, drain, and run under cold water.
- Blanch broccoli for 1 minute. Remove from heat, drain, and run under cold water.
- Place snow peas and broccoli in a large bowl with tomatoes, mushrooms, and olives.
- Cook the two pastas according to package directions. Drain and cool slightly.
- Combine vegetables, pasta, and 1 tablespoon Parmesan cheese. Add dressing and mix well.
- Chill several hours before serving.
- Garnish generously with additional Parmesan cheese and serve.

Dressing:

1 bunch green onions, sliced
⅓ cup red wine vinegar
⅓ cup vegetable oil
⅓ cup olive oil
2 tablespoons fresh parsley, chopped
2-3 cloves garlic, minced
2 teaspoons dried whole basil
1 teaspoon dried dillweed
1 teaspoon salt
½ teaspoon freshly ground pepper
½ teaspoon sugar
½ teaspoon oregano
2 teaspoons Dijon mustard

- Combine all ingredients in blender and mix well.
- Store in a jar.
- When ready to use, shake vigorously until mixed.

Add a small amount of dressing to pasta salad while pasta is still hot to prevent sticking.

Spring Pasta Salad with Pesto

1   (16-ounce) box seashell pasta
1½ cups carrots, sliced
2   cups broccoli florets
¼   cup pine nuts

- Cook seashell pasta as directed on package.
- Steam carrots until crisp tender. Set aside. Blanch broccoli until crisp tender. Refresh under cold water. Drain.
- In a large bowl, toss pasta, vegetables, and ¼ cup pine nuts.
- Add Creamy Pesto Dressing and mix to coat.
- Cover and refrigerate.
- Before serving, add salt and pepper to taste.

Creamy Pesto Dressing:

3   cloves garlic
1   tablespoon fresh basil
1   tablespoon red wine vinegar
¼   cup pine nuts
1   cup mayonnaise
¼   cup Parmesan cheese, grated
¼   cup parsley, chopped
½   teaspoon salt
¼   teaspoon pepper

- Combine garlic, basil, and vinegar in a food processor.
- Add ¼ cup pine nuts and blend.
- Add mayonnaise, Parmesan cheese, parsley, salt, and pepper. Blend well.

Olive oil may be substituted for mayonnaise. Use 1 cup olive oil for 1 cup mayonnaise. Or, use ½ cup olive oil and ½ cup mayonnaise. Pine nuts may be found in specialty stores, but are easily replaced with walnuts.

Broccoli and Cauliflower Salad

Easy
8-12 Servings

   1   bunch broccoli, cut into bite-
         sized pieces
   1   head cauliflower, cut into bite-
         sized pieces
   1   small red onion, thinly sliced
10-12 slices crisp bacon, crumbled

Dressing:
   ½   cup Parmesan cheese
   ¼   cup sugar
   1   cup mayonnaise
         Salt and pepper to taste

Great picnic or potluck dish!

- In a large bowl, mix together broccoli, cauliflower, and onion. Add bacon.
- Mix dressing ingredients in a small bowl until blended.
- Pour dressing over vegetables and mix well. Refrigerate overnight before serving.

Broccoli Salad

Easy
6-8 Servings

Dressing:
   ¾   cup mayonnaise
   3   tablespoons fresh lemon juice
   ½   teaspoon sugar
         Salt and pepper to taste

   1   bunch broccoli, cut into very
         small florets with stalks
         discarded
   4   hard-cooked eggs, chopped
   1   small onion, diced
   ½   pound fresh mushrooms, sliced
   ¾   cup pimiento stuffed olives,
         chopped
   1   cup zucchini, chopped (optional)

- In a small bowl, mix dressing ingredients.
- Combine remaining ingredients in a large bowl. Pour dressing and toss well.
- Serve in a large decorative bowl or individually on bed of greens.
- If preferred, broccoli may be blanched and refreshed before tossing with dressing.

Lettuceless Salad

Dressing:

1   egg
1   tablespoon white vinegar
2   teaspoons Dijon mustard
1   small clove garlic, halved
1   teaspoon dill seed
¾   teaspoon salt
½   teaspoon thyme
½   teaspoon marjoram
½   teaspoon basil
½   teaspoon celery salt
¼   teaspoon white pepper
½   cup vegetable oil
1   cup buttermilk
2   cups mayonnaise, preferably
    homemade

- Combine first eleven ingredients in food processor or blender. With machine running, pour oil, then buttermilk, and process until smooth and thick.
- Transfer to large bowl and whisk in mayonnaise.

Salad:

1   head broccoli, florets
1   head cauliflower, florets
1   pound Cheddar cheese, cubed
4   celery stalks, chopped
3   large carrots, chopped
1   cucumber, cubed
1   red apple, unpeeled, cored, and
    cubed
1   small onion, diced
1   green bell pepper, sliced
⅓   cup raisins
1   cup salted roasted sunflower
    seeds

- Combine all ingredients, except sunflower seeds, in large bowl and toss.
- Divide on plates and spoon dressing over each serving.
- Garnish with sunflower seeds and pass additional dressing.

Hard-boiled eggs: Place eggs in a saucepan and cover with cold water. Bring to a rolling boil. Cover and remove from heat. Let sit 20 minutes. Immediately plunge eggs into cold water and refrigerate.

Marinated Vegetable Salad

Easy
8-10 Servings

1 (17-ounce) can early green peas
2 cups fresh green beans, blanched
3 stalks celery, chopped
1 green pepper, chopped
1 (2-ounce) jar pimiento, diced
2 cups broccoli florets
¼ pound mushrooms, sliced
4 spring onions, chopped with tops
¾ cup vinegar
½ cup sugar
½ cup vegetable oil
1 teaspoon salt
Fresh pepper to taste
2 tablespoons water

• Mix all ingredients together in a large bowl. Chill in refrigerator 24 hours.

For a sweeter-tasting raw onion: Slice onions, pour boiling water over them, and drain immediately. Cover with cold water for a few minutes. Drain and serve.

Japanese Cucumber Salad

Easy
4-6 Servings

2 large cucumbers
⅓ cup white wine vinegar
4 teaspoons sugar
1 teaspoon salt
2 slices fresh ginger, slivered
Butter lettuce

• Cut cucumbers in half lengthwise. Remove large seeds. Slice crosswise into very thin slices.
• In a medium bowl, mix vinegar, sugar, salt, and ginger. Marinate cucumber slices in this dressing 3-4 hours in refrigerator.
• To serve, remove from marinade with slotted spoon and place on butter lettuce leaf.

This dish may also be served with shrimp, lobster, or crabmeat sprinkled on top.

Spinach and Strawberry Salad

Easy
4 Servings

1 pound fresh spinach leaves
1 quart fresh strawberries

Dressing:

½ cup olive oil
1½-2 tablespoons strawberry vinegar
or other fruit-flavored vinegar
¼ teaspoon sugar
1 tablespoon strawberry yogurt
Salt and pepper to taste

- Remove stems from spinach, wash well, and dry.
- Remove stems from strawberries, wash, drain, and cut in half.
- Beat all ingredients for dressing; adjust according to taste.
- Combine spinach and strawberries in bowl and toss with sweet and sour dressing.

Apple and Bacon Spinach Salad

Easy
6 Servings

Dressing:

¼ cup olive oil
3 tablespoons red wine vinegar
1 teaspoon sugar
½ teaspoon dry mustard
Dash salt
Dash pepper

Salad:

5 slices bacon
⅓ cup almonds, sliced
½ pound fresh spinach
1 apple, unpeeled
3 green onions, sliced

- In a jar, combine dressing ingredients. Shake well. Refrigerate.
- In a skillet, cook bacon. Drain well. Save 1 tablespoon of drippings.
- In skillet, toast almonds in drippings. Remove and drain well.
- Wash and prepare spinach for salad.
- Cut apple into bite-sized pieces.
- Just before serving, pour dressing over spinach. Toss. Add remaining ingredients and serve.

Spinach and Avocado or Fruit Salad

Easy
12 Servings

Dressing:

1   cup vegetable oil
½   cup sugar
⅓   cup wine vinegar
1   tablespoon dry mustard
1   tablespoon celery seed
1   teaspoon salt
2   green onions, sliced

- Combine first six ingredients in a blender. Blend thoroughly.
- Stir in onions.
- Chill several hours before using.

Spinach and Avocado Salad:

1   pound fresh spinach
2   heads Boston lettuce
2   avocados, peeled and cut in wedges
1   (11-ounce) can mandarin oranges, drained
1   red onion, thinly sliced

- Tear greens into bite-sized pieces. Place in a salad bowl.
- Add remaining ingredients for either Avocado or Fruit Salad. Add dressing to taste.
- Toss and serve.

Spinach and Fruit Salad:

1   pound fresh spinach
2   heads Boston lettuce
1   pound red seedless grapes, halved
½   cup walnuts, chopped
2   grapefruit, peeled and sectioned
3   oranges, peeled and sectioned

Sweet 'n Sour Slaw

Easy
8-10 Servings

1   cup white vinegar
½   cup vegetable oil
2   teaspoons celery seed
1   cup plus 2 tablespoons sugar
1   green pepper, finely chopped
1   red onion, chopped
1   head cabbage, chopped
1   teaspoon salt

- In a small saucepan, mix together vinegar, oil, celery seed, and 2 tablespoons of sugar. Bring to a boil and stir until sugar dissolves. Cool thoroughly.
- Place green pepper, onion, and cabbage together in a large bowl. Pour 1 cup of sugar and salt over vegetables and mix well.
- Pour cooled dressing over vegetables. Chill for several hours before serving.

Caesar Salad

Stars Restaurant

2   heads romaine lettuce
    Cruet of olive oil (about ¾ cup)
4   anchovies
2   cloves garlic, peeled
2   raw eggs, in hot water
1   lemon, halved with net to strain
      out seeds
½   teaspoon dry mustard
    Freshly ground pepper to taste
¼-½   cup garlic croutons
½   cup freshly grated Parmesan
      cheese

- Remove and discard outer leaves of romaine. Wash remaining lettuce and break into bite-size pieces. Wrap in a towel and refrigerate until serving time.
- Put a few drops of oil in the bottom of a large wooden bowl with a little pepper.
- Add anchovies and make a paste using forks.
- Add garlic cloves and blend into paste.
- Break eggs, discarding whites. Add yolks to bowl and whisk until smooth.
- Start adding olive oil very slowly, letting it flow down the side of the bowl. (You will end up making a real mayonnaise.)
- Squeeze in the lemon juice, add the mustard and lots of freshly ground pepper. Mix well.
- Add romaine, croutons and cheese. Toss lightly but thoroughly and serve.

You may want to arrange ingredients in separate bowls and prepare this tableside as it is done at Stars.

German Cole Slaw

2   cups water
2   cups sugar
2   cups vinegar
¼   cup vegetable oil
1   head cabbage, shredded
1   green pepper, chopped
1   onion, thinly sliced
1   (2-ounce) jar chopped pimientos
1   tablespoon salt
2   tablespoons mustard seed

- In a 3-quart saucepan, bring water, sugar, vinegar, and vegetable oil to a boil. Remove from heat and let cool.
- In a large mixing bowl, combine remaining ingredients.
- Pour cooled vinegar mixture over cabbage mixture and cover. Refrigerate for 24 hours or at least overnight.
- To serve, drain thoroughly and serve chilled.

Cole Slaw Salad

Easy
8-10 Servings

1 large head cabbage, shredded
2 cucumbers, peeled and chopped
3 green onions, chopped
2 medium tomatoes, peeled and chopped
1 large green pepper, chopped
Salt and pepper to taste
½ teaspoon sugar
1-2 tablespoons red wine vinegar
¼ cup mayonnaise

• Combine all ingredients in a large serving bowl. Toss and chill until ready to serve.

• If making 4-6 hours ahead, combine all ingredients except mayonnaise and refrigerate. Add mayonnaise before serving.

When preparing cabbage for slaw, remove outer leaves and cut head in halves. Let stand in cold water until crisp, about 30 minutes. Shake off excess water. Shred very finely with sharp knife.

New Potato Salad

Easy
10 Servings

3 pounds new potatoes, unpeeled
1 bunch green onions, chopped
3 stalks celery, chopped
3 boiled eggs, chopped

Dressing:
1 teaspoon salt
1 teaspoon basil
½ teaspoon pepper
1 tablespoon Dijon mustard
2 cloves garlic, minced
3 tablespoons red wine vinegar
½ cup mayonnaise
⅓ cup olive oil

• Boil potatoes in salted water, drain, and cool.

• Quarter potatoes. In a large bowl, mix potatoes with onion, celery, and eggs.

• In a medium bowl, combine salt, pepper, basil, mustard, garlic, and vinegar. Stir in mayonnaise and whisk in oil.

• Pour over potatoes and toss to combine ingredients.

Even better made the day before.

Cobb Salad

Average
6 Servings

1 (8-ounce) bottle French dressing
4 slices bacon, cooked and crumbled
2 ounces bleu cheese, crumbled
6-8 cups lettuce, shredded
2 cups tomatoes, peeled and chopped
2 cups cooked chicken, chopped
1 avocado, peeled and chopped
2 hard-cooked eggs, chopped

- Combine dressing, bacon, and bleu cheese.
- Place lettuce on serving plates. Arrange tomato, chicken, avocado, and eggs on lettuce. Serve with dressing to taste.

To guarantee a ripe avocado at serving time: Purchase one 2-3 days in advance. Store in a brown paper bag in a dark cabinet, checking every day for ripeness. Refrigerate when ready.

Japanese Chicken Salad

Easy
8 Servings

Salad Dressing:

4 tablespoons sugar
2 teaspoons salt
½ teaspoon pepper
4 tablespoons vinegar
½ cup vegetable oil

- In a mixing bowl, combine all ingredients. Mix well.

Japanese Chicken Salad:

4 chicken breasts
1 head leafy lettuce
3 green onions, chopped
1 (3-ounce) can chow mein noodles
1 (4-ounce) package slivered almonds
¼ cup poppy seeds

- Cook chicken and chop.
- Tear lettuce into bite-sized pieces.
- In a large bowl, combine chicken, lettuce, onions, chow mein noodles, almonds, and poppy seeds.
- Pour salad dressing over chicken salad. Toss and serve.

Polynesian Luncheon Salad

Easy
8-10 Servings

4 cups chicken, cooked and chopped
1 cup pineapple chunks
¾ cup strawberry halves
½ cup seedless green grapes
1 cup celery, chopped
½ cup salad dressing, mayonnaise style
Salt and pepper to taste
¼ teaspoon ginger
Lettuce
¼ cup toasted walnuts
Whole strawberries for garnish

- In a large mixing bowl, mix together all ingredients, except lettuce, walnuts, and strawberries. Lightly toss. Chill.
- Serve on a bed of lettuce. Sprinkle walnuts on top and garnish with strawberries.

This is a refreshing twist for chicken salad and a delightful luncheon entrée.

Curried Chicken and Artichoke Salad

Easy
10-12 Servings

1 (8-ounce) package chicken-flavored rice
1 (5.2-ounce) package long grain and wild rice
6 chicken breast halves, cooked, deboned and cubed
1 bell pepper, chopped
16 pimiento-stuffed olives, sliced
4 scallions, sliced
2 (6-ounce) jars marinated artichokes, drained, marinade reserved
1 cup mayonnaise
1 teaspoon curry powder
Salt and pepper to taste
Lettuce
Slivered almonds

- Cook both rice mixes according to package directions. Cool.
- In a large bowl, combine rice, chicken, bell pepper, olives, scallions, and drained artichokes.
- In a separate bowl, mix together marinade, mayonnaise, curry, salt, and pepper. Stir mixture into chicken salad. Refrigerate.
- Serve on a bed of lettuce. Garnish with slivered almonds.

Curried Chicken Salad

Easy
6 Servings

1   (3-pound) chicken
½   cup celery, diced
1   apple, cored and diced
½   cup onion, diced
½   cup seedless grapes, halved
⅓   cup slivered almonds, toasted
2   teaspoons curry powder
1   cup mayonnaise
    Salt and pepper to taste

- Cook chicken and let cool. Cube the meat.
- In a bowl, combine chicken, celery, apple, onion, grapes, and almonds.
- In another bowl, stir together the curry, mayonnaise, salt, and pepper. Stir into chicken mixture.
- Serve chilled.

To peel a summer tomato: Run the back edge of a knife over the skin of tomato. Prick skin and pull off peel.

Hot Chicken Salad

Average
4 Servings

2   cups chicken or turkey, cooked
    and cubed
1   cup celery, chopped
1   cup green pepper, chopped
½   cup green onion, sliced
1   (4-ounce) jar pimiento, drained
    and chopped
½   cup sharp Cheddar cheese,
    grated
½   cup mayonnaise
1   tablespoon fresh lemon juice
1   tablespoon Worcestershire sauce
¼   teaspoon hot pepper sauce
    Bread crumbs
    Butter

- Preheat oven to 350°.
- In a large bowl, combine chicken, celery, green pepper, onion, pimiento, Cheddar cheese, mayonnaise, lemon juice, Worcestershire sauce, and hot pepper sauce.
- Coat a 1½-quart casserole dish with non-stick cooking spray. Fill with the chicken mixture.
- Sprinkle bread crumbs on top and dot with butter.
- Bake for 20-25 minutes.

Vegetable Aspic

1½ cups V-8 juice
2 (3-ounce) packages lemon
    flavored gelatin
¼ cup water
3 tablespoons vinegar
½ teaspoon lite salt
½ cup celery, finely chopped
½ cup cucumber, finely chopped
½ cup small English peas, drained
2 hard-boiled eggs, chopped
1 green pepper, chopped

- In a large saucepan, heat 1 cup V-8 juice. Add gelatin and stir until dissolved.
- Add remaining V-8 juice, water, vinegar, and salt. Chill until syrupy.
- Fold in remaining ingredients. Pour into eight individual molds or a 1½-quart mold. Chill until set.

Roll eggs on counter top to center yolks before cooking for deviled eggs.

Tomato Aspic

2 envelopes unflavored gelatin
4 tablespoons cold water
1 (46-ounce) can V-8 juice
¾ cup celery, finely chopped
¾ cup green pepper, seeded and
    finely chopped
¾ cup onion, finely chopped
9 ounces lemon gelatin
½ cup fresh lemon juice
½ cup cider vinegar
2 tablespoons sugar
3 tablespoons Worcestershire
    sauce
   Dash cayenne pepper

- In a small bowl, combine unflavored gelatin and cold water. Set aside to soften.
- Bring V-8 juice to a boil.
- Add celery, green pepper, and onion and boil for 1 minute.
- In a large bowl, place lemon gelatin and add V-8 mixture. Stir until dissolved.
- Add softened unflavored gelatin to V-8 mixture, making sure all gelatin dissolves.
- Add lemon juice, vinegar, sugar, Worcestershire sauce, cayenne pepper, and salt; allow to cool.
- Lightly oil or spray with cooking spray a 12-cup Bundt pan.
- Pour in cooled liquid mixture and chill until set.
- May be made one day in advance.

Raspberry-Tomato Aspic with Horseradish Sauce

Easy
6 Servings

1 (16-ounce) can tomatoes
1 (3-ounce) package raspberry
   gelatin
6 drops hot pepper sauce
   Salt and pepper to taste
   Onion powder to taste

Horseradish Sauce:

½ pint sour cream
½-1 tablespoon horseradish
¼ teaspoon sugar
   Dash Worcestershire sauce
   Pinch of salt

- Purée tomatoes. Then bring to a boil in a small saucepan.
- Place gelatin in a large bowl. Add purée and stir well. Season with hot pepper sauce, salt, pepper, and onion powder.
- Pour mixture into a 1 quart decorative mold. Refrigerate until firm.
- Mix together all ingredients for horseradish sauce in a medium bowl and blend well. Chill before serving.
- Serve on lettuce with horseradish sauce.

Spiced Peach Salad

Easy
8-12 Servings

1 (3-ounce) package lemon gelatin
1 (3-ounce) package orange
   gelatin
½ cup orange marmalade
½ cup ginger marmalade
1 (28½-ounce) jar spiced peaches,
   drained and chopped
1 (16-ounce) can white Royal
   Anne cherries, drained, pitted,
   and chopped
½ cup almonds, chopped

- In a large bowl, dissolve lemon and orange gelatin in 2 cups of boiling water. Add marmalades and blend well. Let cool and then stir in remaining ingredients.
- Pour into a 9x13-inch, lightly greased dish or mold. Chill until set.
- This is also pretty poured into 12 individual molds.

Cranberry Apple Salad

Easy
6-8 Servings

2 cups cranberry juice
1 (3-ounce) package lemon gelatin
Dash of salt
1-2 medium red delicious apples, chopped (about 1½ cups)
½ cup celery, chopped
⅓ cup pecans, chopped
¾ cup seedless red or green grapes, sliced (optional)

- In a small saucepan, heat 1 cup of cranberry juice to a boil. Pour juice over gelatin in a large bowl. Stir until dissolved. Add salt and second cup of cranberry juice. Chill until slightly thickened.
- Fold in remaining ingredients. Pour into 1-quart mold or six individual molds. Chill until set. Unmold and serve.

Picking a good canteloupe: If stem end is barely soft and smells like a canteloupe, it's ripe. Choose one that has a lot of membrane on it, not one that is very smooth. Shaking the fruit should result in hearing the seeds "rattle."

Cranberry Waldorf Salad Ring

Easy
8-10 Servings

2 (1-ounce) packages unflavored gelatin
1 cup orange juice
2 (16-ounce) cans whole berry cranberry sauce
¾ cup apples, peeled and chopped
¾ cup celery, chopped
¾ cup walnuts, chopped
Crisp greens

- In a small saucepan, mix together gelatin and orange juice and set aside for 5 minutes. Place over low heat and stir until gelatin is dissolved.
- Remove from heat and pour into a large bowl with cranberry sauce. Stir well. Chill until partially set.
- Fold in apple, celery, and walnuts. Pour into a 1½-quart ring mold and chill until firm.
- Unmold onto crisp greens.

A wonderful holiday standby!

Remoulade Sauce

3 cups mayonnaise
1 cup creole mustard
3 hard-cooked eggs
1 clove garlic
4 green onions, coarsely chopped
   with tops
2 tablespoons Worcestershire
   sauce
1 tablespoon lemon juice
1 tablespoon vinegar
2 tablespoons anchovy paste
1 tablespoon horseradish
1 tablespoon sherry
2 tablespoons capers
2 tablespoons parsley

- Combine all ingredients in the bowl of a food processor with a steel blade.
- Process on and off until blended. Store in refrigerator until ready to use.

A wonderful dip, dressing, or accompaniment to fish or shellfish!

Hot and Sweet Holiday Mustard

6 ounces Coleman's dry mustard
⅛ teaspoon red pepper, crushed
   Water
¼ teaspoon white pepper
¼ teaspoon black pepper
2 cups sugar
1½ cups white distilled vinegar
1 teaspoon salt
3 eggs
½ cup butter

- Mix mustard and red peppers with enough water to make a paste. Add white and black pepper and set aside.
- In the top of a double boiler, combine the sugar, vinegar, and salt. Heat until the sugar has melted and remove from heat.
- Stir sugar by droplets into the mustard paste. Pour back into the double boiler to keep warm but do not return it to the heat.
- In another bowl, beat eggs well. Stir mustard sauce by droplets into the eggs. Pour into double boiler and return to heat. Bring to a boil, then remove from heat. Add butter immediately, stirring until melted.
- Pour into glass half-pint jars and cool before refrigerating.

Mustard Horseradish Sauce

Easy
2 Cups

1 cup sour cream
½ cup mayonnaise
1 tablespoon horseradish
Pinch of sugar
¼ teaspoon salt
5 tablespoons creole mustard

- In a bowl, combine all ingredients thoroughly.
- Serve chilled as a sauce for tenderloin or on roast beef sandwiches.

Cheese Dressing for Potatoes

Easy
3 Cups

8 ounces extra sharp Cheddar cheese, grated
4 ounces butter, softened
1 cup sour cream
1 tablespoon onion, grated

- Mix ingredients together until well-blended.
- Serve on baked potatoes. Also good with vegetables such as broccoli or asparagus.
- Will keep for several weeks in the refrigerator.

Poppy Seed Dressing

Easy
2 Cups

½ cup sugar
½ teaspoon salt
1 tablespoon dry mustard
1 tablespoon paprika
2 tablespoons poppy seeds
4 tablespoons cider vinegar
2 teaspoons onion, grated
1 cup salad oil

- Blend all ingredients except oil in blender or with mixer.
- Add oil in thirds, beating well after each addition. Mixture will be quite thick.
- Keeps well in refrigerator for several days.

Honey Celery Seed Dressing

SECCA Santa

Easy
2 Cups

⅔ cup sugar
1 teaspoon dry mustard
1 teaspoon celery seed
1 teaspoon paprika
¼ teaspoon salt
⅓ cup vinegar
⅓ cup honey
¼ cup cold water
½ cup vegetable oil

• Place all ingredients except oil in food processor and blend 30 seconds. Add oil very slowly until mixture thickens like mayonnaise. Serve over fresh citrus fruits.

Vinaigrette Aux Fines Herbes

Easy
2½ Cups

½ cup red wine vinegar
1 teaspoon salt
   Pepper to taste
2 teaspoons Dijon mustard
2 cloves garlic, minced
1 tablespoon fresh oregano
      or
2 teaspoons dried oregano
1½ tablespoons fresh parsley
      or
4 teaspoons dried parsley
1 tablespoon fresh chives
      or
2 teaspoons chives
2 cups vegetable oil

• Put all ingredients except oil in food processor or blender, and process until well combined.
• Continue to run processor and add oil in a thin stream until well mixed.
• Refrigerate until ready to use, up to several days.

112

Yogurt Dressing

1 cup plain yogurt
1 small clove garlic, minced
1 teaspoon Dijon mustard
1 tablespoon lemon juice
1 tablespoon minced fresh chives
1 tablespoon minced fresh parsley
¼ teaspoon dried basil or tarragon
2 tablespoons minced cucumber
   Pepper to taste

- Mix all ingredients together in a jar and shake vigorously.

Can substitute buttermilk for yogurt. Add 1 tablespoon diced red bell pepper for color.

Tomato Dressing

1 cup sugar
1 tablespoon salt
1 teaspoon pepper
¾ cup vinegar
1 cup salad oil
1 can tomato soup
2-3 cloves garlic, whole

- In a large jar, combine all ingredients and shake well. Refrigerate.
- Before serving, remove garlic cloves.

Wonderful on home-grown tomatoes.

Drew's Honey Mustard Dressing

½ cup mayonnaise
1 tablespoon Dijon mustard
1 tablespoon honey
1 tablespoon vinegar
   Hot pepper sauce
   Paprika
   Half and half

- In a bowl, combine the mayonnaise, mustard, honey, and vinegar.
- Add a dash of hot pepper sauce and paprika to taste.
- Stir in half and half to taste and the dressing is the right consistency.
- Good as a dressing on spinach or green salad.

113

Bleu Cheese Dressing

1 cup mayonnaise
2 tablespoons onion, finely minced
1 teaspoon garlic, minced
¼ cup fresh parsley, minced
½ cup sour cream
1 tablespoon fresh lemon juice
1 tablespoon white wine vinegar
¼ cup crumbled bleu cheese
Salt and pepper to taste

• Combine all ingredients and chill for at least 1 hour before serving.

Special Salad Dressing
Heritage of Hospitality

1 pint mayonnaise
2 hard-boiled eggs, finely chopped
3 ounces vinegar
2 teaspoons horseradish
2 teaspoons Worcestershire sauce
1 clove garlic, minced
½ teaspoon paprika

• In a bowl, whisk all ingredients together.
• Refrigerate until ready to use in an airtight jar.

May also be used as a dip or dressing for potato salad.

pasta, eggs, cheese

Easter Sunrise Breakfast
Country Ham
Egg and Mushroom Casserole
Moravian Sugar Cake
Moravian Coffee

The Moravian Band, Old Salem

Visitors experience the sights and sounds of the 18th Century as they tour Old Salem. Costumed men and women shape beeswax candles, dye yarn, and hammer tin in the traditions of centuries past. The haunting refrain of the Moravian band echoes through the restored town during the beautiful and moving Easter Sunrise Service and at events such as the annual recreation of an 1800's Salem Christmas.

Photo by Sarah Turner

Lasagna with Fresh Spinach

Easy
8 Servings

8 lasagna noodles
1½ pounds fresh spinach
½ cup onion, chopped
1 clove garlic, minced (optional)
1 cup carrots, grated
2 cups mushrooms, sliced
1 (15-ounce) can tomato sauce
1 (6-ounce) can tomato paste
½ cup black olives, sliced
1½ teaspoons oregano
Salt and freshly ground pepper
   to taste
2 cups cottage cheese or ricotta
   cheese
1 pound Monterey Jack cheese,
   grated
¼ cup Parmesan cheese, grated

- Preheat oven to 375°.
- Cook noodles according to package directions.
- Steam spinach until tender, about 5-6 minutes.
- In a large skillet, sauté onion and garlic until soft.
- Add carrots and mushrooms. Cook until crisp tender.
- Stir in tomato sauce, tomato paste, olives, and oregano. Add salt and pepper.
- In a 13x9x2-inch casserole dish, layer half of the noodles, cottage or ricotta cheese, spinach, sauce mixture, and ⅓ of the Monterey Jack cheese.
- Repeat layering.
- Place remaining ⅓ Monterey Jack cheese on top. Sprinkle with Parmesan cheese.
- Bake for 30 minutes.
- May be made ahead and refrigerated until ready to bake.

Quick Vegetable Lasagna

Easy
10 Servings

1 pound ricotta or small curd
   cottage cheese
1½ cups mozzarella cheese, grated
1 egg
1 (10-ounce) package frozen
   chopped spinach, thawed and
   drained
½ teaspoon salt
¾ teaspoon oregano
⅛ teaspoon pepper
1 (32-ounce) jar spaghetti sauce
8 ounces lasagna noodles,
   uncooked
1 cup water

- Preheat oven to 350°.
- In a large bowl, mix ricotta cheese, 1 cup mozzarella cheese, egg, spinach, salt, oregano, and pepper.
- Grease 13x9x2-inch pan.
- Layer ⅓ cup spaghetti sauce, ⅓ of the noodles, and ½ cheese and spinach mixture in casserole. Repeat layers. Place final ⅓ of noodles over layers. Top with remaining sauce and reserved ½ cup mozzarella cheese.
- Pour water around edges of pan.
- Cover tightly with foil.
- Bake 1 hour and 15 minutes or until bubbly. Let stand 15 minutes before serving.

Shrimp Alfredo

4   tablespoons butter
1   pound large shrimp, shelled and deveined
1   teaspoon shallots, minced
1   small clove garlic, minced
½   pound fettuccine or angel hair pasta, cooked al dente and drained
4   large egg yolks
1   cup half and half
½   cup fresh Parmesan cheese, grated
2   teaspoons fresh parsley, chopped
    Salt and pepper to taste

- Melt butter in a large sauté pan. Add shrimp, shallots, and garlic. Cook, stirring, for 3-4 minutes or until shrimp are pink.
- Reduce heat to medium low and stir in cooked pasta.
- Beat egg yolks, half and half, and Parmesan cheese together.
- Add egg mixture to shrimp and cook, stirring for 3-4 minutes or until thickened. Do not boil.
- Stir in parsley. Season with salt and pepper to taste.

Pasta Primavera with Shrimp

1   pound spaghetti
3-4 tablespoons butter
3   fresh cloves garlic, minced
1   pound fresh shrimp, peeled
2-3 tablespoons oil
1   green pepper, chopped
1   bunch fresh broccoli florets
2   cups fresh mushrooms, sliced
1   cup fresh parsley, chopped
1   cup green onion, chopped
½   sweet red pepper, chopped
1   cup heavy cream
½   cup Parmesan cheese, grated

- Cook pasta according to package directions while preparing shrimp. Keep warm.
- Melt butter in skillet and sauté garlic for 1-2 minutes over medium heat.
- Add shrimp and sauté for 3-4 minutes or until they turn pink.
- Remove to serving dish and keep warm.
- Place oil, green pepper, and broccoli in skillet. Sauté until crisp tender.
- Add mushrooms, ½ cup parsley, onion, and red pepper. Sauté several minutes.
- Add shrimp, garlic, and cream. Simmer briefly, but heat thoroughly to reheat shrimp.
- To serve, place reserved spaghetti on serving platter, pour shrimp/vegetable mixture over spaghetti, and garnish with remaining parsley and Parmesan cheese.

Shrimp and Bay Scallops Marinara

Easy
4 Servings

2 medium onions, chopped
2 cloves garlic, minced
¼ cup olive oil
2 pounds canned plum tomatoes
    or
6 large fresh tomatoes, juiced,
    seeded, chopped
½ cup fresh basil leaves, chopped
2 tablespoons parsley, minced
    Salt and pepper to taste
1 cup dry vermouth
1 pound shrimp
    or
½ pound shrimp and ½ pound
    scallops
    Freshly ground pepper
1 pound linguine, cooked al dente
    Fresh Parmesan cheese, grated

- Sauté onions and garlic in olive oil until tender.
- Add tomatoes, basil, and parsley. Simmer, uncovered, 25 minutes. Season with salt and pepper.
- Heat vermouth in medium-sized pan until almost boiling. Add shrimp/scallops and simmer until shrimp turn pink and scallops lose transparency.
- Add seafood to tomatoes along with ¼ cup of the cooking liquid.
- Serve over hot pasta and top with fresh grated Parmesan cheese.

Spicy Shrimp and Sesame Noodles
The Last Catch Cafe and Bar

Easy
6 Servings

½ pound linguini
36 medium shrimp
2 tablespoons sesame oil
1 teaspoon Vietnamese chili and
    garlic paste*
3 cloves garlic, minced
2 tablespoons soy sauce
2 stalks spring onions, chopped
    (green part only)
    Sesame seeds for garnish

- Cook linguini until al dente. Rinse under cold water and set aside.
- Sauté shrimp over medium heat in sesame oil, adding chili and garlic paste and minced garlic. Cook just until shrimp turn pink. Add soy sauce and linguini. Toss to coat and heat. Sprinkle with chopped spring onions. Place on warmed plates or serving platter. Garnish with sesame seeds and serve.

*Available in oriental grocery stores.

117

Pasta with Clam Sauce for Two

1   (6½-ounce) can minced clams,
       undrained
4   tablespoons butter
½   teaspoon salt
½   teaspoon pepper
       Cayenne pepper to taste
1   teaspoon parsley, minced
1   teaspoon chives, minced
1-2 cloves garlic, crushed
½   teaspoon oregano
3   tablespoons dry white vermouth
4-6 ounces linguini

- In a wok, combine all ingredients, except linguini, and heat to a boil. Lower heat and simmer while linguini is cooking.
- Cook linguini according to package directions for 7 minutes.
- Drain and stir into clam mixture. Cook 3-5 minutes. Serve.

Any vegetables added to pasta dough for color should be well-dried first to prevent a sticky dough. When cooked, pasta should be firm to the bite (al dente).

Vermicelli with Clam Sauce
Heritage of Hospitality

3   cloves garlic
⅔   cup olive oil
1   cup bottled clam juice
¼   teaspoon salt
       Pepper to taste
½   teaspoon oregano
3   (7½-ounce) cans of minced
       clams
½   cup fresh parsley, chopped
½   cup green onions, chopped
1   pound vermicelli
       Parmesan cheese, freshly grated
       Fresh clams for garnish

- In a skillet, sauté garlic in the oil, mashing it as it cooks.
- Stir in clam juice, salt, pepper, and oregano and simmer for 5 minutes. Add clams with their juice, parsley, and onions. Cook, uncovered, for 10 minutes until liquid is reduced.
- Cook vermicelli according to package directions. Toss hot vermicelli with half of the sauce and the Parmesan cheese. Pour remaining sauce on top. Garnish with steamed clams.

Linguini with Salmon Sauce

Easy
2 Servings Main Course
4 Servings First Course

3 tablespoons butter
½ cup scallions, sliced
½ cup ripe tomatoes, peeled, seeded, and chopped (optional)
1 tablespoon lemon juice
¼ cup dry white wine
1 tablespoon tomato paste
1 cup heavy cream
Freshly ground pepper to taste
½-1 cup smoked salmon, coarsely chopped
8 ounces linguini
2 tablespoons fresh parsley, basil, or dill, chopped

- Heat 2 tablespoons of the butter over medium heat. Sauté scallions until limp. If desired, add tomatoes and cook briefly.
- Add lemon juice and wine and reduce by one-third.
- Stir in tomato paste and cream. Cook over medium low heat until slightly reduced and until sauce begins to thicken. Add pepper and salmon.
- Cook linguini al dente. Drain and toss with 1 tablespoon butter in large, warm bowl.
- Pour hot salmon sauce over linguini and toss gently.
- Sprinkle with parsley, basil, or dill for garnish. Serve immediately.

This recipe also works well with freshly cooked salmon or canned red salmon, drained and rinsed.

Pasta with Cream and Fresh Herbs

Easy
6 Servings

1½ cups heavy cream
4 tablespoons unsalted butter
½ teaspoon salt
⅛ teaspoon nutmeg
Pinch of cayenne pepper
¼ cup Parmesan cheese, freshly grated
1 cup fresh herbs, chopped (any combination of chives, parsley, basil, oregano, or mint)
Salt and pepper to taste
1 pound fresh pasta

- Combine cream, butter, salt, nutmeg, and cayenne pepper in a saucepan and simmer over low heat for 20 minutes until thickened.
- Stir in Parmesan cheese and herbs. Season with salt and pepper, if desired, and cook for a few minutes.
- Cook pasta al dente; drain; combine with sauce and serve.

Skiers' Delight Pasta

2 (10-ounce) packages fresh fettuccine
4 tablespoons unsalted butter
12 ounces prosciutto, shredded
½ cup pine nuts
1 cup Parmesan cheese, freshly grated
1 teaspoon nutmeg
  Salt and pepper to taste
1½ cups petite peas
1-1½ cups heavy cream

- Cook fettuccine according to package directions.
- Melt butter in heavy-bottomed, large pot.
- Add cooked pasta to butter and toss well.
- Add prosciutto, pine nuts, cheese, and spices. Mix well. Gently stir in peas.
- Add enough cream so mixture is coated well, but not too runny.
- Heat mixture to serving temperature. Serve.
- Broccoli may be substituted for peas, if desired.

A hearty dish for cold winter nights!

Dixie Pasta

1 cup country ham
2 tablespoons olive oil
1 clove garlic, minced
¼ cup onion, chopped
1 medium zucchini, sliced
½ cup fresh green beans, blanched
1 cup broccoli florets, blanched
½ cup carrots, sliced
1 medium tomato, peeled, seeded, and chopped
½ teaspoon oregano
½ teaspoon basil
⅓ (12-ounce) package fettucine, cooked
⅓ (8-ounce) package linguini, cooked
1 teaspoon butter
½ cup Parmesan cheese, grated

- In large frying pan, brown country ham and remove.
- In same pan, add olive oil, garlic, onion, and zucchini. Sauté for 2 minutes.
- Add beans, broccoli, carrots, and tomato. Season with oregano and basil. Sauté for 3-5 minutes.
- Place hot pasta in warmed bowl.
- Stir in butter and ¼ cup cheese.
- Top with vegetable and ham mixture and ¼ cup cheese.

Fettucine with Zucchini and Mushrooms

Easy
6 Servings

1 pound fettucine
¾ pound mushrooms, thinly sliced
1½ sticks butter
1¼ pounds zucchini, julienned
1 cup heavy cream
¾ cup Parmesan cheese, grated
½ cup fresh parsley, chopped

- Cook the fettucine according to package directions so that it is al dente.
- In a large, deep skillet, melt ½ stick of the butter and sauté the mushrooms for 2 minutes.
- Add the zucchini, heavy cream, and remaining stick of butter, which has been cut into small pieces.
- Bring to a boil and simmer for 3 minutes.
- Add fettucine to vegetables and cream.
- Toss with Parmesan cheese and parsley.

Pasta dough rolls out smoother and easier if allowed to "rest" at least 10 minutes before rolling.

A few drops of oil added to water while cooking pasta will keep the pot from boiling over and the pasta from sticking.

Angel Hair Pasta with Three Caviars

Easy
4-6 Servings

8 ounces angel hair pasta
2 tablespoons vegetable oil
⅓ cup fresh chives, minced
2 hard cooked egg yolks, finely chopped
¼ cup sour cream
2 tablespoons fresh lemon juice
¾ cup heavy cream
3 ounces (or more) each golden, red, and black caviar

- Cook pasta in 4 quarts of water, al dente. Drain, rinse, and drain again.
- Place pasta in large bowl and toss in oil to prevent sticking.
- Gently combine chives and egg yolks (saving some of each for garnish) and add to pasta.
- Just before serving, mix together sour cream, lemon juice, and heavy cream. Stir gently into pasta. Do not refrigerate.
- Arrange on serving platter in small portions and put a serving of each color caviar on top.
- Garnish with reserved chives and egg yolks.

121

Baked Pasta with Chicken and Roasted Red Peppers

Difficult
8 Servings

2 tablespoons olive oil
7 tablespoons unsalted butter
½ pound mushrooms, chopped
½ pound sweet red peppers, roasted and chopped
¾ cup onion, chopped
½ cup carrots, sliced
⅓ cup celery, chopped
1¼ teaspoons garlic, minced
½ teaspoon rosemary, crumbled
1 chicken, cooked, picked, and cut into bite-sized pieces
1 cup white wine
2 teaspoons salt
Pepper to taste
1 cup chicken broth
½ cup sherry
6 tablespoons flour
3 cups milk
1½ cups Parmesan cheese
2 ounces prosciutto, shredded
½ pound mozzarella cheese, grated
1 (8-ounce) box lasagna noodles, cooked according to package directions

- In a small skillet, heat 1 tablespoon of the olive oil and 1 tablespoon of the butter and sauté mushrooms. Remove from heat and add to red peppers. Set aside.
- In another skillet, heat remaining 1 tablespoon of olive oil and 1 tablespoon of butter and sauté onion, carrots, celery, and garlic. Season with rosemary. Add chicken and ½ cup wine. Increase heat to medium high and reduce wine, stirring often. Season with 1 teaspoon of the salt and pepper to taste. Remove from heat and set aside.
- In a saucepan, combine chicken broth, sherry, and remaining ½ cup of wine. Cook over medium high heat for 5 minutes; set aside.
- In a saucepan, melt remaining 5 tablespoons butter over medium heat. Stir in flour. Whisk in milk and let the sauce come just to a boil. Reduce to low heat and simmer until thickened. Stir in reserved broth mixture and ½ cup Parmesan cheese. Add remaining 1 teaspoon salt and pepper to taste. Stir until thickened.
- In a 9x13-inch greased baking dish, spread a small amount of thickened white sauce. Arrange a layer of noodles on top. Layer half of the chicken mixture, half of the shredded prosciutto, half of the mushroom mixture, 1 cup of the white sauce, ½ cup Parmesan cheese, ⅓ cup mozzarella cheese. Repeat layers and top with noodles, remaining sauce, and cheeses.
- Bake for 30 minutes in a preheated 400° oven. Let stand 15 minutes before serving.
- This dish may be assembled one day in advance and refrigerated until ready to bake.

The best pasta is made from Durum wheat flour which has more gluten and elasticity than a soft wheat flour.

Sausage and Vegetable Pasta

Easy
4 Servings

¼   cup green pepper, chopped
¼   cup onion, chopped
½   pound fresh mushrooms, sliced
3   tablespoons butter
1   pound Polish sausage, sliced,
      bite-sized
2   cups zucchini, sliced (can
      substitute peas or broccoli)
2   tomatoes, chopped
      or
1   (16-ounce) can tomatoes, well-
      drained
½   teaspoon garlic powder
1   teaspoon oregano
1   teaspoon Italian seasoning
½   cup Parmesan cheese
1   (8-ounce) package fettucine,
      cooked

- In a large skillet, sauté green peppers, onions, and mushrooms in butter.
- Add sausage, zucchini, tomatoes, garlic powder, oregano, and Italian seasoning. Heat thoroughly, approximately 10 minutes.
- Stir in Parmesan cheese and let melt.
- Serve over hot buttered fettucine.

Never rinse good quality dried pasta or freshly made pasta after cooking. It will not be sticky, and loss of flavor and nutrients may result.

Light Tomato Sauce

Easy
1 Quart

2   tablespoons olive oil
1   medium onion, chopped
1   clove garlic, crushed
1   (15-ounce) can tomato sauce
6   large tomatoes, peeled, seeded,
      and chopped
4   tablespoons fresh parsley,
      chopped
3   tablespoons fresh basil, chopped
1   tablespoon fresh oregano,
      chopped

- In a medium saucepan, sauté onion and garlic in oil until limp. Do not brown.
- Add tomato sauce and tomatoes, blending well.
- Add seasonings, reserving 2 tablespoons parsley and 1 tablespoon basil, and simmer over low heat for 45 minutes.
- Before serving, stir in remaining parsley and basil.
- Serve over hot pasta.

Jim Kroncke's Famous Spaghetti Sauce

Easy
6-8 Servings

¼   cup olive oil
½   cup onion, chopped
1   clove garlic, minced
½   pound fresh mushrooms,
      chopped
2   tablespoons dried parsley
½   pound ground chuck
1   pound sausage, Italian or regular
1   (28-ounce) can tomatoes
1   (16-ounce) can tomatoes
1   (12-ounce) can tomato paste
1   teaspoon dried basil
2   teaspoons dried oregano
¼   teaspoon pepper
2   tablespoons sugar
1-2 teaspoons salt

- In a large skillet, slowly sauté onion, garlic, mushrooms, and parsley in oil for 5 minutes. Remove mixture to a bowl and set aside.
- In the same skillet, brown ground chuck and sausage. Drain well.
- Combine mushroom mixture with beef and sausage in a Dutch oven. Add remaining ingredients and bring to a boil.
- Simmer, covered, for 3-3½ hours, stirring often.
- Serve over hot spaghetti noodles.

Fresh wet pasta cooks in 30 seconds, fresh dried pasta in 3 minutes, and commercial dried pasta in 8-15 minutes.

Pasta with Uncooked Sauce

Easy
4-6 Servings

½   cup olive oil
1½ pounds fresh tomatoes, peeled,
      seeded, and chopped
      Few flakes red pepper seeds
½   cup black olives, chopped
2   tablespoons parsley, minced
1   clove garlic, minced
3-4 tablespoons fresh basil or
      oregano, chopped
      Fresh ground pepper to taste
1   pound rotelle or farfalle pasta

- In a large bowl, combine first eight ingredients and set aside at room temperature for at least 2 hours.
- Cook pasta al dente and drain. Place in a warm serving bowl. Pour sauce over and toss to combine. Serve.

Great hot weather dish.

Tomato Herb Pasta with Carrot Sauce

Difficult
4 Servings

Pasta:

1½ cups unbleached flour
4 tablespoons parsley, minced or combination of parsley, basil, and oregano
1 small clove garlic, minced
2 eggs
2 tablespoons tomato paste
1 tablespoon olive oil

- Place flour, herbs, and garlic in the bowl of a food processor. Process to combine.
- Add eggs, tomato paste, and olive oil. Process until a ball is formed, adding more flour as necessary.
- Remove dough from machine and let rest for 5 minutes.
- Roll and cut dough using a hand-crank pasta machine on thinnest widths.
- Dry pasta on a towel or hang on a rack until ready to cook.
- Cook pasta in 4 quarts of boiling water for 30 seconds if still wet and 3 minutes if dry. Drain and serve with Carrot Sauce.

Carrot Sauce:

3 tablespoons butter
½ pound fresh mushrooms, chopped
3 shallots, diced
4 baby carrots, cut in 1-inch julienned lengths
2 tablespoons fresh chopped parsley, some reserved
1 tablespoon fresh chopped basil, some reserved
Pepper to taste
2 tablespoons Madeira or Port
⅛ teaspoon freshly grated nutmeg
½ cup reduced chicken stock (boiled down from 1 cup)
½-¾ cup cream
2 tablespoons fresh lemon juice
1 cup freshly grated Parmesan cheese

- Melt butter in a medium sauté pan. Add mushrooms and shallots. Sauté for 5 minutes.
- Add carrots, herbs, and pepper. Sauté 5 more minutes.
- Add Madeira, nutmeg, chicken stock, and cream. Simmer until sauce is reduced by a third (about 10 minutes). Flavor with lemon juice and reserved herbs. Serve over pasta and top with Parmesan cheese.

Tomato Pasta may be topped simply and deliciously with butter, Parmesan cheese, and fresh parsley!

Ann's Canneloni

Besciamellia Sauce:

6	tablespoons unsalted butter
6	tablespoons flour
1½	cups whole milk
1½	cups heavy cream
½-1	teaspoon salt
¼	teaspoon white pepper
½	teaspoon nutmeg

- Melt butter in a heavy saucepan. Add flour and cook for 2 minutes over medium heat. Do not brown.
- Stir in milk and then cream. Cook over medium heat until thickened, stirring constantly.
- Remove from heat and add salt, white pepper, and nutmeg. Set sauce aside.

Canneloni Filling:

4	tablespoons butter
⅓	cup onion, finely chopped
2	cloves garlic, finely chopped
1	(10-ounce) package frozen chopped spinach, thawed, drained, and chopped again
1½	pounds ground round beef
4	chicken livers
10	tablespoons Parmesan cheese, freshly grated
2	tablespoons heavy cream
2	eggs, lightly beaten
1	teaspoon oregano
½	teaspoon salt
1	teaspoon pepper
2	(8-ounce) boxes manicotti shells
1	tablespoon salt
1	tablespoon olive oil
2	cups extra thick and zesty bottled spaghetti sauce

- Melt 2 tablespoons of the butter in a large sauté pan. Add onion and garlic and sauté over medium heat until onion is translucent.
- Add spinach and sauté for 5 minutes or until moisture has been removed from spinach. Transfer mixture to large bowl.
- In the same pan, melt 1 tablespoon of the butter and cook beef until lightly browned, breaking up any lumps. Drain and add to spinach mixture.
- Melt remaining 1 tablespoon of butter in sauté pan. Add chicken livers and sauté until browned, but slightly pink inside. Remove from pan, cool, and chop coarsely. Add to spinach mixture.
- Add to spinach mixture 6 tablespoons of the Parmesan cheese, cream, eggs, oregano, ½ teaspoon salt, and pepper. Mix well.

Assembly instructions on next page.

With excess summer tomatoes: Peel and place on cookie sheet in freezer until frozen. Then store in ziploc bags in freezer. Great during the winter for soups, spaghetti sauce, etc.

To Assemble:
- Cook manicotti shells in boiling water with salt and oil. Cook a few minutes less than package directions instruct. Drain and rinse shells. Set aside.
- Preheat oven to 375°.
- Pour 1 cup tomato sauce in a 3½-quart casserole (15x10x2).
- Fill 20 manicotti shells with ⅓ cup filling each. Place filled manicotti in tomato sauce in two rows of 10 each.
- Pour Besciamellia Sauce over stuffed shells and sprinkle with 4 tablespoons Parmesan cheese.
- Pour remaining cup tomato sauce in two lines lengthwise across shells.
- Bake in preheated 375° oven for 25-30 minutes until heated through and bubbly.
- Can be frozen.

Divine Italian Pie

Easy
6 Servings

Crust:
- 6 ounces vermicelli, cooked and drained
- ¼ cup butter
- ½ cup Parmesan cheese, grated
- 1 egg, beaten
- 1 teaspoon dried basil

Filling:
- 1 pound lean ground beef
- ¼ pound ground sausage
- 1 medium onion, chopped
- 1 (15½-ounce) jar "best" prepared spaghetti sauce
- 1 (8-ounce) package shredded mozzarella cheese

Crust:
- Combine all crust ingredients in a bowl. Chop mixture and press into bottom and sides of a 10-inch pie plate.

Filling:
- Brown beef, sausage, and onion in a skillet. Drain well.
- Combine meats and spaghetti sauce in a mixing bowl.
- To assemble pie, sprinkle ¼ cup of cheese over crust. Pour meat mixture on top. Sprinkle with remaining cheese. Bake in a preheated 350° oven for 30 minutes or until golden brown.

SECCA Santa Spanakopeta

3 packages frozen, chopped spinach, thawed
4 tablespoons butter
2 bunches green onions, chopped
½ cup chopped parsley
1 pound feta cheese, drained and crumbled
1 cup small curd cottage cheese
7 eggs, well beaten
3 sticks butter, melted
1 pound phyllo leaves, thawed

- Preheat oven to 350°.
- Squeeze excess water from spinach. Sauté onions in butter until soft. Add spinach. Let cool. Add cheeses, parsley, and eggs.
- Butter a baking dish 17x11½x2-inches. Place 8-10 phyllo leaves in pan, brushing each with melted butter. Spread with the spinach mixture. Cover with 8-10 more leaves, again brushing each first with melted butter.
- With a sharp knife, cut through top to mark 24 squares.
- Bake for 1 hour or until golden brown and puffy. Serve.

When cutting mold off cheese, dip knife in vinegar first to prevent mold from returning. Store cut cheese, wrapped in plastic wrap, in a jar.

Fabulous Ham and Cheese Soufflé

16 slices white bread, crust cut off and cubed
½ pound ham, cubed
   or
1 pound sausage, cooked and drained
1½ cups Swiss cheese, cut into small cubes
4 cups (1-pound) sharp Cheddar cheese, grated
6 eggs
3 cups milk
½ teaspoon onion salt
½ teaspoon dry mustard
¼ cup butter, melted
3 cups corn flakes, crushed

- Preheat oven to 375°.
- Grease a 9x13-inch baking dish.
- Spread half of bread cubes evenly on bottom. Add ham (or sausage) and both cheeses. Cover with remaining bread cubes.
- In a medium bowl, mix eggs, milk, onion salt, and dry mustard. Pour evenly over bread cubes. Refrigerate overnight.
- Combine corn flakes and butter for topping. Spread over casserole.
- Bake for 40 minutes.

Egg and Mushroom Casserole

Easy
10-12 Servings

12 slices day-old white bread, crusts removed
6 tablespoons butter, softened
½ pound fresh mushrooms, sliced
1½ pounds New York sharp cheese, grated
6 eggs
2 cups half and half
1 cup heavy cream
1½ teaspoons dry mustard
¼ teaspoon salt
½ teaspoon paprika

- Preheat oven to 350°.
- Spread bread slices with butter and cut into 1-inch strips. Place in a 9x13-inch casserole dish.
- Sauté mushrooms with remaining butter in a small skillet. Set aside to cool.
- Mix grated cheese with mushrooms and their liquid. Pour evenly on top of bread.
- In a medium bowl, beat eggs lightly. Add remainder of ingredients except the paprika and blend. Pour over top of cheese and mushroom mixture. Sprinkle with paprika.
- Bake for 30 minutes.
- This dish can be prepared the day before. Cover and refrigerate. Bring it to room temperature before baking.

To peel an egg: Put a tiny hole in larger end of egg before boiling. Chill after boiling for easier peeling.

Brunch Casserole

Easy
12 Servings

4 cups day-old white or French bread, cubed
2 cups Cheddar cheese, shredded
10 eggs, lightly beaten
1 quart milk
1 teaspoon dry mustard
1 teaspoon salt
¼ teaspoon onion powder
Freshly ground pepper to taste
8-10 slices bacon, cooked and crumbled
½ cup mushrooms, sliced
½ cup tomatoes, peeled and chopped

- Generously butter a 9x13-inch baking dish.
- Arrange bread cubes in baking dish and sprinkle with cheese.
- In a bowl, add the next six ingredients and mix. Pour evenly over bread.
- Sprinkle mixture with bacon, mushrooms, and tomato. Cover and chill up to 24 hours.
- To bake, preheat oven to 325° and bake, uncovered, for 1 hour or until set. Tent with foil if top begins to overbrown.

Garlic Cheese Grits
Heritage of Hospitality

1   cup quick-cooking grits
1   teaspoon salt
¼   pound butter
1   (6-ounce) roll garlic cheese
2   eggs
½   cup milk
1   cup cornflakes, buttered

- Preheat oven to 350°.
- Cook grits in 4 cups salted water until thick.
- In a small saucepan, melt butter and cheese together. Add to cooked grits.
- Beat eggs and milk together in a small bowl. Gradually add this to grits mixture. Blend well.
- Pour into a buttered medium casserole. Top with cornflakes.
- Bake for 45 minutes.

Lightly mash garlic clove with edge of knife before peeling. Peel will come off easily. Then mash garlic again for easier mincing.

Sausage and Cheese Grits

1   pound sausage
    Hot pepper sauce to taste, about
       4 drops
1   clove garlic, minced
½   teaspoon salt
⅛   teaspoon pepper
1   cup quick-cooking grits
1   cup extra sharp Cheddar cheese,
       grated
2   large eggs, well beaten

- Preheat oven to 350°.
- Brown sausage in a large skillet and drain off grease.
- Add hot pepper sauce, garlic, salt, and pepper to sausage and stir well. Set aside.
- Cook grits according to package directions. Add to sausage and blend.
- Add Cheddar cheese and eggs. Mix well. Pour into a well buttered 9x9-inch baking dish.
- Bake, uncovered, for 1 hour.

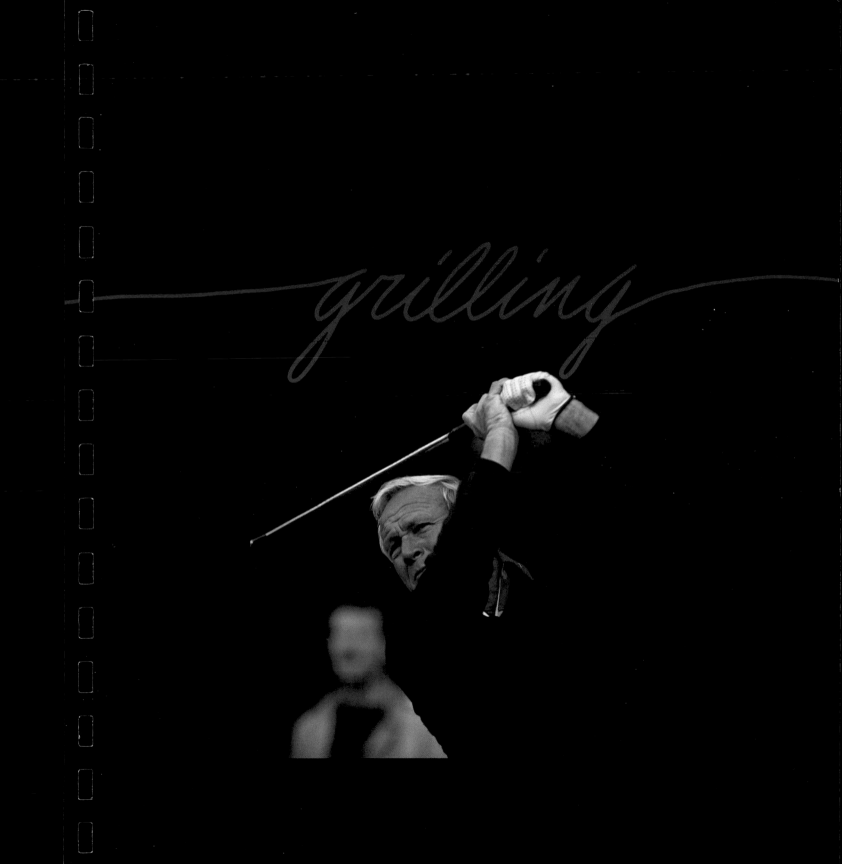

Steeplechase Picnic
Angels on Horseback
Party Lamb Pitas
Grilled Salmon Steaks
Vegetable Brochettes
Grilled Pineapple
Raspberry Buttermilk Sherbet

Arnold Palmer at the recent Vantage Championship held at Tanglewood

The mild days of winter and balmy summer breezes provide the perfect climate for year-round recreational activities in Winston-Salem. The city boasts numerous public and private golf courses, tennis courts, swimming pools, recreation centers, and parks.

Tanglewood, the largest and one of the most beautiful of the city/county parks, was once the estate of William and Kate Reynolds. Now a public park complete with winding trails, camping facilities, a tennis center, swimming pool, and fishing and boating, Tanglewood also features hotel accommodations and two 18-hole championship golf courses, one of which served as home for the 1974 PGA Championship. Tanglewood hosts the annual million-dollar Vantage Championship Senior PGA Tour event.

Photo by D. Michael O'Bryon

THE ART OF GRILLING

There are few pleasures in life that equal the wonderful aroma of freshly grilled foods and very few that satisfy the senses as well as remain simple and healthy to eat. Grilling is an ancient art first mastered by early man well over 100,000 years ago. The Spanish introduced this simple technique of cooking meats over hot coals to Mexico and the American Southwest in the 1800's where it quickly became a popular way to feed the hungry cattle-rancher and cowboy. Grilling became part of American tradition first at large-scale outdoor barbecues featuring spit-roasted pig and "Texas" ribs and later, when Americans moved to the suburbs, at small, patio cookouts. Today the value of grilling has been rediscovered by Americans who are demanding fresh, flavorful food that is low in fat and calories and, at the same time, elegant. Grilling incorporates the best in eating traditions to become a permanent culinary art.

Today's grilling techniques are as simple as those our ancestors used with no special requirements other than a well-prepared fire and the freshest of ingredients. This section on grilling contains a selection of recipes that can be prepared over coals, gas, or even indoors. We hope they will serve as a starting point for creative, healthy approaches to eating! To assist in mastering the simple art of grilling, we've listed below some basic tips:

—Allow 30-45 minutes for coals to reach a medium hot stage. Coals should be covered with a layer of gray ash with occasional red glow visible.

—Consider using hardwood charcoals (mesquite, hickory, oak, cherry) instead of standard charcoal briquets. Hardwood charcoal is made directly from whole pieces of wood with no additives or filler. It burns hotter and cleaner, imparts flavor, and can be re-used.

—For extra flavor and aroma, add soaked hardwood chips, aromatic herbs, or grapevine cuttings directly to the fire.

—Foods thicker than 1½ inches or requiring a longer cooking time than 15 minutes should be grilled covered for a more even and moist result.

—Grill foods at room temperature.

—Always oil the grill rack before cooking fish or poultry to prevent sticking.

—For ease in turning delicate foods such as seafood, use a well-oiled, hinged grill rack.

—Seafood should not be marinated more than 30 minutes or in heavily acid mixtures which tend to break down the fibers and actually "cook" the fish.

—Use small amounts of sugar or honey in marinades or basting sauces as they have a tendency to burn when hot.

—Do not salt meats prior to or during the grilling process, as the salt will draw out the meat's moisture and cause drying.

—If using wooden skewers or picks, pre-soak for 20 minutes to prevent burning.

—Gas grills have permanent briquet-shaped rocks which heat up easily and quickly. Gas fires are hotter than a charcoal briquet fire, but less hot than a hardwood charcoal fire. Gas grills make grilling easier but compromise in flavor.

—A kettle-type grill with a domed hood reflects heat off all inside surfaces and results in food cooked more quickly and evenly than on an open grill.

—An open grill does not have a hood, is the least expensive, and is best used for quick cooking of food that is no more than 1½ inches thick.

—Special tools: fireproof mitt
long-handled tongs, spatula, fork, and basting brush
spray bottle for flare-ups
wire brush for scraping racks clean
skewers for threading meats, fish, and vegetables
hinged grill rack
non-aluminum pan for marinating
electric firestarter

—Many people have experimented with a special variation of grilling—smoking. This technique involves a long exposure of foods to smoke and heat generated from slow-burning woods. The results are deliciously moist meats, fish, and poultry with a distinctive smokey flavor.

—We have included several recipes using the smoking method in our grilling section.

—For successful smoking:

• Be sure to have coals at their hottest point before topping with wood, adding food and covering smoker.

• Various soaked woods placed over charcoal enhance the flavors of smoked foods. Hickory for pork and poultry, and cherry or apple for fish are excellent choices.

Danish Cheese Melt

1 pound combination Danish cheeses, cut into ¼-inch thick slices (use a mixture of Danish fontina, svenbo, creamy havarti, or any of the spiced creamy havartis)
1 (8-ounce) can dried green chilies
Hot jalapeño peppers, as desired

Suggested items for dipping:
    Raw vegetables, cubed
    Cooked new potatoes
    Tortilla chips
    Potato chips
    Rounds of French bread

- Arrange overlapping slices of cheese in cast iron or ceramic skillet 10-12-inches in diameter and 2-inches deep. Sprinkle drained chilies over cheese.
- Place pan on grill over hot coals or on burner over low heat. Let cheese melt slowly, removing pan from heat occasionally if bubbling seems too vigorous.
- When heating on grill, dipping can begin as soon as cheese in center of skillet begins to melt. During serving, if cheese begins to firm up, simply return to heat until cheese is melted.

Grilled Bleu Cheese Burgers

2-3 pounds lean ground beef
1 teaspoon salt
½ teaspoon freshly ground pepper
6 ounces cream cheese, softened with small amount of milk
2 tablespoons bleu cheese, crumbled
2 tablespoons onion, minced
2 teaspoons creamy horseradish sauce
2 teaspoons mustard
½ pound mushrooms, sliced and sautéed in butter

- Combine beef, salt, and pepper in a large bowl and blend well. Shape into 12-16 thin patties, about 4-inches in diameter. (Each will be half the final burger.)
- Combine cheeses, onion, horseradish, and mustard in a small bowl. Mix well.
- Put cheese filling on top half of each patty, spreading to within ½-inch of edge. Top with remaining patties, pressing edges together to seal.
- To grill, first sear patties to seal in juices. Then raise rack to about 3 inches from fire and broil to desired doneness.
- Top hamburgers with sautéed mushrooms.

Burgers may be made and filled one day ahead.

Herbert Smith's Grilled Beef Tenderloin

Easy
10-12 Servings

1   (4-5 pound) whole beef
      tenderloin, trimmed of fat
    Garlic salt
    Dijon mustard

- Pat meat dry and have at room temperature 30 minutes before grilling.
- Rub meat lightly on all sides with garlic salt and mustard.
- Grill over medium hot coals 30 minutes, turning once, for medium rare.

Meat can be cut in half for easier grilling.

Barbecued Beef Brisket

Easy
4-6 Servings

1   (3-4 pound) beef brisket
2   tablespoons liquid smoke
1   teaspoon garlic, minced
1   teaspoon onion, minced
2   teaspoons celery salt
2   tablespoons Worcestershire
      sauce
1   cup barbecue sauce

- Cover brisket with liquid smoke, garlic, onion, celery salt, and Worcestershire sauce. Marinate overnight in refrigerator.
- Place brisket in a roasting pan, cover, and bake in a preheated 300° oven for 4-5 hours.
- The last hour, put brisket on grill and baste often with barbecue sauce.

Zesty Grilled Flank Steak

Easy
4 Servings

¾   cup vegetable oil
¼   cup soy sauce
¼   cup honey
2   tablespoons red wine vinegar
2   tablespoons green onion,
      chopped
1   large clove garlic, minced
1½ teaspoons ginger
1½ pounds flank steak

- Combine the first seven ingredients to make marinade. Pour marinade over flank steak and marinate in refrigerator for at least 4 hours or preferably overnight. Turn steak several times.
- Remove steak from marinade. Grill for 7 minutes per side.
- To serve, slice thinly across the grain.

Grilled Flank Steak with Wine Sauce
Heritage of Hospitality

Easy
4 Servings

1½-2 pounds flank steak, lightly scored
1 teaspoon salt
1 teaspoon pepper
1 teaspoon crushed thyme
Soy sauce to taste
1 cup shallots, chopped
or
¾ cup green onions, chopped, including tops
1¼ cups red wine
1 stick butter
2 tablespoons chopped parsley

• On steak rub in salt, pepper, and thyme. Brush on soy sauce with pastry brush until lightly coated on one side. Allow to stand at room temperature for 30-45 minutes.

• In a medium saucepan, combine shallots and red wine. Bring to a boil. Add butter and parsley; heat until butter melts. Set sauce aside.

• To grill steak, first sear to seal in juices. Then raise rack to about 3-inches from fire; broil meat for about 4-7 minutes on each side, depending on desired doneness.

• Remove from rack and slice in thin, diagonal strips. Arrange on platter and serve with warm wine sauce.

Lemon Grilled Chuck Steak

Easy
8 Servings

1 teaspoon lemon peel, grated
⅔ cup lemon juice
⅓ cup vegetable oil
2 green onion tops, chopped
1½ teaspoons salt
⅛ teaspoon pepper
1 teaspoon Worcestershire sauce
1 teaspoon prepared mustard
1 (4-pound) chuck steak, 1½- inches thick

• Combine first eight ingredients to make marinade. Pour marinade over chuck steak and marinate for 3 hours at room temperature, 6 hours in refrigerator, or overnight in refrigerator.

• Grill over coals for 12 minutes per side for rare or 15 minutes per side for medium.

• To serve, slice thinly across the grain.

London Broil with Honey Ginger Marinade

1   (2½-pound) London Broil

Marinade:

3   tablespoons honey
1½ teaspoons ginger
1½ teaspoons garlic powder
¾   cup vegetable oil
1   green onion, chopped
¼   cup soy sauce
2   tablespoons vinegar

- In a bowl, whisk together the honey, ginger, and garlic powder. Stir in oil, onion, soy sauce, and vinegar.
- Place meat in a shallow dish and pour the marinade over it. Refrigerate for at least 8 hours, turning meat two or three times.
- Grill meat over hot coals to the desired doneness, basting frequently. Slice meat thinly on a diagonal.

Grilled London Broil

2   pounds London Broil,
      1½-inches thick
½   cup red wine vinegar
¼   cup olive oil
¼   cup soy sauce (or less)
      Black peppercorns, crushed

- Place meat in a non-aluminum pan.
- Mix together the vinegar, oil, and soy sauce and pour over meat.
- Cover and refrigerate for 4-6 hours, turning once.
- Bring meat to room temperature 30 minutes before grilling.
- Remove meat from marinade and coat all sides with crushed peppercorns.
- Grill over medium hot coals 6-7 minutes per side for medium rare.

When grilling chicken, place in sauce or marinade and bake in the oven (with your other food) for 20-30 minutes; then grill it. The chicken will cook on the grill faster.

Grilled Beef Brochettes

1	(0.6-ounce) package Italian dressing
¼	teaspoon oregano
1	cup red wine vinegar
½	cup water
¼	cup olive oil
⅓	cup soy sauce
2-3	pounds top sirloin, cubed
18-20	large fresh mushrooms
12	small onions
2	green peppers, cut into 12 sections
12	cherry tomatoes

- Combine first six ingredients. Pour over beef and marinate 4-5 hours.
- Parboil mushrooms, green peppers, and onions for 5 minutes.
- Alternate beef and vegetables on skewers.
- Place on grill over medium coals. Baste with marinade frequently and turn every few minutes until desired doneness is reached.

Marinated Chicken Sandwiches with Hot Mustard Sauce

Marinated Chicken Sandwich:

8	chicken breasts, skinned and boned
1	cup soy sauce
½	cup pineapple juice
¼	cup sherry
¼	cup firmly packed brown sugar
¾	teaspoon fresh garlic, minced
8	slices Monterey Jack cheese
8	Kaiser rolls or pita bread halves
	Hot Mustard Sauce

- Place chicken in shallow dish. Combine soy sauce, pineapple juice, sherry, brown sugar, and garlic. Pour over chicken and marinate 30 minutes.
- Grill chicken over hot coals for 25 minutes, basting with marinade and turning every 5 minutes.
- Place cheese slices on chicken during last 5 minutes of grilling.
- Serve chicken on Kaiser roll or pita bread with Hot Mustard Sauce.

Hot Mustard Sauce:

½	cup dry mustard
⅔	cup white vinegar
⅔	cup sugar
1	egg

- Combine all ingredients in a blender.
- Place in double boiler. Bring water to a boil and reduce heat to low. Stir constantly until sauce thickens, about 7 minutes.
- Cool before using and store in refrigerator.

Lemon Barbecued Chicken

2 (3-pound) fryers, each cut up
   into 8 pieces
1 cup vegetable oil
½ cup fresh lemon juice
⅛ teaspoon salt
¼ teaspoon pepper
1 teaspoon paprika
1 teaspoon rosemary
2 teaspoons basil
2 teaspoons parsley
2 teaspoons onion powder
½ teaspoon thyme
1 clove garlic, minced

- Place chicken pieces in a non-aluminum pan.
- Mix remaining ingredients together and pour over chicken. Cover tightly with plastic wrap and marinate in refrigerator for 6-8 hours, turning occasionally.
- Remove from refrigerator 1 hour before grilling.
- Grill 20-25 minutes per side or until done, basting often.

Memphis Outdoor Barbecued Chicken

½ cup vinegar
1 cup ketchup
1 tablespoon hot pepper sauce
1 tablespoon steak sauce
1 tablespoon Worcestershire sauce
1 lemon, sliced
1 stick margarine or butter
¼ teaspoon black pepper
¼ cup mustard
¼ cup cola
15-20 mixed pieces of chicken

- Mix together first ten ingredients in saucepan. Bring sauce mixture to a low boil. Cook for 1 hour, stirring occasionally.
- Grill chicken over medium low heated coals for 30 minutes, turning frequently.
- Begin basting with sauce and continue grilling for an additional 25 minutes. Total cooking time 55 minutes. Serve.

Chicken on the grill is delicious but often arduous for the chef on a hot summer day. Shorten the process by cooking the chicken in the microwave before grilling. The shortened grilling time prevents the chicken from burning and still gives that grilled flavor and appearance.

Grilled Ginger Chicken Breasts

Easy
6-8 Servings

6 chicken breast halves, boned
¼ cup soy sauce
3 tablespoons dry white wine
2 tablespoons lemon juice
2 tablespoons cooking oil
¾ teaspoon fine herbs, crushed
½ teaspoon ginger root, grated
1 clove garlic, minced
¼ teaspoon onion powder
 Dash of pepper
 Cherry tomatoes for garnish
 Fresh parsley for garnish

• Arrange chicken breasts in a shallow, 9x13-inch baking dish.
• Combine remaining ingredients in a small bowl. Mix well and pour over chicken. Cover and chill for 4 hours, turning every hour.
• Place chicken on rack and grill over hot coals for 5 minutes per side, basting twice with the marinade mixture.
• Transfer chicken to a warm platter and garnish.
• Garnish with cherry tomatoes and parsley.

Sesame Chicken Kebobs

Easy
4 Servings

1 large green pepper, cut into 1-inch pieces
2 medium onions, quartered
½ cup vegetable oil
¼ cup soy sauce
¼ cup dry white wine
¼ cup light corn syrup
1 tablespoon sesame seeds
2 tablespoons lemon juice
¼ teaspoon garlic powder
¼ teaspoon ground ginger
4 chicken breast halves, skinned, boned, and cut into 1-inch cubes
1 small pineapple, cut into 1-inch cubes
3 small zucchini, cut into 1-inch pieces
½ pound fresh mushroom caps

• In a small amount of water, blanch green pepper and onion in microwave for 2½ minutes.
• Combine next eight ingredients and mix well.
• Add chicken, cover, and marinate at least 2 hours in the refrigerator.
• Remove chicken and reserve marinade.
• Alternate chicken, pineapple, and vegetables on skewers.
• Grill about six inches from medium hot coals for 15-20 minutes or until done, basting with marinade frequently.

Grilled Cornish Hens with Hot Pepper Jelly

Easy
6-8 Servings

6-8 Rock Cornish game hens
¼ cup butter or margarine
¾ cup hot pepper jelly
2 tablespoons lime juice
　 Salt and pepper to taste

- Using poultry shears, cut hens in half. Rinse birds and pat dry.
- Combine butter and jelly in a saucepan and heat until melted. Add lime juice and set aside.
- Sprinkle birds with salt and pepper. Place birds skin side up on a grill approximately six inches over a bed of medium low coals.
- Grill birds, turning several times, until skin is brown and meat is no longer pink at the bone, 30-40 minutes. Baste with jelly mixture during last 15 minutes of cooking, using all. Serve.

Tom's Grilled Pork Chops

Easy
6 Servings

6 (¾-1 inch) thick pork chops
½ cup honey
½ cup vinegar
½ cup soy sauce

- Place pork chops in a casserole dish.
- In a bowl, stir together the honey, vinegar, and soy sauce. Pour over pork chops.
- Marinate for 8-12 hours in the refrigerator, turning and basting several times.
- Grill pork chops for 15 minutes, turning and basting once.

Pork Satés

Easy
6 Servings

½ cup chutney, puréed or chopped
　 very fine
¼ cup ketchup
1 tablespoon soy sauce
4 drops hot pepper sauce
2 tablespoons vegetable oil
2 pounds boneless pork loin, cut
　 ¾-inch thick in 1-inch squares
¾ cup salted peanuts, very finely
　 chopped

- Combine chutney, ketchup, soy sauce, hot pepper sauce, and vegetable oil in a medium bowl. Mix well.
- Pour this mixture into a shallow dish. Add meat squares and marinate for several hours, turning occasionally.
- Lace meat on skewers. Grill over medium coals for 15 minutes, turning to brown both sides, or place under a preheated broiler and broil the same.
- After meat has browned, immediately roll in finely chopped peanuts. Serve as an appetizer or entrée.

A Far Eastern spiciness permeates these delightful pork kabobs.

Pork Loin Lahaina

1 (6-pound) bone-in center cut pork loin roast
1 tablespoon safflower oil
1 clove garlic, minced
1 (1¼-inch) slice fresh ginger
1 (20-ounce) can sliced pineapple in juice
1 tablespoon soy sauce
1 tablespoon honey

- Have butcher remove chine bone.
- In a skillet, heat oil. Add garlic and ginger and sauté until lightly browned.
- Drain pineapple and reserve ½ cup juice. Add pineapple juice, soy sauce, and honey to skillet and heat through. Cool marinade to room temperature.
- Add ⅛ cup marinade to reserve pineapple and chill.
- Marinate pork roast in remaining marinade for 4 hours in refrigerator.
- To grill, place roast on rotisserie and grill to internal temperature of 170° or grill directly on rack turning every 20-30 minutes, basting frequently.
- Remove roast from grill and let sit for 10 minutes. Slice halfway between each chop and insert pineapple slice.
- Brush roast with marinade from pineapple slices and serve.

Lamb Chops Teriyaki

4 lamb chops, 1-inch thick
⅓ cup brown sugar, firmly packed
¼ cup soy sauce
2 tablespoons ketchup
1 tablespoon lemon juice
½ teaspoon salt
½ teaspoon ground ginger
¼ teaspoon pepper
⅛ teaspoon garlic powder

- To make sauce, combine all ingredients except lamb chops in a small bowl. Mix until smooth.
- Place lamb chops on rack about 3 inches from the heat and grill about 5 minutes per side. Brush often with sauce.

Party Lamb Pitas

1	(6-pound) leg of lamb, boned and butterflied
4	cloves garlic, minced
⅔	cup fresh lemon juice
⅓	cup dry white vermouth
2	tablespoons rosemary
1	teaspoon salt
1	teaspoon pepper
¼	cup olive oil
¼	cup Worcestershire sauce
⅔	cup Dijon mustard
20-30	(4-inch) round pitas, halved

- With a sharp knife, remove the skin, membrane, and fat from the leg of lamb. Place lamb in a cooking bag.
- Combine garlic, lemon juice, vermouth, 1 tablespoon of the rosemary, salt, pepper, olive oil, and Worcestershire sauce. Pour over the lamb.
- Refrigerate for 24 hours, turning lamb several times.
- Remove lamb from the bag 2 hours before cooking and reserve the marinade. Brush lamb with Dijon mustard.
- Sprinkle 1 tablespoon of rosemary over medium hot coals. Grill lamb, turning every 10-15 minutes and basting liberally with the reserved marinade. Cook until the internal temperature is 170°, about 40 minutes to 1 hour.
- Let lamb cool completely and then carve into thin slices.
- Warm pitas in a 350° oven for 5-7 minutes. Stuff with slices of lamb and serve with Cucumber Yogurt Sauce.

Cucumber Yogurt Sauce:

1	cup plain yogurt
1	medium cucumber, peeled, seeded, and chopped
½	teaspoon fresh lemon juice
¼	teaspoon dill

- Combine ingredients and refrigerate overnight.

6-inch or 8-inch packaged pitas may be used to make delicious entrée sandwiches.

Angels on Horseback

24 fresh oysters
    Juice of one lemon
 1 teaspoon oregano
    Fresh ground pepper
24 3″ strips of bacon
12 wooden skewers, soaked

- Sprinkle each oyster with lemon, oregano and pepper.
- Pre-cook bacon strips in microwave to soften— 45-60 seconds. Cool.
- Wrap each oyster in bacon and thread two per skewer. Refrigerate until ready to cook.
- Grill over hot coals until bacon is crispy. Serve as an appetizer.

Savory Swordfish

 6 swordfish steaks
¾ cup fresh lemon juice
½ cup butter, melted
1½ teaspoons basil, chopped
    Paprika
    Salt and pepper to taste

- Place swordfish steaks in pyrex dish. Pour lemon juice and butter over fish.
- Sprinkle with basil, paprika, salt, and pepper.
- Grill fish on an oiled rack over low heat.

Marinade for Swordfish Steaks

½ cup soy sauce
¼ cup vegetable oil
 3 tablespoons brown sugar
 1 clove garlic, finely chopped
 2 green onions, chopped
 1 teaspoon ginger root, grated
 1 tablespoon wine vinegar

- Combine all ingredients and marinate swordfish steaks 2 hours, or less, before broiling or grilling.
- Baste with marinade while cooking.

This versatile marinade can also be used for fresh shrimp.

Oriental Grilled Swordfish Steaks
Cumberland Cafe

6 (7-ounce) swordfish steaks,
   2-2½ inches thick

Marinade and Dipping Sauce:
½ cup sesame oil
¼ cup soy sauce
   Juice of 3 limes
   Juice of 1 lemon
3 cloves garlic, sliced
1 tablespoon fresh ginger, grated
2 tablespoons rice wine vinegar*
2 tablespoons fish sauce*
1 tablespoon fresh cilantro* or
   Chinese parsley, chopped
1 teaspoon Vietnamese chili* and
   garlic paste (optional)

Garnish:
2 tablespoons butter
1 large red onion, sliced
1 green, red, or yellow pepper,
   sliced (or combination)
2 teaspoons fresh cilantro,
   chopped

- Mix all marinade ingredients until blended.
- Place swordfish in marinade making sure both sides are coated well. Refrigerate for 4-24 hours, turning from time to time to ensure even marinating.
- Grill fish over open fire or broil 4 minutes on the first side and 2 minutes on the second side. Baste each steak with marinade at least once on each side.
- To prepare garnish, melt butter in a sauté pan. Sauté onions and peppers until crisp tender. Add cilantro.
- Arrange steaks on plates or platter. Top each with pepper/onion mixture. Serve with a small bowl of marinade for dipping.

*Available at oriental grocery store.
Tuna, grouper, or fresh wahoo steaks may be substituted for swordfish.*

Teriyaki Swordfish

⅓ cup soy sauce
⅓ cup bourbon
2 tablespoons brown sugar
½ teaspoon fresh ginger, grated
4 swordfish steaks, 1-inch thick

- Combine first four ingredients.
- Marinate swordfish steaks for 2 hours.
- Grill over medium hot coals for 5-7 minutes per side. Baste with extra marinade. Serve.

Grilled Seafood with Coriander Oil
La Chaudière Restaurant

Easy

Cobia, tuna, swordfish, grouper, or other firm, light-colored fish
1 tablespoon coriander seeds
1 cup safflower oil
¼-⅓ cup lime juice
Salt and pepper to taste

- Crush half of the coriander seeds.
- Combine crushed and whole seeds with oil in a bottle. (Best if prepared at least 24 hours in advance.)
- Before grilling fish, combine flavored oil and lime juice. Season with salt and pepper to taste.
- Grill fish and place on serving platter. Brush with coriander oil and serve with steamed spinach, tomatoes sautéed in garlic butter, and boiled new potatoes. Fish may be garnished with spring onions steamed and tied in a knot.

Sesamed Shrimp Ke-Bob Kelly
The Bingham School Inn, Mebane

Easy
4 Servings

2 pounds shrimp, peeled and deveined
Medium-size wooden skewers
½ cup butter, melted
¼-½ cup sesame seeds
1-2 teaspoons soy sauce

- Place 5-6 shrimp on each skewer.
- Brush one side of the shrimp with butter. Press sesame seeds into shrimp. Turn shrimp over and repeat butter and sesame seeds. Sprinkle with soy sauce.
- Grill over medium hot coals, turning occasionally.
- Remove from skewers and serve immediately with extra soy sauce.

Shrimp Kebobs

1 pound large fresh shrimp, peeled and deveined
1 (15¼-ounce) can pineapple chunks, undrained
1 (8-ounce) bottle Italian salad dressing
1 (8-ounce) can tomato sauce
2 tablespoons brown sugar
1 teaspoon prepared mustard
1 medium green pepper, cut into 1-inch cubes

- Drain pineapple chunks, reserving ¼ cup juice.
- In a small bowl, combine pineapple juice, Italian dressing, tomato sauce, brown sugar, and mustard. Mix well.
- Combine marinade and shrimp in a plastic bag. Toss gently.
- Marinate 2 hours in the refrigerator, turning bag occasionally.
- Remove shrimp and save marinade. Alternate shrimp, pineapple, and green peppers on four skewers.
- Grill over medium hot coals, 3-4 minutes on each side, or until done, basting with marinade.

Lemon Shrimp Brochettes

½ cup fresh orange juice
¼ cup white wine vinegar
¼ cup salad oil
¼ cup soy sauce
¾ pound fresh shrimp, peeled and deveined
Lemon wedges

- In a large bowl, combine first four ingredients. Add shrimp and marinate several hours.
- Alternate shrimp and lemon wedges on skewers.
- Grill over medium coals 3-4 minutes or until done, basting frequently with marinade.
- Heat remaining marinade and serve with shrimp.

To insure even cooking when grilling kebobs, slightly separate items on skewer.

Grilled Salmon Steaks

Easy
6 Servings

¼ cup butter, melted
1½ teaspoons soy sauce
1 tablespoon fresh lemon juice
1 teaspoon Worcestershire sauce
Dash of garlic salt
6 salmon steaks

- Mix butter, soy sauce, lemon juice, Worcestershire, and garlic salt. Brush on salmon steaks.
- Grill 10 minutes on one side. Baste and turn fish. Grill for 8-10 minutes more.
- Cooking time will depend on the thickness of the fish.
- Baste the fish frequently during grilling.

Grilled Salmon with Garlic and Lime

Easy
6-8 Servings

3-4 pounds of salmon filets
   or steaks
3 large cloves garlic
1 tablespoon salt
3 limes
   Melted butter for basting
   Lime slices

- Place salmon in a single layer in a large pyrex dish.
- Make a paste of the garlic and salt by mashing together. Spread on fish. Squeeze the juice and pulp of the limes over the fish. Marinate for 2 hours at room temperature.
- Oil grill. Grill fish over white coals for 5 minutes on one side. Turn fish and brush with melted butter. Grill for 10 more minutes.
- Garnish with lime slices.

Sprinkle rosemary on coals while cooking fish. Grouper may be used instead of salmon.

Grilled Grouper Filets

Easy
4 Servings

2 tablespoons lemon juice
2 tablespoons vegetable oil
1 tablespoon fresh dill, parsley,
   or fennel
   Freshly ground pepper to taste
4 (6-ounce) grouper filets

- In a small bowl, combine lemon juice, oil, herbs, and pepper and mix well.
- Brush fish with herb mixture.
- Spray grill rack or hinged fish rack well with no-stick cooking spray.
- Grill fish over medium high coals 5 minutes per side, basting once before turning.

147

Grilled Rainbow Trout with Pesto Mayonnaise

Easy
4 Servings

Grilled Rainbow Trout:

4 fresh rainbow trout,
approximately 1 pound
each, boned
Vegetable oil or olive oil

2 lemons, sliced thinly

8 sprigs fresh dill weed, fennel,
basil, or parsley, or
combination of these
Black pepper, freshly ground

- Wash and dry well insides and outsides of trout. Brush outsides with oil to prevent sticking on grill.
- Fill each cavity with lemon slices, 2 sprigs of herbs, and the pepper. Press fish together.
- Place fish directly over oiled grill rack or place in an oiled, hinged fish rack.
- Grill over medium high coals approximately 5 minutes per side until skin is nicely browned and fish is cooked through.
- Serve with Pesto Mayonnaise.

Pesto Mayonnaise:

1 cup mayonnaise (homemade
preferred)

4 tablespoons pesto sauce

2 tablespoons fresh lemon juice

- Stir together all three ingredients to form Pesto Mayonnaise.

Grilled Salmon with Honey, Ginger and Dark Soy
Jay's Restaurant

Easy
6 Servings

Marinade:

⅛ cup honey

¾ tablespoon fresh ginger, minced

⅛ cup dark soy sauce

⅛ cup white wine

1 tablespoon Pommery mustard

⅛ cup chopped parsley
Juice of ½ lemon

1 tablespoon salad oil

1 tablespoon vinegar
Salt and pepper to taste

6 (6-8 ounce) salmon steaks

- Combine marinade ingredients in a blender.
- Grill salmon on a very hot grill just to sear both sides of fish. Transfer to a baking dish.
- Spoon marinade over steaks. Bake in a preheated 400° oven for 5-8 minutes.
- Transfer salmon to a serving platter. Drizzle with marinade and serve.

148

Flounder Filets

Easy

Flounder filets
Butter
Mayonnaise
Lemon, sliced
Tomato, sliced
Onion, sliced
Parsley
Aluminum foil

- Preheat oven to 350° or grill.
- Wash filets and pat dry.
- Cut foil in large enough pieces to cover each filet easily. Butter or oil and place a filet on each.
- On each filet, lightly spread mayonnaise and cover with slices of lemon, tomato, and onion. Sprinkle with parsley.
- Wrap aluminum foil loosely around each filet.
- Cook approximately 15 minutes in oven or on the grill. If prepared in the oven, open foil and broil last 5 minutes.

Seafood Brochettes

Easy
6 Servings

2 pounds swordfish steaks, cut into 1-inch cubes
1 pound sea scallops
12 large shrimp, peeled, deveined
½ cup fresh lime juice
¼ cup vegetable oil
1 medium clove garlic, minced
1 tablespoon fresh parsley, minced
1 tablespoon fresh oregano, minced
24 cherry tomatoes
2 large green peppers, cut into 1-inch cubes

- Place swordfish, scallops, and shrimp in a large bowl.
- Combine remaining ingredients and pour over seafood. Cover with plastic wrap and let marinate 30 minutes to 2 hours in refrigerator.
- Alternate seafood and vegetables on skewers.
- Grill over medium coals, 5 minutes on each side, basting once.

Parboil new potatoes before using on shish-kebob with other vegetables.

Grilled Sea Scallops with Cilantro Sauce
Jay's Restaurant

Cilantro Sauce:

3 shallots, chopped
¾ cup white wine
8 ounces unsalted butter, cubed
½ cup cilantro, chopped
Artificial sweetener (optional)

4½ ounces scallops per person

3¼ inch strips roasted red pepper

- Place shallots and wine in a sauce pan. Reduce to 2 tablespoons of liquid.
- Add half of the cubed butter to pan and whisk until melted.
- Add cilantro and remaining butter stirring until butter is melted. Keep at room temperature until ready to use.
- If sauce seems bitter add up to ½ package of a granulated artificial sweetener.
- Thread scallops on skewers. Grill two minutes per side.
- Remove scallops from skewers and place on serving plate. Spoon a portion of sauce over scallops and on plate. Garnish with red pepper strips and serve.

Grilled Wild Duck Breasts
Heritage of Hospitality

Easy

Wild duck
Salt and pepper
Melted butter
Lemon juice
Worcestershire sauce

- Breast ducks and skin. Salt and pepper. Baste with melted butter, lemon juice, and Worcestershire sauce.
- Place breasts on grill, fleshy side up. Cook close to hot charcoal at 10 minutes per side.

Vegetable Brochettes

3 ears corn, quartered to
      1-1½ inches
3 medium zucchini, quartered
      to 1-1½ inches
½ cup butter, melted
2 tablespoons chives, minced
2 tablespoons parsley
½ teaspoon garlic salt

• On four large skewers, alternate corn and zucchini.
• Combine remaining ingredients and brush on vegetables.
• Cook on grill or broil in oven for 8 minutes, basting every 2 minutes.

Corn on the Grill

6 ears of corn
½ cup butter, melted
1 tablespoon parsley, chopped
1 tablespoon chives, chopped
¼ teaspoon salt
      Pepper to taste

• Combine melted butter with parsley, chives, salt, and pepper.
• Brush corn with butter and wrap each ear in foil.
• Grill over hot coals for 10-15 minutes on each side.

Grilled Potatoes

2 large baking potatoes, peeled
      and sliced into ¼-inch rounds
⅓ cup butter, melted
1 tablespoon fresh rosemary,
      chopped
      Freshly ground pepper to taste
1 tablespoon fresh parsley,
      chopped

• Pat potatoes dry on both sides.
• Combine next four ingredients.
• Brush one side of potatoes with butter mixture. Place potatoes buttered side down on grill rack over medium high coals. Grill approximately 10 minutes a side, basting several times and turning once.
• Potatoes should be nicely browned and crisp.

Grilled Whole Baby Squash

Easy
4 Servings

4 tablespoons butter, melted
2 tablespoons fresh herbs,
    chopped
    Freshly ground pepper to taste
4 baby yellow or zucchini squash,
    ends trimmed

- In a small bowl, combine butter with seasonings.
- Brush all sides of squash with butter mixture.
- Place squash on grill rack. Grill approximately 15 minutes or until lightly browned, turning and basting frequently.

Mustard-Garlic Marinade

Easy
¾ Cup

¼ cup Dijon mustard
3-4 cloves garlic, crushed
1 tablespoon cracked black pepper
¼ cup red or white wine
¼ cup olive oil

- Mix together all ingredients and spread on meat.
- Marinate in the refrigerator at least overnight.
- To vary, use 1 teaspoon rosemary.
- This marinade is best for lamb or pork.

Marinade for Beef

Easy
3 Cups

½ cup ketchup
1 teaspoon salt
2 tablespoons A-1 sauce
2 tablespoons sugar
2 cups white vinegar
2 tablespoons Worcestershire
    sauce
¼ cup water
2 tablespoons oil

- Mix all ingredients together, stirring thoroughly.
- Pour marinade into a plastic bag and add the meat. Fasten bag securely. Refrigerate overnight.
- Excellent for chicken or beef shish-kebobs or steaks.

Admiral Parson's Barbecue Sauce

Easy
3 Cups

1 cup water
¼ cup vinegar
½ cup butter
4 tablespoons brown sugar
4 tablespoons hot mustard
4 teaspoons salt
1 bay leaf
¼ teaspoon cayenne pepper
1 teaspoon hot pepper sauce
½ teaspoon mustard seed
1 large onion, grated or minced
　Juice of one-half lemon and
　　grated rind
⅛ teaspoon rosemary
4 teaspoons parsley, chopped
1 teaspoon black pepper
¼ teaspoon ground coriander
½ teaspoon liquid smoke (optional)
1 cup ketchup
4 tablespoons Worcestershire
　sauce

- Combine water and vinegar in a large saucepan.
- Over medium heat, add butter and stir until melted.
- Add remaining ingredients, except for ketchup and Worcestershire sauce. Bring to boil and simmer for 20 minutes.
- Add ketchup and Worcestershire sauce and simmer for 10 minutes.
- Use for baking or broiling, indoors or outdoors. Can be stored in refrigerator for several weeks.

Smoked Whole Salmon

Easy
10 Servings

1 (4-6 pound) salmon
　Peanut oil

- Using a smoker, use a full pan of charcoal with added apple tree or mesquite chips for flavor. If smoker has a water pan, use it as the steam keeps the salmon moist.
- Rub peanut oil on the skin and inside salmon.
- Place on the grill when coals are the hottest. Cover and smoke approximately 3 hours for a 4-pound salmon, 4 hours for a 5-pound salmon, and 5 hours for a 6-pound salmon.

Smoked Salmon Filet

1 (7-8 pound) salmon
Salt
Dark rum
Brown sugar

- Have seafood market filet one side of salmon, leaving the skin on.
- Salt both sides of salmon. Cover and refrigerate for 8 hours.
- Wash salt off, pat dry, and refrigerate for another 8 hours.
- Combine rum and brown sugar (amount according to taste) and brush on salmon 1 hour before smoking.
- Prepare smoker with hickory chips. Place on grill when coals are past their hottest.
- Smoke for 2½-3 hours.

Grilled Pineapple
Anne Byrd, professional cooking instructor

1 fresh pineapple
1-2 cups Kirsch liqueur
½-1 cup brown sugar

Kirsch Cream:
½ cup heavy cream
2 tablespoons confectioners sugar
1-2 teaspoons Kirsch liqueur

- Leaving the crown on, slice the pineapple lengthwise into quarters.
- Marinate the quarters in Kirsch for 12 hours, adding more Kirsch if necessary. This will depend upon the absorbency of the pineapple.
- After marinating, press brown sugar into the pineapple.
- Grill pineapple on both sides over hot coals, until the brown sugar caramelizes.
- Spoon extra brown sugar and Kirsch on top of the warm pineapple.
- In a small bowl, whip ingredients for Kirsch Cream to soft peaks.
- Top pineapple with dollop of Kirsch Cream.

meats

Traditional Christmas Dinner

Cream of Spinach Soup
Crown Roast of Pork with Cranberry Stuffing and Dijon
Mustard Sauce
Butternut Squash Soufflé
Green Bean and Carrot Sauté
Wild Rice and Almond Casserole
Cranberry Waldorf Salad Ring
Orange Raisin Muffins
Bûche de Noël

The White Hall Dining Room—from a c. 1818 Low Country, South Carolina plantation house, now installed in the Museum of Early Southern Decorative Arts.

Located within the restored village of Old Salem, the Museum of Early Southern Decorative Arts (MESDA) is the only museum in the country dedicated to exhibiting and researching the regional decorative arts of the early South. Nineteen rooms, dating from 1690 to 1820, and six galleries feature the furniture, paintings, textiles, ceramics, and silver of a particular period or region.

Photo by Smith/Weiler/Smith

Veal Scallopine with Tomatoes and Olives

Easy
4-6 Servings

8	slices veal scallopine
¼	cup flour
	Salt and freshly ground pepper to taste
1	egg, beaten with 1 tablespoon water
2	tablespoons vegetable oil
7	tablespoons butter
1	cup red or green bell pepper, thinly sliced
2	teaspoons garlic, minced
½	cup onion, chopped
½	cup pear-shaped tomatoes, chopped and drained
24	small stuffed green olives, sliced
1	teaspoon oregano
2	tablespoons red wine vinegar or dry red wine
3	tablespoons fresh parsley, chopped

- Pound each piece of veal lightly between two pieces of wax paper until ⅛-inch thick.
- Mix flour, salt, and pepper together. Coat veal with flour mixture. Shake off excess flour and dip in egg mixture.
- Heat oil and 1 tablespoon of the butter in large skillet. Add veal and sauté over medium heat until lightly browned, about 2-3 minutes per side. Remove to warm platter.
- Clean skillet. Add remaining 6 tablespoons butter and melt. Add bell pepper, garlic, and onion. Sauté about 5 minutes or until tender.
- Add tomatoes and olives and cook 1 minute. Add oregano and vinegar and cook 30 seconds over high heat.
- Pour hot vegetable mixture over veal and garnish with parsley.

Veal Cushions Capocelli
Valentino Gourmet Italian Restaurant

Easy
4 Servings

12	thin slices prosciutto ham
12	thin slices mozzarella cheese
12	(4-inch) medallions of veal, thinly sliced
½-¾	cup butter
½	cup Marsala wine
2	teaspoons butter
	Salt and pepper to taste

- Place a slice of prosciutto and a slice of cheese on a piece of veal. Fold veal over like an envelope. Secure with a wooden pick. Repeat procedure for all twelve pieces.
- Melt ½ to ¾ cup butter in a skillet and brown veal pockets well, for about 5 minutes. Remove them to a hot platter. Cover and set aside.
- Scrape the skillet well and add wine, 2 teaspoons butter, salt, and pepper to taste. Heat thoroughly. Pour over veal and serve.

155

Veal Chops with Morels

Easy
4 Servings

12-15 pieces dried morel mushrooms
    Salt and white pepper to taste
 4 (8-ounce) rib veal chops
    All purpose flour
 6 tablespoons clarified butter
 2 shallots, peeled and chopped
 ⅔ cup Madeira
 1⅓ cups heavy cream
 ½ cup beef broth

- Soak morels in cold water overnight. Drain and rewash six times. Pat dry.
- Preheat oven to 425°.
- Lightly salt and pepper the veal chops, then dust with flour. Shake off excess flour.
- In large skillet with oven-proof handle, heat 4 tablespoons butter over medium heat. Lightly brown the veal on both sides. Place pan in oven and cook 12 minutes. Remove veal to serving platter and cover.
- Degrease pan well. Return to heat and add 2 tablespoons butter. Add shallots and cook, stirring for a few seconds. Add morels and sauté for a few seconds.
- Add Madeira and reduce to ⅓ the volume. Add heavy cream and beef broth. Reduce sauce until it has obtained a light substance of its own.
- Uncover pan and pour sauce over veal. Serve immediately.

Veal Roast with Sour Cream Gravy

Easy
4 Servings

 1 (3-pound) veal roast
 4-6 small onions, skinned
 ½ teaspoon thyme
 1 teaspoon basil
 1 teaspoon oregano
 ½ cup dry white wine
 ⅓ pound fresh mushrooms, trimmed

Gravy:
 1 tablespoon butter
 2 tablespoons flour
 2 cups broth
 2 tablespoons sour cream

- Place veal and onions in a crock pot. Sprinkle with thyme, basil, and oregano. Pour in wine.
- Cook for 8 hours on low.
- Add mushrooms 30 minutes or so before serving.
- Mix all ingredients for gravy in a medium saucepan and heat. Serve warm with veal roast.

A pretty garnish for this roast is thin slices of lemon.

156

Grapefruit Sauce
La Chaudière Restaurant

Average
2½ Cups

1 cup fresh grapefruit juice
1 tablespoon grapefruit zest
⅓ cup chicken stock
2 sticks butter, softened

- Combine grapefruit juice, zest, and chicken stock in a saucepan. Heat over high heat and reduce liquid by half. Whisk butter into reduction by tablespoons until all is incorporated. Keep warm until ready to serve.
- Serve over pan sautéed fish, chicken, or veal scallops.

Perfect Tenderloin

Easy
10 Servings

1 whole tenderloin of beef, at room temperature
3-4 tablespoons butter
⅓-½ cup teriyaki sauce
1 clove garlic, minced

- Preheat oven to 400°.
- Place tenderloin on a rack in shallow roasting pan. Spread butter on top.
- Pour teriyaki sauce over tenderloin.
- Sprinkle with minced garlic.
- Bake for exactly 40 minutes. Remove from oven and let sit for 10 minutes before slicing. Tenderloin will be medium rare.

Marinated Roast Tenderloin

Easy
8-10 Servings

5-8 pounds tenderloin
    Lemon pepper to taste
2 cloves garlic, crushed
1½-2 cups soy sauce
½ cup bourbon
3 strips bacon
1 medium onion, sliced

- Sprinkle lemon pepper over tenderloin and place in a large plastic bag.
- In a small mixing bowl, combine garlic, soy sauce, and bourbon. Pour mixture over tenderloin.
- Marinate at room temperature for 2 hours or overnight in the refrigerator.
- Allow tenderloin to come to room temperature if marinating in refrigerator. Remove from bag and place on a rack in a shallow roasting pan.
- Place bacon strips on top. Pour marinade over roast and put slices of onion on top.
- Place in a preheated 450° oven; immediately reduce heat to 400° and roast 40-45 minutes. Allow to sit for 15 minutes before slicing.
- Slice thinly and serve with cocktail rolls for hors d'oeuvres or as desired for entrée.

Beef Tenderloin with Vegetables

⅓ pound fresh snow peas, strings removed
1 teaspoon sugar
2½ tablespoons soy sauce
1 tablespoon dry sherry
1½ teaspoons corn starch
3 tablespoons vegetable oil
5 large fresh mushrooms, quartered
½ (6-ounce) can water chestnuts, sliced
2 slices fresh ginger root
1 pound beef tenderloin, cut into 1-inch cubes

- Drop peas into a saucepan of boiling water and cook for 1 minute until they turn bright green. Drain and run them under cold water.
- Combine sugar, soy sauce, sherry, and corn starch in a small bowl.
- Pour 1 tablespoon of oil into a moderately hot wok. Add mushrooms, peas, and water chestnuts. Stir-fry for 2 minutes. Remove vegetables and set aside.
- Pour remaining 2 tablespoons of oil into wok. Add ginger root. Heat to high. Drop in beef and stir-fry 2-3 minutes until lightly brown. Remove ginger root.
- Return vegetables to wok to reheat briefly.
- Serve over rice.

For a more economical meal, substitute 1 pound of top round, cut in thin strips for tenderloin.

Civet "Beef and Wine"
The Stocked Pot and Company

½ cup butter (¼ cup oil may be substituted)
3 medium onions, sliced thick
3 pounds top round or sirloin beef, sliced in 2x½-inch strips
3 medium tomatoes, cored and peeled
10 whole cloves
1 cinnamon stick, broken in half
1 teaspoon salt
½ teaspoon fresh ground pepper
½ cup semi-dry white wine
3 scallions, chopped

- In a heavy skillet, melt butter. Add onions and sauté over medium heat until transparent.
- Add beef and sauté until lightly browned.
- Add tomatoes, cloves, cinnamon, salt, and pepper. Cook until tomatoes dissolve into mixture.
- Add wine and continue cooking until desired thickness of sauce.
- Remove to serving dish. Sprinkle scallions on top.
- Serve with rice.

Sauerkraut Stew
Old Salem Tavern

4   pounds meaty beef shortribs
    Flour seasoned with salt
      and pepper
2   large carrots, sliced
2   large onions, sliced
3-4 cloves garlic, sliced
4   cups water
1   small head of cabbage, shredded
12 ounces sauerkraut, rinsed and
      drained
8   cups of beef or veal stock
1   (12-ounce) can plum tomatoes
3   bay leaves
1   teaspoon thyme leaves
    Worcestershire sauce
    Salt and pepper to taste
1   pound Kielbasa sausage, sliced
    Chopped parsley
    Sour cream

- Cut ribs into pieces and toss with seasoned flour. Place in a baking pan with carrots, onions and garlic. Roast at 400° until lightly browned. Transfer all ingredients to a large kettle.
- Add water to baking pan and scrape up any browned bits. Add to the kettle.
- Add cabbage, kraut, stock, tomatoes and seasonings. Simmer gently until the meat is very tender and vegetables are completely cooked. Check seasoning.
- Add sliced Kielbasa and heat thoroughly. Serve bowls of stew garnished with chopped parsley, sour cream and black bread.

Substitute red wine for half water when called for in stews and pot roasts to produce a more flavorful dish.

Rib Roast Perfection

Easy

1   standing rib roast, any size

- Preheat oven to 350°.
- Place roast of any size in roasting pan. Cook in oven for 1 hour. Turn oven off. Do not open oven.
- Forty-five minutes before serving, turn oven back on to 325° and cook until ready to serve. Roast will be medium rare every time!

Beef Strips Oriental

Easy
4 Servings

1   pound flank steak, sliced thin across grain
⅓   cup soy sauce
⅓   cup dry white wine
1   teaspoon sugar
2-3   tablespoons corn starch
1   medium onion, sliced
1   cup mushrooms, sliced
¼   cup green pepper, sliced
¼   cup red pepper, sliced
1   can sliced water chestnuts

- Place steak strips in a shallow, 2-quart glass baking dish. Combine soy sauce, wine, and sugar. Pour over meat. Marinate for 1 hour or longer in refrigerator.
- Add corn starch, onion, mushrooms, peppers, and water chestnuts to meat mixture. Stir well.
- Cook in microwave on full power for 8-10 minutes, until sauce is thickened, stirring halfway through cooking time. Serve over rice.

So quick and easy!

Use peanut oil when cooking in a wok. You can heat to a higher temperature for stir-frying without oil smoking.

Marinated Beef Brisket

Easy
8-10 Servings

1   (4-5 pound) beef brisket
2   teaspoons unseasoned meat tenderizer
½   teaspoon celery salt
½   teaspoon seasoned salt
½   teaspoon garlic salt
¼   cup Worcestershire sauce
¼   cup liquid smoke

- Place beef brisket on heavy duty aluminum foil.
- Sprinkle beef with tenderizer, celery salt, seasoned salt, garlic salt, Worcestershire sauce, and liquid smoke. Roll tightly in aluminum foil and marinate overnight in refrigerator.
- Place foil wrapped brisket in crock pot, cutting brisket in half if necessary.
- Cook on low setting for 8-10 hours.
- Chill brisket and then slice across the grain.
- Serve with reheated sauce.

Makes a great Reuben sandwich.

Cheesy Chili Casserole

Easy
6 Servings

1 pound ground beef
1 medium onion, chopped
1 green pepper, chopped
1 (28-ounce) can tomatoes, undrained
1 cup cooked macaroni
1 (16-ounce) can light kidney beans
 Salt and pepper to taste
1 cup sharp Cheddar cheese, cubed

- Preheat oven to 350°.
- Brown beef in a large skillet. Drain and return to pan.
- Add onion and green pepper. Cook until softened over medium low heat.
- Add tomatoes, macaroni, and kidney beans. Season with salt and pepper.
- Pour into 2½-quart casserole and top with cheese.
- Bake for 30-45 minutes until heated through.
- Omit macaroni and add chili powder to taste for a great chili.
- Freezes well.

Individual Barbecued Beef Loaves

Easy
4-6 Servings

Barbecue Sauce:
½ cup ketchup
6 tablespoons vinegar
3 tablespoons brown sugar
2 beef bouillon cubes

Beef Loaves:
1½ pounds ground chuck beef
2 tablespoons onion, finely chopped
1½ teaspoons salt
¼ teaspoon pepper
1 cup dry bread crumbs
1 cup evaporated milk

- Preheat oven to 350°.
- Combine all ingredients for barbecue sauce and simmer for 1 minute. Set aside.
- In a mixing bowl, lightly mix together all ingredients for beef loaves. Avoid over mixing.
- Shape mixture into 6-8 loaves and arrange side by side in a 1½-quart baking dish.
- Pour barbecue sauce over loaves and bake for 45 minutes. Serve hot.

When short on time, try baking your meat loaf or salmon loaf recipe in muffin tins to reduce baking time from 50-60 minutes to 20-25 minutes. Leftovers freeze easily and are convenient to pull out of the freezer.

161

Taco Casserole

1 pound ground beef
1 (15-ounce) can kidney beans,
   drained
1 small onion, chopped
5 ounces sharp Cheddar cheese,
   grated
1 small head iceberg lettuce, torn
   into bits
½ cup mayonnaise
½ cup taco sauce
1 (7¼-ounce) bag tortilla chips

- Preheat oven to 350°.
- In a large skillet, brown beef. Drain and place in a mixing bowl.
- Add kidney beans, onion, cheese, and lettuce to beef.
- In a separate bowl, mix together mayonnaise and taco sauce.
- Add sauce to beef mixture and blend well.
- Crush chips coarsely and gently stir into beef mixture.
- Pour into a 2-quart casserole dish and heat, uncovered, for about 30 minutes or until heated thoroughly. Serve.

How to remove onion odor from hands: Turn on cold water and rub hands over spigot.

Ryan's Rack
Ryan's Restaurant

Herbed Coating:
1 cup bread crumbs
½ teaspoon garlic powder
½ teaspoon dry mustard
½ teaspoon white pepper
½ teaspoon salt
¼ teaspoon oregano
¼ teaspoon thyme
1 teaspoon rosemary
4 tablespoons butter, melted

6 rib baby racks of lamb
6 tablespoons Dijon mustard

- Preheat oven to 425°.
- Prepared herbed coating by combining all ingredients in a mixing bowl.
- Brush racks with Dijon mustard.
- Pat well with herbed coating and place on a broiling rack.
- Place in a preheated oven:
    6-8 minutes - rare
    10 minutes - medium rare
    14 minutes - medium
    17 minutes - medium well
    20 minutes - well done

Roast Lamb with Herbed Mustard

Easy
8 Servings

1 (6-pound) leg of lamb
½ cup Dijon mustard
2 tablespoons soy sauce
1 clove garlic, minced
1 teaspoon ground rosemary or thyme
¼ teaspoon powdered ginger
2 tablespoons olive oil

- Preheat oven to 350°.
- Blend the mustard, soy sauce, garlic, herb, and ginger together in a small bowl. Beat in the olive oil by droplets to make a mayonnaise-like cream.
- Paint the lamb with the mixture, using a spatula. Meat will pick up more flavor if it is coated several hours before roasting.
- Set lamb on the rack of a roasting pan.
- Bake lamb 20 minutes per pound, or until internal temperature is 170 to 175°.

Roast Lamb with Barbecue Sauce

Easy
8 Servings

1 (5-7 pound) leg of lamb
2 cups tomato juice
¾ cup vinegar
1 tablespoon sugar
2 tablespoons Worcestershire sauce
¼ teaspoon dry mustard
¼ teaspoon cayenne pepper
¼ teaspoon black pepper
¼ teaspoon salt
1 clove garlic, crushed

- Whisk together all ingredients except lamb.
- With a brush, coat lamb thickly and evenly with this mixture. Let stand at room temperature for 2-3 hours.
- Place lamb on a rack in a roasting pan and roast in a preheated 375° oven for approximately 30 minutes per pound. Internal temperature for well done should be 175-185°. For medium rare, it should be 160-165°.

163

Navarin Printanier

3½   pounds lamb, cut from shoulder
      or leg
3-4   tablespoons cooking oil
  1   tablespoon sugar
  1   teaspoon salt
  ¼   teaspoon pepper
  4   tablespoons flour
  5   cups beef stock
  3   tablespoons tomato paste
  2   cloves garlic, mashed
  ¼   teaspoon thyme
  1   bay leaf

Vegetables:

  8   small boiling potatoes, peeled
      and trimmed to ovals
  8   small turnips, peeled and cut in
      1½-inch lengths
  8   carrots, peeled and cut in
      1½-inch lengths
16   pearl onions, peeled and scored
  1   (8-ounce) package frozen peas,
      thawed
  1   cup green beans, cut in 1-inch
      pieces, blanched
  2   tablespoons fresh parsley,
      chopped

- Trim fat from lamb and cut into 1-inch cubes. Pat pieces dry with paper towel.
- Heat oil in a sauté pan. Brown lamb on all sides. Transfer to a heavy Dutch oven as meat is cooked.
- When all meat is browned, sprinkle with sugar and toss over medium high heat for 3-4 minutes until sugar is slightly caramelized. Add salt, pepper, and flour. Toss to coat well. Reduce heat to low.
- Remove excess fat from browning skillet. Add 1 cup of stock and reduce over high heat. Scrape browned bits from bottom. Add to Dutch oven with remaining stock and bring to a simmer.
- Add tomato paste, garlic, thyme, and bay leaf. Cover and place in a 350° oven for 1 hour or slowly simmer on top of stove.
- When done, remove stew from oven. Using a colander, strain liquid into a bowl. Reserve lamb and remove bay leaf.
- Wash Dutch oven and skim excess fat from cooking liquid.
- Recombine meat and liquid in Dutch oven.
- Add potatoes, turnips, carrots, and onions. Stir to combine, cover, and simmer 1 hour until meat and vegetables are tender.
- Five minutes before serving, add thawed peas and blanched beans. Cover and simmer until ready to serve.
- If stew seems thin, thicken with 1 tablespoon flour and 1 tablespoon softened butter kneaded together. Stir into stew and cook until thickened.
- Garnish with chopped parsley and serve.

Sausage and Pepperoni Pizza

Easy
4 Servings

Sauce:

- 1 (15-ounce) can whole, peeled tomatoes, chopped, undrained
- 1 (6-ounce) can tomato paste
- 1 teaspoon basil
- 1 teaspoon oregano
- ½ teaspoon marjoram
- ½ teaspoon garlic salt
- 1 teaspoon fennel seeds
- ½ pound sausage, mild or hot and spicy

- In a large saucepan, combine tomatoes and their juice, tomato paste, and seasonings. Simmer over low heat.
- Lightly brown sausage in a skillet, drain, and add it to sauce mixture in pan. Simmer 30-45 minutes, uncovered, stirring occasionally.
- Place pizza dough in a 14-inch, deep dish pizza pan or on a large cookie sheet and roll edges of dough. Spread sauce over crust. Top with mozzarella cheese slices, mushrooms, pepperoni, and Parmesan cheese.
- Bake in a 400° oven for 20-25 minutes.
- Sauce makes one deep dish pizza or two thin pizzas.
- Pizzas will freeze well.

Toppings:

Mozzarella cheese, sliced
Fresh mushrooms, sliced
Pepperoni, sliced
Parmesan cheese, grated

Crust:

- 1 (1-ounce) package dry yeast
- 1 teaspoon sugar
- 1 cup warm water (105-115°)
- 1 teaspoon salt
- ⅛ cup olive oil
- 3½ cups flour

- Stir yeast and sugar in 1 cup water until dissolved. Pour yeast mixture into large mixing bowl.
- Add salt and olive oil. Add 2 cups flour and beat until smooth. Add remaining flour and mix well.
- Turn dough out on board and knead well.
- Let dough rise until double in bulk (about 1 hour).
- Punch dough down and press into pizza pan.

To prevent mushrooms from drying out, lightly brush them with olive oil just before baking.

165

Lemon Sage Pork Chops

Easy
4 Servings

4 pork chops, 1-inch thick
    Juice of 1 lemon
2 tablespoons fresh chopped sage
    or
2 teaspoons dried sage
    Pepper to taste

- Preheat oven to medium broil.
- Sprinkle one side of each pork chop with half the lemon juice, sage, and pepper.
- Broil 5 minutes.
- Turn pork chops and sprinkle other side with remaining lemon juice, sage, and pepper.
- Broil an additional 5-7 minutes, until meat is nicely browned and cooked through.

Baked Italian Pork Chops with Tomato Sauce

Easy
6 Servings

Italian Tomato Sauce:

3 tablespoons corn oil
1 large clove garlic, minced
1 medium yellow onion, chopped
1 (32-ounce) can pear-shaped tomatoes, roughly chopped, undrained
1 stalk celery, chopped
1 carrot, diced
½ teaspoon basil
¼ teaspoon oregano
    Black pepper, freshly ground

- Heat oil in large saucepan over medium heat. Add garlic and onion and sauté for 5 minutes.
- Add remaining ingredients and simmer, uncovered, for 25-30 minutes until sauce thickens.
- If desired, sauce can be puréed for a smoother texture.

Pork Chops:

6 (¾-inch) center cut loin pork chops, trimmed of fat
    Black pepper, freshly ground
½ teaspoon oregano
1 small yellow onion, thinly sliced into rings
1 green bell pepper, thinly sliced
1 recipe Italian tomato sauce
6 tablespoons Parmesan cheese, freshly grated

- Preheat oven to 350°.
- Layer pork chops in a 9x13-inch baking dish. Season with black pepper and oregano.
- Cover pork chops with onion rings and green pepper slices.
- Spoon most of the Italian Tomato Sauce over the pork chops and spoon the extra sauce around the sides. Sprinkle Parmesan cheese over all.
- Bake 45 minutes, covered. Remove cover and bake an additional 15 minutes.
- Serve with rice.

Chinese Casserole

½ pound ground beef
½ pound sausage
1 cup onion, chopped
1 cup celery, chopped
½ cup green pepper, chopped
2 (10½-ounce) cans cream of
    chicken soup
1 cup uncooked rice
1 cup water
1 (4-ounce) can mushrooms,
    undrained
1 (8-ounce) can bean sprouts,
    drained
1 (8-ounce) can sliced water
    chestnuts, drained

- Preheat oven to 350°.
- In a large skillet, brown beef and sausage. Drain.
- Add onions, celery, and green pepper to beef and cook 5 minutes. Place in a large mixing bowl.
- Add remaining ingredients to meat mixture and blend well.
- Place in a 9x13-inch baking dish.
- Bake for 1 hour. Serve.

Instead of using fat to pan fry a steak or pork chops, heat the frying pan for 2-3 minutes and shake in 1 teaspoon of salt. This helps seal in the juices.

Pork Chops Capri

6 pork chops, 1½-inches thick
2 tablespoons butter
1 tablespoon flour
2 teaspoons Dijon mustard
1 cup beef broth
1 teaspoon salt
¼ teaspoon pepper
¾ cup sour cream
2-3 teaspoons capers

- Brown pork chops in butter in large sauté pan. Remove from pan after browned.
- Add flour and Dijon mustard to the pan drippings. Brown lightly.
- Add broth, salt, and pepper. Bring to a boil.
- Return pork chops to broth sauce. Lower heat and simmer, covered, for 50-60 minutes.
- Just before serving, stir in sour cream and reheat, but do not boil.
- Garnish with capers and serve.

Crown Roast Pork with Cranberry Stuffing and Dijon Mustard Sauce

1   crown roast of pork
     (approximately 18 chops)

Cranberry Stuffing:

3   (6-ounce) boxes long grain and
     wild rice
4   cups raw cranberries
1   cup butter, melted
7   tablespoons sugar
4   tablespoons onion, grated
1¼ teaspoons salt (or to taste)
1   teaspoon marjoram
2   cloves garlic, minced
1   teaspoon pepper
1   teaspoon mace
1   teaspoon thyme
1   teaspoon dill weed

Mustard Sauce:

6   tablespoons butter
6   tablespoons flour
1½ cups dry white wine
2   cups chicken broth
1   cup heavy cream
4½ tablespoons Dijon mustard
1½ teaspoons dry mustard
     Salt and pepper to taste

Garnishes:

Orange slices, spiced peaches, watercress, paper frills for chops

---

- Preheat oven to 325°.
- Trim any excess fat from roast.
- Cover bone ends of crown roast with foil to prevent burning. Place a piece of heavy foil around bottom of roast to prevent stuffing from leaking out.
- Place roast on a rack in a large roasting pan. Roast 45 minutes per pound.
- One hour before roast has completed cooking, fill the middle of the crown with cranberry stuffing, piling it quite high. (Extra stuffing may be put in a buttered baking dish, covered, and heated 30-45 minutes.) Return roast to oven for remaining hour. If stuffing becomes too brown, cover with foil.

Cranberry Stuffing:
- Prepare rice according to package directions.
- Coarsely chop cranberries in a food processor.
- Combine all stuffing ingredients in a large pot. Stir carefully to mix well.
- Cook over medium low heat 10-15 minutes or until heated thoroughly. Allow to cool.

Mustard Sauce:
- Melt butter in a medium saucepan. Blend in flour and cook, stirring, over low heat for 3 minutes.
- Add wine and cook until thickened.
- Stir in chicken broth and cream. Cook 5 minutes.
- Stir in mustards and season with salt and pepper. Serve warm.

To Serve:
- Place roast on a serving platter.
- Remove foil tips and decorate with chop frills. Garnish with orange slices or spiced peaches and sprigs of watercress. Pass mustard sauce separately.

A wonderfully elegant replacement for the traditional holiday turkey dinner. The stuffing may also be used in pheasant or any kind of game.

Marinated Pork Roast

3 tablespoons vegetable oil
⅛ teaspoon granulated garlic
1 teaspoon dried mustard
1 teaspoon dried thyme
1 teaspoon dried rosemary
1 teaspoon minced parsley
½ teaspoon salt
½ teaspoon pepper
1 (4-5 pound) boneless pork loin
  roast
1 cup white wine

• Combine oil, garlic, mustard, thyme, rosemary, parsley, salt, and pepper. Rub seasoning mixture on roast and wrap in foil. Refrigerate overnight.
• Preheat oven to 325°.
• Remove roast from foil. Place roast, fat side up, on a rack in a shallow baking pan lined with foil.
• Bake, uncovered, for 2½-3 hours, basting frequently with wine. Slice and serve with a spoonful of basting sauce from the pan.

Stir-Fried Pork

½ pound lean pork
4 tablespoons oil
¼ pound broccoli, cut in small
  pieces
¼ pound Chinese snow peas
¼ pound carrots, sliced on diagonal
¼ pound mushrooms, sliced (or
  black Chinese mushrooms)
½ teaspoon salt
1 scallion, cut into ½-inch slices
1 clove garlic, minced
1 slice ginger root, shredded
1 tablespoon sherry
½ cup beef stock
4 teaspoons soy sauce
2 teaspoons corn starch
2 tablespoons cold water

• Slice pork into thin strips against the grain.
• Heat 2 tablespoons of the oil in a wok. Add broccoli, snow peas, carrots, and mushrooms and stir-fry to soften slightly, about 1 minute. Remove from the pan.
• Heat remaining 2 tablespoons oil in the wok. Add salt, scallion, garlic, and ginger root. Brown lightly.
• Add pork to the wok and stir-fry until pork begins to brown, approximately 3 minutes. Sprinkle with sherry and stir-fry for another 30 seconds.
• Return vegetables to wok. Add beef stock and 2 teaspoons of the soy sauce. Simmer, covered, 1-2 minutes.
• Meanwhile, blend corn starch, cold water, and remaining 2 teaspoons soy sauce in a bowl to form a paste. Stir into pork until thickened.
• Serve at once over steamed rice.

Pork Roast and Herbs

Easy
8-10 Servings

1 (4-6 pound) pork roast, boned and rolled
1 cup brown sugar
1 cup natural stone ground mustard
2 tablespoons sage
2 tablespoons rosemary
1 tablespoon garlic powder
1 teaspoon salt
½ teaspoon pepper

- Preheat oven to 350°.
- In a medium bowl, mix brown sugar, mustard, sage, rosemary, garlic powder, salt, and pepper.
- Unroll pork roast and spread half of sauce inside. Re-wrap and spread the other half of sauce on top and around roast.
- Bake roast, uncovered, for approximately 3 hours. Allow 45 minutes per pound. Internal temperature should register 185°.
- Sauce may be spread on roast several hours ahead of time. Wrap roast and refrigerate until ready to cook.

Country Ham
Heritage of Hospitality

Easy

Country ham
1 cup vinegar
1½ cups brown sugar
1 cup molasses

- Preheat oven to 500°.
- Wash ham thoroughly.
- Place ham in a large pan and add the vinegar, 1 cup brown sugar, and molasses. Cover with water and cover the pan.
- Bake until boiling. Reduce heat to 300° and continue baking for 1½ hours.
- Turn off oven and do not open door. Let stay in oven overnight.
- To serve, remove ham from pan, trim, and place on the rack of a broiling pan. Pat top with ½ cup brown sugar. Place under the broiler for a few minutes until sugar melts.

Best Baked Ham Ever

1	(10-15 pound) semi-boneless, fully cooked ham
2	cups sugar
1	cup cider vinegar
1	stick cinnamon
12	whole cloves
6	allspice berries
	Additional cloves to stud ham
	White pepper to taste
1½	cups brown sugar
1	cup sherry

- Preheat oven to 350°.
- Wash ham and place in large roasting pan with lid. Add sugar, vinegar, cinnamon stick, cloves, and allspice berries. Fill pan with water, cover, and place in oven.
- Cook 15 minutes per pound, turning ham often. Remove from oven and cool.
- Lower oven temperature to 250°.
- Remove top skin, but leave fat on ham. Place ham in washed and dried roasting pan and stud at intervals with cloves. Sprinkle liberally with white pepper and spread brown sugar all over. Pour sherry into pan and bake, uncovered, for 1 hour. After 30 minutes of cooking time, baste every 10 minutes with pan juices.
- Remove from oven and keep covered and warm until serving time.
- Serve with optional mustard sauce.

Mustard Sauce

2	teaspoons dry mustard
¼	teaspoon salt
1	teaspoon sugar
2	tablespoons flour
¾	cup water
2	tablespoons vinegar, warmed
2	egg yolks, beaten
2	tablespoons butter, melted

- Combine mustard, salt, sugar, and flour. Place in top of double boiler.
- Add water and vinegar, stirring until smooth and creamy.
- Add egg yolks and butter, stirring until thickened. Do not boil or eggs will curdle.
- Can be prepared one day ahead and reheated to serve.

Bob Neuman's Ham

Easy
20-25 Servings

1   (10-12 pound) whole cooked
      ham
½   cup brown sugar
1   tablespoon hot mustard
1   teaspoon cinnamon
      Cloves
      Cinnamon

- Preheat oven to 325°.
- Cut off all fat from ham.
- Mix sugar, mustard, and cinnamon. Rub into all sides of ham. Stick cloves into ham and sprinkle generously with cinnamon.
- Bake for 15 minutes per pound, uncovered, for a crispy outer crust.
- Slice very thinly to serve.

Spinach and Ham Roll-Ups

Average
12 Servings

1   can cream of celery soup
1   cup sour cream
2   tablespoons Dijon mustard
1   cup Minute rice, uncooked
1   (10-ounce) package frozen
      chopped spinach, thawed and
      drained
1   cup small curd cottage cheese
2   eggs
½   cup onion, finely chopped
¼   cup flour
18 slices boiled ham (about 1½
      pounds)
      Parsley
      Buttered bread crumbs
      Paprika

- Preheat oven to 350°.
- In a small bowl, blend soup, sour cream, and mustard.
- In a medium bowl, combine half of soup mixture, rice, spinach, cottage cheese, eggs, onion, and flour. Mix well.
- Place about 2 tablespoons of spinach mixture on each ham slice. Roll up.
- In an 11x7-inch baking dish, place ham rolls close together, seam side down. Spoon remaining soup over rolls. Top with parsley, bread crumbs, and paprika.
- Bake, uncovered, for 30-35 minutes. Let stand 10 minutes before serving.

172

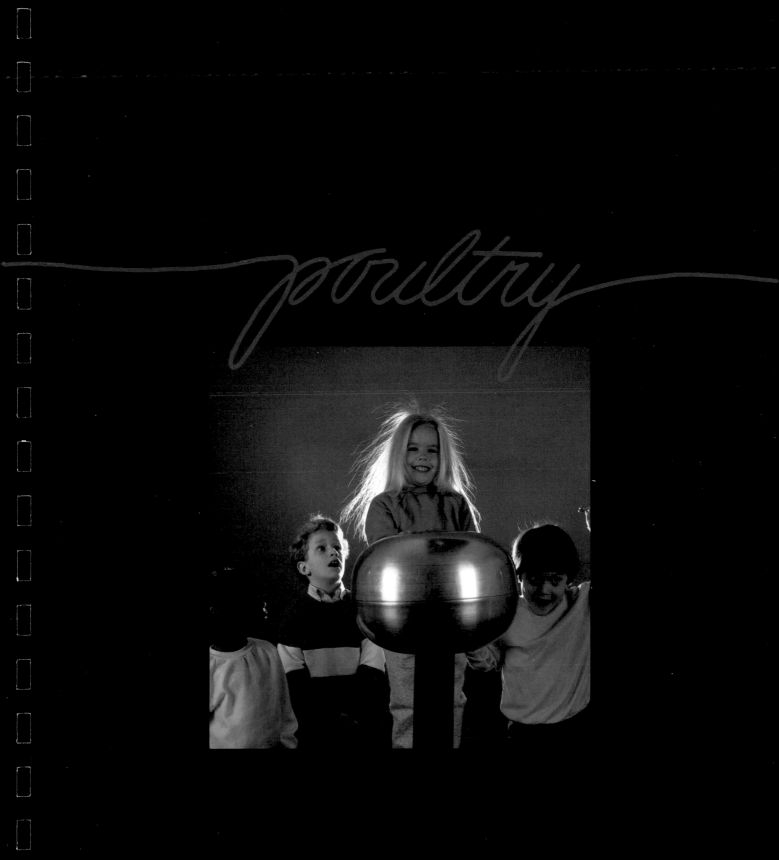

poultry

Guild Luncheon
Mint Tulips
Cold Poached Tarragon Chicken
with Horseradish Cream
Spinach and Avocado Salad
Zucchini Bread
Cheesecake Squares

The Nature Science Center's hair-raising electro-static generator

Whether exploring the mysteries of the laser, star-gazing in the planetarium, or making frozen shadows, visitors to the Nature Science Center encounter endless opportunities for exploring the natural and physical sciences. The hands-on museum offers children and adults a variety of entertaining and intriguing programs and exhibits such as a tidal pool complete with spiny sea urchins and a petting barnyard which includes pygmy goats and a miniature horse.

The Nature Science Center was founded in 1962 by the Junior League of Winston-Salem which continues to provide volunteers to assist in the Center's programs.

Photo by Smith/Weiler/Smith

Honey-Baked Chicken

2 (1½-2 pound) chickens, cut up
  or
8 chicken breast halves
½ cup butter
½ cup honey
¼ cup Dijon mustard
1 teaspoon salt
1 teaspoon curry powder

• Preheat oven to 350°.
• Place chicken pieces in shallow baking pan, skin side up.
• In a small saucepan, melt butter. With a whisk, mix in honey, Dijon mustard, salt, and curry until well mixed.
• Pour over chicken. Bake for 1¼ to 1½ hours, basting every 15 minutes, until chicken is tender and nicely browned.

The honey-Dijon sauce is great for baking chicken wings for appetizers.

Chicken Cacciatore a La Capocelli
Valentino Gourmet Italian Restaurant

2 whole chickens, cut up
½ cup olive oil
1 clove garlic, mashed
½ teaspoon fresh rosemary, crushed
  Salt and pepper to taste
6 anchovy filets, minced
⅔ cup red wine vinegar
1 cup red Chianti wine
3 tablespoons tomato paste
⅓ cup chicken broth or water
1 pound mushrooms, sliced
2 tablespoons butter

• In a large skillet, cook chicken in oil over high heat for 5 minutes, stirring constantly.
• In a mixng bowl, combine garlic, rosemary, salt, pepper, anchovies, vinegar, and wine. Pour over chicken and simmer for 10 minutes, or until liquid is reduced by one-third.
• Mix tomato paste in broth or water. Pour over chicken and simmer for 5 minutes.
• In a separate pan, sauté mushrooms in butter. Add mushrooms to chicken mixture, cover, and simmer over low heat for 20 minutes. Serve chicken with steamed white rice. Spoon extra sauce over rice.

This recipe may be halved easily for a smaller group.

Spicy Oven Fried Chicken

Easy
4 Servings

1 (3-3½ pound) fryer, quartered
6 tablespoons butter
½ teaspoon salt
2 teaspoons Worcestershire sauce
2 teaspoons curry powder
1 teaspoon oregano
½ teaspoon dry mustard
½ teaspoon garlic powder
   (optional)
¼ teaspoon paprika
3 dashes hot pepper sauce
1 cube chicken bouillon

• Preheat oven to 375°.
• Wash chicken and pat dry. Place skin side down in an oven-proof baking dish.
• Melt butter in a small saucepan. Add remaining ingredients.
• Brush chicken generously with sauce.
• Bake, uncovered, for 20 minutes.
• Turn chicken skin side up and brush with sauce.
• Continue baking until chicken is tender and nicely browned, about 50-60 minutes. Baste during cooking with remaining sauce.

A roast chicken is done when legs wiggle easily, and if pricked with a fork, the juices run clear yellow, not pink.

Barbecued Chicken

Easy
4 Servings

½ cup vinegar
   Juice of 1 lemon
1 teaspoon Worcestershire sauce
1 teaspoon black pepper
1 teaspoon sugar
2 teaspoons hot pepper sauce
¼ pound butter
1 tablespoon prepared mustard
   Pinch cayenne pepper
2 teaspoons paprika
1 whole chicken, cut up
   Salt
½ cup water

• Preheat oven to 350°.
• In a saucepan, heat first ten ingredients, just until butter is melted.
• Place chicken in roasting pan and sprinkle lightly with salt. Add water to pan, cover, and let steam for 15 minutes in oven.
• Drain any water still in pan and pour heated sauce over chicken.
• Cover chicken and bake for 1 hour, basting often. Serve.

This recipe comes from the files of Jessie Payne, now deceased. She was a very popular and well-known caterer from Lexington, N.C.

Chicken-Artichoke Casserole

2 cans artichoke hearts, drained
and quartered
½ cup butter
½ pound mushrooms, sliced
½ cup flour
3 cups rich chicken stock
4 cups Cheddar cheese, grated
⅛ teaspoon thyme
Nutmeg to taste
Salt and pepper to taste
4-5 cups chicken, cooked, chopped
½ cup bread crumbs

- Preheat oven to 350°.
- Place artichokes in greased 11x13-inch casserole.
- In a sauté pan, melt butter and sauté mushrooms. Remove mushrooms with a slotted spoon and sprinkle over artichoke hearts.
- Add flour to sauté pan. Cook for 3 minutes using a whisk to prevent lumping. Add chicken stock. Cook, stirring, until thickened. Add 3 cups of cheese and season with thyme, nutmeg, salt, and pepper.
- Add cooked chicken to the casserole.
- Pour sauce over chicken. Sprinkle with bread crumbs and remaining cheese.
- Bake for 30 minutes or until lightly browned.

Blanched broccoli may easily be substituted for artichoke hearts.

Chicken and Wild Rice Casserole

1 (6-ounce) box wild rice with
herbs
4 cups cooked chicken or turkey,
diced
1 (10¾-ounce) can cream of
celery soup
1 medium onion, minced
1 (2-ounce) jar pimiento, drained
2 (8-ounce) cans sliced water
chestnuts, drained
2 (10-ounce) packages French-
cut green beans, thawed and
drained
2 cups mayonnaise
Parmesan cheese
Paprika

- Preheat oven to 350°.
- Cook rice according to package directions.
- Combine rice with remaining ingredients except Parmesan cheese and paprika.
- Pour into a greased 3-quart casserole.
- Sprinkle with Parmesan cheese and paprika.
- Bake for 45 minutes. Serve.
- This dish may be prepared one day ahead and refrigerated until baking time or frozen prior to baking.

Oriental Chicken on Golden Cheese Strata

Oriental Chicken:

2	teaspoons cornstarch
1	teaspoon cold water
½	cup butter or margarine
½	cup flour, heaping
1	tablespoon salt
1	cup heavy cream
3	cups milk
2	cups chicken stock
2	cups chicken, diced
½	cup mushrooms. sautéed
½	cup blanched, slivered almonds
1	cup water chestnuts, sliced
¼	cup pimiento strips
¼	cup sherry

- Combine cornstarch and cold water.
- Melt butter in top of double boiler; add flour and salt. Cook until bubbly.
- Add cream, milk, chicken stock, and cornstarch mixture. Stir until smooth. Cook approximately 30 minutes, stirring occasionally.
- Add chicken, mushrooms, almonds, chestnuts, pimiento, and sherry. Heat thoroughly.
- Serve Oriental Chicken on Golden Cheese Strata or pastry shell.

Golden Cheese Strata:

5	slices bread
4	eggs
2	cups milk
1	teaspoon dry mustard
1	teaspoon salt
½	pound Cheddar cheese, grated

- Preheat oven to 350°.
- Remove crusts from bread; cube it and place in greased 9x13-inch casserole.
- Blend eggs, milk, mustard, salt, and cheese.
- Pour over bread cubes in greased casserole; refrigerate at least 1 hour or overnight.
- Place casserole in shallow pan of water and bake for 1 hour.

To fry chicken, have lard very hot. Drop in a small piece of bread to test. When it browns quickly, lower heat and place chicken in pan. Grease should half-cover pieces of chicken. Cover and turn chicken once to brown. Be sure to prick livers with fork.

Chef's Choice Royale

1 bunch broccoli
8 tablespoons unsalted butter
2 cups fresh bread crumbs
1¼ cups onion, chopped
4 tablespoons flour
1½ cups milk
1½ cups half and half
4 cups turkey, ham, or chicken, cooked and cubed
½ teaspoon black pepper
1½ teaspoons salt (omit if using ham)
¼ teaspoon nutmeg (omit if using ham)
4 cups rice, cooked
10 (1-ounce) slices Cheddar cheese

- Preheat oven to 350°.
- Cut broccoli into bite-size pieces using as much of the stem as possible. Steam until fork tender and set aside.
- Melt butter in a large pan. Remove 2 tablespoons butter and toss with bread crumbs.
- In remaining butter, sauté onion until translucent. Stir in flour and cook 2 minutes.
- Add milk and half and half and stir until thickened.
- Add turkey, ham, or chicken and season with salt, pepper, and nutmeg.
- To assemble casserole, spread rice in the bottom of a 3½-quart dish. Arrange broccoli evenly over rice. Pour meat and sauce on top and smooth evenly.
- Place cheese slices to form next layer and top with buttered bread crumbs.
- Bake for 25-30 minutes or until heated through and golden. Serve.
- This recipe may be cut in half easily.

Crescent Chicken Squares

1 (3-ounce) package cream cheese, softened
3 tablespoons margarine, melted
2 cups chicken breasts, cooked, cubed
¼ teaspoon salt
⅛ teaspoon pepper
2 tablespoons milk
1 tablespoon onion, chopped
1 tablespoon pimiento, chopped
1 (8-ounce) can refrigerated crescent dinner rolls
1 tablespoon margarine
¾ cup seasoned croutons, crushed

- Preheat oven to 350°.
- Blend softened cream cheese and margarine until smooth.
- Add chicken, salt, pepper, milk, onion, and pimiento.
- Separate rolls into 4 rectangles; seal perforations.
- Spoon ½ cup chicken mixture into center of each rectangle; pull corners of dough to center and seal.
- Brush tops with 1 tablespoon margarine and dip into croutons.
- Bake on ungreased cookie sheet 20-25 minutes and serve.

Melt-In-Your-Mouth Chicken Pie

Easy
4-6 Servings

2½-3 pounds chicken breasts
  2 stalks celery
  1 onion halved
  2 cups chicken broth, reserved
  1 (10¾-ounce) can cream of
     chicken soup

Batter for Crust:
  1 stick margarine, melted
 ½ teaspoon black pepper
  1 teaspoon salt
  1 cup self-rising flour
  1 cup buttermilk

- Preheat oven to 400°.
- Place chicken in a stock pot. Add water to cover. Add celery and onion. Simmer until chicken is tender, about 25-30 minutes.
- Discard onion and celery; reserve the broth.
- Remove meat from bone, chop, and place in an 8x11½x2-inch baking dish.
- Combine 2 cups reserved broth and soup in a saucepan. Bring to a boil and pour over chicken.
- In a mixing bowl, combine margarine, pepper, salt, flour, and buttermilk. Mix thoroughly.
- Spoon batter over chicken mixture.
- Bake for 25-30 minutes or until bubbly and lightly browned.

Garden Chicken Pie

Average
10-12 Servings

  4 tablespoons butter
 ½ cup onion, finely chopped
  6 tablespoons flour
  2 teaspoons instant chicken
     bouillon
 ½ teaspoon salt
 ¼ teaspoon pepper
1½ cups half and half
 ½ cup water
  4 cups cooked chicken, chopped
  1 cup carrots, thinly sliced
  1 (9-ounce) package frozen peas,
     thawed
  1 (4-ounce) jar sliced mushrooms,
     drained
  1 stick butter, melted
10 sheets phyllo pastry

- Preheat oven to 375°.
- Melt butter in a saucepan. Add onion and sauté until wilted.
- Blend in flour, chicken bouillon, salt, pepper, half and half, and water. Cook, stirring, until slightly thickened.
- Add chicken, carrots, peas, and mushrooms. Stir to combine. Remove from heat.
- Brush baking dish lightly with melted butter. Layer 5 sheets of phyllo in baking dish, brushing each sheet with butter. Keep phyllo sheets that you are not working with under a damp cloth to keep from drying out. Spread chicken filling over pastry sheets. Layer remaining 5 sheets of phyllo over chicken, brushing each sheet with butter.
- Bake pie for 25-35 minutes or until golden. Serve.

If phyllo sheets are 14 inches by 18 inches, only use 5 sheets and cut each sheet in half.

Savory Chicken Pie

Crust:

1	cup sour cream
1	egg
½	cup butter, softened
1	teaspoon salt
1	teaspoon baking powder
1	cup flour
½-1	teaspoon ground thyme

Filling:

2	tablespoons butter, melted
½	cup onion, chopped
½	cup celery or green pepper, chopped
½	cup carrots, sliced
½	cup pimiento, chopped
½	cup mushrooms, sliced
2	cups chicken or turkey, cooked and chopped
1¼	cup cream of chicken soup
1	cup Cheddar cheese, shredded

Crust:
- Preheat oven to 400°.
- Cream sour cream, egg, and butter.
- Add salt, baking powder, flour, and thyme. Blend well.
- Spread flour mixture over bottom and sides of a 9-inch pie pan.

Filling:
- Sauté onion, celery/green pepper, and carrots in melted butter.
- Add pimiento, mushrooms, chicken/turkey, and soup; stir together thoroughly.
- Spoon filling into crust and sprinkle with cheese.
- Bake for 25-30 minutes.

Chicken Piccata

½	cup flour
1	teaspoon salt
¼	teaspoon pepper
	Dash of paprika
8	chicken breast halves, skinned and boned
¼	cup butter, clarified
1	tablespoon olive oil
2-4	tablespoons dry Madeira or water
3	tablespoons fresh lemon juice
3-4	tablespoons capers
¼	cup parsley, chopped

- In a small bowl, combine flour, salt, pepper, and paprika.
- Pound chicken breasts between two sheets of waxed paper. Dredge in flour mixture, shaking off excess.
- Heat butter and oil in a large, heavy skillet over medium heat. Sauté chicken for 2-3 minutes on each side; do not overcook. Remove skillet from heat.
- Stir in wine or water and lemon juice. Return to heat and cook until juices thicken.
- Add capers and parsley. Heat thoroughly and serve.

Cold Poached Tarragon Chicken
with Horseradish Cream

Easy
8-12 Servings

Tarragon Chicken:

8   chicken breast halves, boned
      and skinned
      Paprika
      Freshly ground black pepper
2   tablespoons butter
2   tablespoons vegetable oil
1   cup dry white wine
1½-2 teaspoons tarragon
      Lettuce

- Dust the chicken breasts with paprika and pepper.
- In a large skillet, heat the butter and oil over medium-low heat. Sauté chicken for 3 minutes on each side until lightly browned. Remove the chicken from the pan and set aside.
- Add the wine to the skillet and stir, scraping up the browned bits. Let wine reduce slightly.
- Stir in the tarragon and return the chicken to the pan. Cover and let simmer for 5 minutes or until chicken is done.
- Let the chicken cool in the liquid and then chill in the refrigerator.
- Slice chicken breasts and arrange on a bed of lettuce. Spoon some of the poaching liquid over the chicken and serve with Horseradish Whipped Cream.

Horseradish Whipped Cream:

½   cup heavy cream
1   tablespoon prepared horseradish
      mustard
8-12   cherry tomatoes

- Whip the cream until soft peaks are formed. Stir in the horseradish mustard.
- Serve in cherry tomatoes which have been scooped out.

Blossom Hill Chicken

Easy
4-6 Servings

8   chicken breast halves
      Salt and pepper to taste
4   tablespoons butter
½   cup Chablis or Sauterne
⅓   cup currant jelly
½   cup Swiss cheese, grated
¼   cup slivered almonds, toasted
      Dash paprika

- Rub chicken breasts with salt and pepper.
- In a skillet, melt butter. Add chicken and gently brown on all sides.
- In a separate bowl, mix wine and currant jelly. Beat until well blended with rotary beater or whisk.
- Pour mixture over breasts. Simmer, covered, about 45 minutes or until tender.
- Remove chicken and place on the rack of a broiler pan. Sprinkle with grated cheese, almonds, and paprika. Broil 5-6 inches from broiler heat until cheese is melted and tops are golden brown.

Chicken Sauté with Variations

4 chicken breast halves, skinned and boned
2 tablespoons butter
2 tablespoons scallions, chopped
4 mushrooms, thinly sliced
3 tablespoons fresh lemon juice
Fresh parsley, chopped

- Rinse chicken and dry thoroughly with paper towels. Flatten slightly with your hand.
- In a 12-inch skillet, melt 1 tablespoon butter over medium-high heat until butter foam subsides. Sauté chicken for 3 minutes on each side or until it is slightly firm. Remove the chicken from the pan and keep warm.
- Lower heat to medium and use the same skillet to sauté the scallions until translucent.
- Add the mushrooms and cook for 3 minutes. Stir in the lemon juice and reduce slightly. Remove from the heat and stir in the remaining 1 tablespoon of butter.
- Serve sauce over the chicken and garnish with parsley.

Variations:

1. Sauté 2 teaspoons finely chopped garlic. Stir in ¼ cup Balsamic vinegar. Reduce slightly and serve over chicken.
2. Add ⅓ cup dry white wine or ¼ cup vermouth to pan. Reduce while stirring. Add 1-2 teaspoons Dijon mustard and ½ cup heavy cream. Reduce by one-third.
3. Add ¼ cup Balsamic vinegar or red wine, 1 tablespoon tomato paste, and ½ teaspoon fresh thyme. Reduce slightly.
4. Add ⅓ cup chicken broth, 2 tablespoons fresh lemon juice, 1 tablespoon snipped chives, and freshly ground pepper to taste. Reduce. Stir in 1 tablespoon butter.

Bone chicken breasts and thighs before frying. Saves time and kids prefer it.

181

Chicken Wellington

1 (6-ounce) package long grain
    wild rice
2 teaspoons orange peel, grated
12 chicken breast halves, skinned
    and boned
    Salt and pepper to taste
2 eggs, separated
12 sheets phyllo pastry
6-8 tablespoons butter, melted

Sauce

2 (10-ounce) jars red currant jelly
1 tablespoon prepared mustard
3 tablespoons port wine
¼ cup lemon juice

- Cook rice according to package directions. Add orange peel and cool.
- Pound chicken breasts to flatten. Season with salt and pepper. Beat egg whites until soft peaks form and fold into rice mixture. Spread approximately ¼ cup rice on each breast. Roll up jelly roll fashion.
- Brush a single sheet of phyllo pastry with butter. Fold top of pastry over chicken and pat to seal. Fold in each side of pastry. Roll up chicken breast to form a neat packet. Brush with melted butter and place on a cookie sheet.
- Repeat this procedure with remaining breasts, pastry, and butter. Breasts may be frozen at this point. Thaw in refrigerator for 30 minutes only. Bake in a preheated 375° oven for 40-45 minutes. Or bake immediately in a preheated 375° oven for 35 minutes. If pastry browns too quickly, cover loosely with foil. Serve lightly coated with sauce.

Sauce:
- Heat current jelly in a saucepan; gradually stir in mustard, port wine, and lemon juice. Serve.

Creamy Baked Chicken Breasts

8 chicken breast halves, skinned
    and boned
8 (4x4-inch) slices American
    cheese
8 slices Monterey Jack cheese
1 (10¾-ounce) can cream of
    chicken soup
¼ cup dry white wine
1½ cups herb seasoned stuffing mix
¼ cup margarine, melted

- Preheat oven to 350°.
- Arrange chicken in a greased 13x9x2-inch baking dish. Top with cheese slices.
- Combine soup and wine, stirring well. Spoon over chicken and sprinkle with stuffing. Drizzle margarine over crumbs.
- Bake for 45-55 minutes.

Chicken Bombay

Filling:

¼	cup butter
¼	cup onion, chopped
1	small apple, peeled and chopped
½	cup raisins
⅛	teaspoon ground ginger
1-2	teaspoons curry powder
¼	teaspoon salt
½	cup slivered almonds, toasted
1½	cups cooked rice
8-10	chicken breast halves, boned
	Melted butter to taste
	Salt, pepper, and paprika to taste

Sauce:

1	(10¾-ounce) can cream of chicken soup
1	teaspoon curry powder
¼	cup chutney

Special, but not difficult!

- Preheat oven to 350°.
- Melt butter in a saucepan. Add onion, apple, and simmer until tender.
- Remove pan from heat and add raisins, spices, salt, almonds, and rice. Blend well.
- Pound chicken breasts flat so that filling can be placed in center of breast.
- Place filling in center of each chicken breast. Fold ends so that filling will not fall out. Use toothpicks if necessary.
- Place breasts in baking pan and brush well with melted butter. Add salt, pepper, and paprika to taste.
- Bake, covered, for 1 hour. Then remove cover and bake 30 minutes more. Serve with sauce.

Sauce:
- Combine all ingredients and heat thoroughly.

Chicken Parmesan with Herbed Tomato Sauce

¾	cup dry bread crumbs
⅓	cup fresh Parmesan cheese, grated
4	chicken breast halves
2	eggs, beaten
¼	cup olive oil
1	clove garlic, crushed
8	ounces tomato sauce
¼	teaspoon oregano
¼	teaspoon thyme
¼	teaspoon basil
4	slices mozzarella cheese

- Preheat oven to 350°.
- Combine the bread crumbs and Parmesan cheese in a bowl. Wash chicken and dip in egg, then coat in bread crumb mixture.
- Heat oil in a skillet and sauté garlic over medium heat. Add chicken and brown 5 minutes on each side. Remove chicken and drain on paper towels.
- Arrange chicken in 5x8-inch casserole. In a small bowl, stir seasonings into the tomato sauce and pour over chicken. Top with mozzarella slices.
- Cover casserole and bake for 20 minutes. Uncover and bake an additional 10 minutes. Serve.

Yogurt Parmesan Chicken

Easy
8 Servings

Sauce:

- ½ cup plain yogurt
- ¼ cup mayonnaise
- ¼ cup green onion, chopped
- ½ teaspoon Worcestershire sauce

- 8 chicken breast halves
  Salt and pepper to taste
- ½ teaspoon thyme
- ½ cup lemon juice
- ½ cup Parmesan cheese

- Preheat oven to 375°.
- Sauce: Blend well the yogurt, mayonnaise, onions, and Worcestershire sauce.
- Place chicken in a 13x9-inch baking dish. Sprinkle with salt, pepper, and thyme. Pour lemon juice over it.
- Pour yogurt sauce over chicken. Then sprinkle with Parmesan cheese.
- Bake for 1 hour. Serve.

Sour Cream Chicken Breasts

Easy
8-10 Servings

- 2 cups sour cream
- 1 tablespoon Worcestershire sauce
- ½ teaspoon hot pepper sauce
  Garlic salt to taste
- 1½ teaspoons paprika
- 8-10 chicken breast halves, deboned and skinned
  Fine bread crumbs or cracker crumbs

- Mix together sour cream, Worcestershire sauce, hot pepper sauce, garlic salt, and paprika. Marinate chicken in mixture overnight.
- To cook, preheat oven to 325°.
- Remove chicken from marinade and roll in fine bread or cracker crumbs.
- Place chicken in baking dish and bake for 1 hour.
- Each baked breast may be placed on a slice of country ham before serving.

Chicken Veronique

Easy
4 Servings

- 4 chicken breast halves, boned and skinned
- 1 tablespoon flour
- ⅓ cup chicken broth
- 2 tablespoons butter
- 1 cup fresh mushrooms, sliced
- 2 tablespoons green onion, sliced
- 1 cup seedless grapes, halved
- ¼ cup dry white wine

- Cut chicken breasts into 1-inch cubes; set aside.
- In a small bowl, stir together flour and chicken broth.
- Melt butter over medium heat in a wok or large skillet. Sauté mushrooms and onions until soft, about 2 minutes. Add chicken and cook until done, about 5 minutes, stirring often. Stir in chicken broth and cook until thickened.
- Stir in grapes and wine and cook for another minute.
- Serve over wild rice.

184

Chicken Kiev

¾ cup butter or margarine,
    softened
1 tablespoon fresh parsley,
    chopped
1 tablespoon fresh chives,
    chopped
1 tablespoon green onion,
    chopped
½ teaspoon salt
⅛ teaspoon pepper
12 chicken breast halves, skinned
    and boned
    Salt and pepper to taste
1 egg
1 tablespoon water
1 cup flour
⅔-1 cup bread crumbs
¼ cup butter

- Combine first six ingredients. Mix well, form into a stick, and wrap in foil. Chill or freeze 45 minutes.
- Pound each breast between sheets of wax paper to ¼-inch thickness.
- Cut butter stick into six equal portions and place in center of each breast. Fold long sides to center and ends over. Secure with toothpick. Sprinkle with salt and pepper.
- Beat together egg and water. Dredge each chicken breast in flour; dip in egg; roll in bread crumbs.
- Chill 1 hour on cookie sheet.
- Preheat oven to 400°.
- In a skillet, melt butter. Add chicken and gently brown on all sides.
- Transfer to a 13x9x2-inch baking dish and bake for 15-20 minutes until tender.

Pennsylvania Dutch Chicken Sauté

¼ cup butter
4 chicken breast halves, skinned,
    but not boned
1 medium onion, sliced
1 clove garlic, minced
2 tablespoons flour
½ teaspoon salt
½ teaspoon pepper
    Pinch of basil
2 chicken bouillon cubes
1 cup hot water
¼ cup red wine

- Melt the butter in a large skillet over medium heat. Sauté chicken breasts on both sides until browned. Add onion and garlic. Cook for 5 minutes.
- In a small bowl, combine flour, salt, pepper, and basil.
- Dissolve bouillon cubes in hot water and stir into the flour mixture. Pour over chicken.
- Cook slowly, covered, for 25-30 minutes. Stir in wine. Continue to cook for 5 minutes.
- Transfer chicken to a serving platter. Garnish with watercress sprigs or parsley. Serve sauce on the side.

Chicken Breasts with Vegetables

Easy
2 Servings

Vegetable oil
1 small onion, sliced
2 chicken breast halves, skinned and boned
1 teaspoon mayonnaise
1 teaspoon Dijon mustard
2 small carrots, cut in julienne strips
1 small zucchini, thinly sliced
1 (3-ounce) can sliced mushrooms, drained
Salt and pepper to taste
1 tablespoon butter
Basil
Garlic power
Paprika

- Preheat oven to 450°.
- Tear off two 12x18-inch sheets of aluminum foil and rub them lightly with vegetable oil. Place onion slices on each sheet.
- Flatten chicken breasts to ¼-inch thick and place over onions.
- Combine mayonnaise and mustard. Spread over each chicken breast. Top with carrots, zucchini, and mushrooms.
- Season with salt and pepper. Dot with butter. Sprinkle with basil, garlic powder, and paprika.
- Seal edges tightly to form a small package. Put directly on oven rack. Bake for 25 minutes.
- To serve, cut an "x" in top and fold back edges.

Champagne Chicken

Easy
4 Servings

2 tablespoons flour
½ teaspoon salt
Pepper
4 chicken breast halves, skinned and boned
2 tablespoons butter, melted
1 tablespoon olive oil
¾ cup champagne, or dry white wine
¼ cup mushrooms, sliced
½ cup heavy cream

- Combine flour, salt, and pepper. Lightly dredge chicken in flour.
- Heat butter and oil in a large skillet over medium heat. Add chicken and sauté for 4 minutes on each side.
- Add champagne and continue cooking over medium heat for 12 minutes or until chicken is done. Remove chicken to platter and keep warm.
- Add mushrooms and heavy cream to sauté pan. Cook over low heat, stirring constantly, until thickened. Return chicken to sauce. Baste chicken with sauce until warmed through. Serve.

This is a quick company dish that is lovely served on a bed of fresh cooked spinach.

Chicken Alouette
Newmarket Grille

4   chicken breasts, skinned and
    boned
4   tablespoons alouette cheese or
    creamy herb garlic cheese
¾   cup flour
2   eggs, beaten
¾   cup bread crumbs
3   tablespoons butter
1   tablespoon vegetable oil
    Dill Butter Sauce

- Pound chicken breasts to flatten, taking care not to puncture holes in meat.
- Spread 1 tablespoon softened cheese evenly over inside of each breast. Fold each in half and pat to seal.
- Dredge each breast in flour and then coat with beaten egg. Roll in bread crumbs and coat evenly. May be refrigerated at this point until ready to sauté. (If held overnight, an additional coating of bread crumbs may be needed.)
- Heat butter and oil in a skillet until foamy. Sauté chicken 2-3 minutes per side or until golden. Remove to an ovenproof dish. Bake in a 350° oven for 20 minutes. Serve, topping each with a tablespoon of Dill Butter Sauce.

Dill Butter Sauce:

1   tablespoon shallot, minced
3   tablespoons dry white wine
2   tablespoons heavy cream
1   tablespoon fresh Parmesan
    cheese, grated
    Dash Worcestershire sauce
    Dash hot pepper sauce
⅛   teaspoon seasoning salt
½   teaspoon lemon juice
½   teaspoon dill weed
1   stick butter

- Combine shallots and wine in a saucepan. Simmer to reduce liquid to 1 tablespoon.
- Add next seven ingredients and whisk to combine.
- Over medium low heat, add pieces of butter gradually to the sauce, whisking constantly. Do not boil.
- Transfer sauce to a double boiler and keep warm until ready to serve.

Slices of orange with a dab of currant jelly on each make a good garnish for roast poultry.

Holiday Roast Turkey Breast with Fruit Stuffing

Stuffing:

7	tablespoons dried apricots, diced
3½	tablespoons currants
4	tablespoons unsalted butter, at room temperature
½	medium onion, chopped
6	tablespoons slivered almonds
2	tart green apples, peeled, cored, and diced
1	tablespoon chopped parsley
2¼	cups dry bread crumbs
½	teaspoon salt
½	teaspoon pepper
¼	teaspoon sage, crumbled
3-4	tablespoons chicken broth

- Soak apricots and currants in boiling water to cover until they are plumped, about 15 minutes. Drain well and set aside.
- In a medium size skillet, melt 1 tablespoon butter over medium heat. Sauté onion until softened, stirring occasionally. Drain on paper towels and set aside.
- In the same pan, melt 1 tablespoon butter over medium heat. Add almonds and sauté until golden, about 2 minutes. Drain on paper towels and set aside.
- In the same pan, melt 2 tablespoons butter over medium heat. Sauté apples until softened, about 5 minutes. Drain apples on paper towels.
- In a large mixing bowl, combine apricots, currants, onion, almonds, apples, parsley, bread crumbs, salt, pepper and sage. Stir in chicken broth. Season with salt to taste.
- Stuffing can be made one day ahead and refrigerated.

Crème Fraiche:

2	cups heavy cream
1	tablespoon buttermilk

- Combine cream and milk in a jar. Cover the jar tightly and shake for at least 1 minute. Let cream set at room temperature for at least 8 hours, or until thick. Store in the refrigerator. Makes 2 cups. Keeps 4-6 weeks.

To Prepare Turkey:

1 (5-6 pound) fresh whole turkey breast, boned and butterflied (do not remove skin)
3 cups apple cider
½ cup apple jack brandy
2 tablespoons butter

- Preheat oven to 350°.
- Gently pound turkey breast between sheets of waxed paper of ½-¾-inch thickness. Sprinkle with salt.
- Spread stuffing on each breast leaving a ½-inch border around. Starting with the long edge, roll the turkey into a 16x3-inch cylinder. Tie at 1-2-inch intervals with twine and secure the ends with toothpicks.
- Combine cider and apple jack brandy.
- Rub turkey with remaining 2 tablespoons of butter and set on a rack in a roasting pan. Roast until browned and the juices run clear when pricked, about 1 hour. Baste every 15 minutes with ½ cup cider mixture. Let the turkey stand for 15 minutes.
- Skim grease from the roasting juice and add enough of the remaining cider mixture to make 1½ cups liquid. Return this liquid to the pan and cook over high heat, scraping up browned bits.
- Stir in the crème fraiche and boil until sauce thickens. Strain sauce and season with salt.
- Cut turkey into ½-¾-inch slices, discarding twine and toothpicks. Arrange slices on a platter and garnish with sage, or arrange slices on a platter covered with watercress and garnish with sage and lemon slices. Serve sauce on the side.

Cashew Chicken

2 teaspoons chicken-flavored
    instant bouillon (or 2 cubes)
1¼ cups boiling water
2 tablespoons soy sauce
1 tablespoon cornstarch
2 teaspoons light brown sugar
½ teaspoon ginger
4 chicken breast halves, skinned,
    boned, and cut into bite-size
    pieces
2 tablespoons vegetable oil
2 cups mushrooms, sliced (about
    8 ounces)
½ cup green onions, sliced
1 small green pepper, sliced
1 (8-ounce) can water chestnuts,
    drained and sliced
½ cup cashew nuts
    Hot, cooked rice

- In a small saucepan, dissolve bouillon in water.
- Combine soy sauce, cornstarch, sugar, and ginger. Stir into bouillon mixture.
- In a large skillet, brown chicken in oil. Add bouillon mixture. Cook and stir until slightly thickened. Add remaining ingredients except nuts and rice. Simmer, uncovered, 5-8 minutes, stirring occasionally.
- Remove skillet from heat. Add ¼ cup nuts.
- Serve over rice. Garnish with remaining nuts.

Sautéed Chicken Livers with Apples and Onions

12 fresh chicken livers
½ teaspoon salt
¼ teaspoon paprika
    Flour
4 tablespoons butter
¼ cup sherry
½-1 Spanish onion, cut in rings
1 Pippin or Granny Smith apple,
    cored, unpeeled, and sliced
2 tablespoons sugar

- Rinse and drain chicken livers. (If large, cut in half.) Season with salt and paprika. Sprinkle lightly with flour.
- Heat 2 tablespoons of the butter in skillet. Cook livers gently until browned. Remove livers from pan.
- Add ¼ cup sherry to pan. Stir to lift glaze. Bring to a boil. Turn off heat and return livers to pan, spooning glazed sauce over.
- In a separate pan, sauté onion rings until tender in 1 tablespoon of the butter.
- In another separate pan, sauté apple with sugar in the remaining tablespoon of butter.
- To serve, layer livers, onions, and apples and spoon sauce over layers.

Turkey Tonnato

1-1½   pounds cooked turkey breast
1   (7-ounce) can tuna in oil
5   flat anchovy filets
1¼   cups olive oil
3   tablespoons lemon juice
3   tablespoons tiny capers
1½   cups mayonnaise, preferably homemade
  Salt to taste
  Lemon slices, olive slices, capers, and fresh parsley for garnish

- Slice turkey in ¼-inch thick slices. Set aside.
- In food processor, blend tuna, anchovies, olive oil, lemon juice, and capers until creamy. Fold into the mayonnaise by hand. Add salt to taste.
- To assemble, smear bottom of large, shallow platter with sauce. Arrange turkey slices in single layer, edge to edge. Cover turkey layer with half of the remaining sauce. Repeat.
- Refrigerate, covered with plastic wrap, for at least 24 hours.
- To serve, bring to room temperature and garnish.

Kingdom Come Duck

4   ducks
2   apples
2   celery stalks, coarsely chopped
2   (10½-ounce) cans consommé, undiluted
1   can water

Sauce:

1½   cups butter
⅔   cup sherry
½   cup bourbon
1   (5-ounce) jar currant jelly
4   tablespoons Worcestershire sauce
  Crumbled bacon for garnish

- Preheat oven to 350°.
- Stuff ducks with apple and celery. Place breast side down in a roaster. Add consommé and water. Cover tightly and cook 3 hours or until very tender.
- Slice breast away (use only the breasts). Ducks may be prepared ahead to this point and refrigerated in cooking liquid.
- Place duck breasts in a lightly greased, shallow casserole.
- Combine sauce ingredients and heat to melt butter and jelly. Pour over ducks, cover, and bake at 350° just until hot.
- Place breasts on a mound of rice and sprinkle with bacon. Serve sauce on the side.
- Sauce may be thickened with flour if too thin.

Before carving roast chicken: Remove from oven and lay breast side down on carving surface for 10-15 minutes. This allows juices to be absorbed into breast meat and it will stay moist.

Roast Goose with Apricot Stuffing

Average
4-6 Servings

1   wild goose, cleaned
    Salt and pepper

Stuffing:
2   cups dried apricots
2   tablespoons sugar
2   cups bread crumbs
½   cup butter, melted

Glaze:
1   cup currant jelly
2   cups orange juice
6   tablespoons apricot brandy

- Parboil goose for 15 minutes. Remove, pat dry, and rub inside and out with salt and pepper.
- Cut apricots in halves or quarters with kitchen scissors. Place in a bowl and cover with hot water. Set aside for 15-20 minutes. Drain.
- Combine stuffing ingredients with enough water to moisten and stuff goose.
- Place goose in a roasting pan and roast at 350° for 20 minutes per pound or until juice runs clear when pierced. Baste frequently with melted butter.
- Combine glaze ingredients and heat. Pour 1 cup of glaze over goose during last 20 minutes of cooking. Continue to baste frequently with glaze.
- Serve goose and stuffing with remaining sauce on the side.

Baked Goose with Potato Stuffing

Easy
4-6 Servings

Potato Stuffing:
4   boiled potatoes, diced
¼   pound raw bacon, cut into small pieces
1   tablespoon butter
1   cup onion, chopped
½   cup celery, chopped
4   slices white bread, crumbled
    Salt and pepper to taste
    Poultry seasoning to taste

1   wild goose, cleaned
    Chicken stock for basting

- In a bowl, combine potatoes and bacon.
- In a skillet, melt butter and sauté onion and celery until partially cooked. Stir into potatoes. Add remaining ingredients and blend.
- Stuff goose lightly.
- In a preheated 500° oven, place goose on a rack in a baking pan, uncovered, and cook for 30 minutes. Reduce heat to 300°. Cover and continue baking for 2-3 hours, basting frequently with chicken stock.

fish & shellfish

Pre-Symphony Cocktail Buffet
Black-Eyed Susans
Cheese Roll-Ups with Mustard Sauce
Smoked Whole Salmon
Marinated Roast Tenderloin
Cheese Tart with Apples
Avocado Pinwheel
Cherry Tomatoes Stuffed with Pesto
Double Chocolate Crinkles
Lemon Hearts

Stevens Center of the North Carolina School of the Arts

Founded in 1947, the Winston-Salem Symphony provides an exhilarating series of concerts for audiences of diverse interests and musical backgrounds. Subscription series such as the premier Classical Series and the Lollipops Concerts for Children are set in the elegant Stevens Center of the North Carolina School of the Arts.

Formerly a classic movie palace of the late 1920's, the Stevens Center was renovated by the North Carolina School of the Arts and is now the school's primary performance facility. This premier theater accommodates all facets of theatrical productions, including the Piedmont Opera Theatre and the Symphony.

Under the direction of Maestro Peter Perret, the Symphony also sponsors the popular Music at Sunset concerts, the Sunday at the Pops series, and accompanies the enchanting performances of the Nutcracker Ballet produced by the North Carolina School of the Arts.

Photo by Smith/Weiler/Smith

Trout Moutardé
Jay's Restaurant

Average
Single Serving

Blackened Spice:
1	tablespoon paprika
¾	teaspoon white pepper
¾	teaspoon black pepper
2½	teaspoons salt
1	teaspoon onion powder
1	teaspoon garlic powder
1	teaspoon cayenne pepper
½	teaspoon thyme leaves
½	teaspoon oregano

Dijon Hollandaise:
3	egg yolks
¾	pound warm butter, clarified
1	tablespoon lemon juice
	Salt and pepper to taste
2	ounces Dijon mustard

1	trout (8-10 ounces) per person
¼	cup flour
2	tablespoons butter
	Toasted sliced almonds

- Combine all ingredients for blackened spice mix.
- Prepare mustard hollandaise. Place egg yolks in a blender. Turn to slow speed until yolks are lightly whipped. Turn blender on high and slowly add melted butter. Add remaining ingredients. Set aside.
- Clean trout, removing fins. Lightly dust fish with blackened spice mix. Sprinkle with flour.
- Heat butter in a sauté pan. When butter is hot, place trout in pan belly side down. Sauté for 3 minutes being careful not to burn. Flip fish and cook 1½ more minutes. Remove from pan and place on an oven-proof plate.
- Spoon 3-4 tablespoons of mustard hollandaise over trout and place in a 250° oven for one minute. Remove to a serving plate, garnish with toasted almonds and serve.

A fish is fresh when its eyes are bright and clear, its scales tight, its flesh firm, its gill cavities red, and it smells clean.

Spinach Stuffed Trout

Average
4 Servings

4 tablespoons unsalted butter
2 shallots, finely minced
6-8 ounces fresh spinach, chopped and dried
2 tablespoons fresh parsley, chopped
½ teaspoon tarragon
½ teaspoon oregano
Black pepper, freshly ground
3 tablespoons tomato sauce
1 tablespoon fresh lemon juice
4 small trout, boned, washed, and dried
2 tablespoons vegetable oil
4 tablespoons dry white wine
1 cup tomatoes, chopped
2 tablespoons fresh parsley, chopped

- Melt 2 tablespoons of butter in a medium saucepan. Add shallots and sauté briefly. Add spinach, herbs, and pepper; continue sautéing until the liquid has evaporated.
- Stir in tomato sauce and lemon juice and cook until the moisture is almost gone. Set aside to cool.
- Fill each trout with spinach mixture and secure opening with small skewers or toothpicks.
- Heat the oil and 2 tablespoons butter in a large skillet over medium heat. Add trout and sauté for 5 minutes on each side or until golden brown. Remove trout and keep warm.
- Add wine to skillet and cook on high heat until reduced by half. Add tomatoes and parsley and sauté for 3 minutes.
- Place trout on top of tomato mixture and serve.

Baked Grouper with Pesto Tomatoes and Mushrooms
Jay's Restaurant

Easy
6 Servings

6 grouper filets, 6-8 ounces each

Flour
Oil
½ cup pesto sauce preferably fresh (store bought can be used)
½ cup mushrooms, sliced
3 tomatoes, peeled, seeded and diced
Juice of 1 lemon
½ cup white wine
Salt and pepper to taste
3 tablespoons unsalted butter

- Preheat oven to 400°.
- Lightly dust fish with flour. Sauté in oil in a hot pan for 1 minute on each side.
- Transfer fish to a baking dish. Add remaining ingredients.
- Bake for 10-12 minutes. Spoon mixture over fish and serve.

Grouper St. Charles
The Last Catch Cafe and Bar

Average
6 Servings

2 tablespoons butter
2 tablespoons vegetable oil
2 eggs
½ cup milk
6 grouper filets, 6-ounces each
1 cup flour, seasoned with salt
   and pepper
12 large shrimp, peeled and
   deveined
12 mushrooms, quartered
2 large tomatoes, coarsely
   chopped
1 bunch green onions
2 ounces dry sherry
1 ounce lemon juice
   Salt and pepper to taste
1 tablespoon butter

- Preheat oven to 400°.
- Heat butter and oil in a pan.
- In a bowl, combine eggs and milk and mix.
- Dip grouper filets in egg mixture, then in flour.
- Place filets in the pan with melted butter and oil and brown on both sides.
- Transfer filets to a baking sheet, saving liquid in pan, and cook in oven approximately 7-10 minutes, depending on thickness of filets.
- Reheat pan and add shrimp and mushrooms. Sauté 1 minute or until shrimp turn pink. Add tomatoes and onions.
- Deglaze with sherry. Add lemon juice, salt, pepper, and butter. Let reduce.
- To serve, remove filets from oven and place on plates. Top with sauce. Serve with rice pilaf.

Baked Grouper Provençale

Easy
6-8 Servings

3 pounds grouper filets, triggerfish
   or swordfish
⅓ cup fresh lemon juice

Sauce Provençale:
1 onion, chopped
1 small clove garlic, minced
1 green pepper, chopped
2 large tomatoes, peeled, seeded,
   juiced, and chopped
2 tablespoons olive oil
   Salt and pepper to taste
   Basil, sage to taste
¾ cup Parmesan cheese, grated

- Marinate fish in lemon juice for 2 hours in refrigerator.
- Preheat oven to 425°.
- Sauté onion, garlic, green pepper, and tomatoes in oil for 5 minutes. Stir in basil, sage, salt, and pepper and sauté for 30 seconds more. Set aside.
- Remove fish from juice and place skin side down in a 13x9-inch baking dish that has been brushed with olive oil.
- Spoon sauce evenly over each filet. Top with Parmesan cheese.
- Bake uncovered for 15-20 minutes or until fish flakes. Serve.

Baked Whole Red Snapper

1   (3-4 pound) red snapper,
     cleaned, with head and tail
     intact
     Fresh lemon juice
     Black pepper to taste
     Fresh thyme, chopped
     Fresh parsley, chopped
     Butter, softened
½   cup dry white wine

- Preheat oven to 425°.
- Dry fish inside and out. Sprinkle the cavity with the lemon juice and pepper. Fill the cavity with thyme and parsley.
- Rub the outside of the fish well with butter and place it in a well-greased baking pan. Pour the wine over the fish.
- Bake the fish, uncovered, for 10 minutes per inch of thickness. Baste the fish with the pan juices several times during baking.
- Serve with Lemon Rice Stuffing as a side dish or bone the fish and fill the cavity with the stuffing and bake.

Lemon Rice Stuffing:

3   tablespoons butter
¼   cup green pepper, diced
¾   cup celery, diced
½   cup yellow onion, diced
3   cups white rice, cooked
⅓   cup plain yogurt or sour cream
2   tablespoons lemon zest,
    chopped
1   teaspoon paprika
½   teaspoon thyme
2   tablespoons fresh parsley,
    chopped

- In a medium saucepan, melt the butter and sauté green pepper, celery, and onion until soft.
- Remove from heat and stir in remaining ingredients. Transfer to a buttered, ovenproof casserole.
- Bake, covered, for 3 minutes, or spoon stuffing loosely into the cavity of the fish, sew together, and bake as directed above.

Canadian method of cooking fish: Cook all fish (broiled, grilled, poached, sauteed, or baked) 10 minutes per inch of thickness measured at its thickest point. This method is the most dependable and results in fish that is moist without being overcooked.

Cheesy Broiled Flounder

Easy
6 Servings

2 pounds flounder filets
2 tablespoons fresh lemon juice
½ cup Parmesan cheese, grated
¼ cup butter, softened
3 tablespoons mayonnaise
3 green onions, chopped
¼ teaspoon salt
Dash of hot pepper sauce
Lemon twists
Fresh parsley, chopped

- Place filets in a single layer on the greased rack of a broiler pan. Brush fish with lemon juice.
- Combine the next six ingredients in a bowl; set aside.
- Broil filets 4-6 minutes until firm.
- Remove from oven and spread with cheese mixture. Broil an additional 30 seconds or until cheese is lightly browned and bubbly.
- Garnish with lemon twists and parsley.

Striped Bass (Rock Bass)
Heritage of Hospitality

Average
6 Servings

¼ pound butter
2 tablespoons onion, chopped
Salt and pepper to taste
5 pounds or more bass filets
1¼ cups fish stock
½ cup dry white wine
2 tablespoons flour
1 cup heavy cream
2 egg yolks
¼ cup water
Juice of ½ lemon
Cayenne pepper

- Preheat oven to 450°.
- Generously grease a baking dish with 1 tablespoon of butter and sprinkle with onion, salt, and pepper. Put filets with skin side down in baking dish and dot with 2 tablespoons of butter. Pour ½ cup of the fish stock and white wine over the fish.
- Cover with foil and cook for 10-15 minutes until fish flakes easily. Do not overcook.
- Meanwhile, melt 2 tablespoons of butter in saucepan. Stir in flour and remaining fish stock with a whisk. When well blended, simmer 10 minutes longer, stirring occasionally.
- Pour cooking liquid from fish into a separate saucepan and boil until reduced by half. Add cream sauce and heavy cream. Bring to a boil, keep hot, and set aside.
- In heavy saucepan, whisk egg yolks vigorously and add water and lemon juice. Do not overcook or eggs will curdle. Off heat beat in 3 tablespoons of butter and cayenne pepper. Add to cream sauce.
- Pour final sauce over fish and run the dish under the broiler until it is golden and lightly glazed.

Baked Salmon with Sour Cream Sauce

Average
10 Servings

1 (6-7 pound) whole salmon
4 slices bacon
2 lemons, sliced

Sauce:
10 tablespoons butter
5 tablespoons flour
2½-3 cups half and half
2 large onions, chopped
1 cup dry sherry
1 cup sour cream at room
temperature
2 tablespoons salmon juice
from baking
1 tablespoon fresh lemon juice
Parsley
Lemon wedges

- Preheat oven to 350°.
- Cover salmon with bacon and lemon slices. Wrap in heavy duty foil and bake for 1 hour and 15 minutes or until salmon flakes easily. Do not overcook. Reserve 2 tablespoons baking juices.
- Serve with sauce.

Sauce:
- Melt 6 tablespoons butter in a heavy saucepan. Stir in flour gradually and cook on low heat for 2 minutes, stirring constantly.
- Slowly whisk in the half and half and cook until sauce is thickened. Set aside.
- Sauté onions in 4 tablespoons of butter until soft. Add sherry and cook until liquid is absorbed.
- Reheat cream sauce and stir in sautéed onions.
- Before serving, stir in sour cream, salmon juice, and lemon juice.
- Garnish with parsley and lemon wedges.

Marinated Salmon Steaks

Easy
2 Servings

2 (8-ounce) salmon steaks, 1¼ to
1½-inches thick
½ cup green onion, sliced with tops
½ cup Chablis or other dry white
wine
1½ teaspoons fresh dill weed
or
½ teaspoon dried dill weed
¼ teaspoon mace
¼ teaspoon pepper
Lemon slices for garnish
Fresh dill weed for garnish

- Place salmon steaks in an 8-inch baking dish.
- Add next five ingredients and cover.
- Chill 30 minutes, turning one time.
- Remove salmon steaks from refrigerator and let stand at room temperature for 20 minutes.
- Preheat oven to 350°.
- Bake, uncovered, for 35 minutes or until fish flakes easily with a fork. Baste with marinade during cooking.

This recipe is equally delicious with swordfish.

Salmon Loaf with Cucumber-Dill Sauce

Easy
6 Servings

Salmon Loaf:
1 (16-ounce) can of salmon, deboned, drained, and flaked
 or
1 pound fresh salmon, poached and flaked
¾ cup Italian seasoned bread crumbs
⅔ cup evaporated milk
¼ cup onion, diced
¼ cup green pepper, diced
1 egg, lightly beaten
1 tablespoon lemon juice
¼ teaspoon celery salt
¼ cup celery, chopped
¼ teaspoon pepper
½ teaspoon Worcestershire sauce

• Preheat oven to 375°.
• Combine all of the loaf ingredients and mix well.
• Press into an 8x5x3-inch greased loaf pan and bake for 45 minutes.
• Remove from pan and slice. Serve with Cucumber-Dill Sauce.

Cucumber-Dill Sauce:
¾ cup sour cream
½ cup cucumber, peeled, seeded, and mashed
¼ cup mayonnaise
1 tablespoon onion, diced
1 teaspoon parsley, chopped
¼ teaspoon fresh dill weed, chopped
⅛ teaspoon salt
2 dashes hot pepper sauce

Sauce:
• Combine ingredients in a bowl and mix well.
• Cover and chill for 30 minutes.

Poached Salmon with Basil Sauce

Average
4 Servings

4 (8-ounce) salmon filets
1 tablespoon plus 1 teaspoon
     butter
3 tablespoons shallots, minced
   Salt and pepper to taste
½ cup dry white wine
2 sprigs parsley
1 bay leaf
½ cup heavy cream
½ cup fresh basil, chopped
1 teaspoon fresh lemon juice
⅛ teaspoon cayenne pepper

- Remove any bones from the fish.
- Melt 1 teaspoon of butter in a large skillet.
- Sprinkle shallots in skillet.
- Arrange salmon in one layer on top of the shallots and sprinkle with salt and pepper.
- Dot salmon with the remaining tablespoon of butter.
- Add wine, parsley, and bay leaf.
- Cover skillet tightly and simmer for 10 minutes. Do not overcook.
- Remove salmon to platter and cover to keep warm.
- Bring poaching liquid to a boil and reduce to ¼ cup.
- Add cream and any juice from poached salmon.
- Remove parsley and bay leaf.
- Return sauce to a boil and cook for 2 minutes longer or until sauce is reduced to ¾ cup.
- Add basil, lemon juice, and cayenne pepper.
- Lightly sauce salmon and serve.

Place lemons and limes in tightly closed jar, and they will stay fresher longer.

Smoked Salmon Timbales with Coulis de Tomatoes

Average
4 Servings

Timbales:
¾ pound smoked salmon, thinly sliced
½ cup Crème Fraiche (recipe page 188)
4 teaspoons red salmon caviar
¼ teaspoon cayenne pepper

Coulis de Tomatoes:
4 ripe tomatoes, peeled and seeded
Salt and pepper to taste
Fresh chives for garnish

• Line four timbales or deep molds (3-4 inches in diameter) with salmon. Trim any overhanging salmon.
• In a food processor, purée any remaining salmon scraps.
• In a small bowl, beat Crème Fraiche until it holds soft peaks. Gently add puréed salmon, caviar, and cayenne pepper.
• Divide mixture into the molds. Cover with plastic wrap and refrigerate at least 1 hour.
• In a food processor fitted with a steel blade, purée tomatoes (for a finer sauce force through a sieve). Season well with salt and pepper to taste. Makes about 1 cup.
• To serve, unmold molds by running around edge of each mold with a thin knife and invert molds with a sharp rap onto four plates.
• Surround each mold with Coulis de Tomatoes. Sprinkle with snipped chives for garnish.

Scalloped Oysters

Easy
8 Servings

1 cup bread crumbs
1 cup butter, melted
1 quart oysters, drained, reserving 8 tablespoons liquid
Salt and pepper to taste
4 tablespoons heavy cream
2 cups saltines, crushed

• Preheat oven to 450°.
• Mix bread crumbs with melted butter and sprinkle in a buttered shallow dish.
• Place half of oysters gently over the bread crumbs.
• Season with salt and pepper. Sprinkle oysters with half of oyster liquid and half of cream. Repeat with one more layer.
• Top with crushed saltines and bake for 30 minutes.

Battered-Fried Shrimp with Tangy Sauce

Easy
4 Servings

2 pounds shrimp in shells
½ teaspoon garlic powder

- Peel shells from shrimp, leaving on the tail. With a sharp knife, cut the shrimp almost in half lengthwise to butterfly. Place on plate and dust lightly with garlic powder. Cover and refrigerate. (This step can be done several hours ahead of time.)

Sauce:

1 (12-ounce) jar orange marmalade
2 tablespoons orange juice
3 tablespoons lemon juice
1½-2 tablespoons prepared horseradish
1½ teaspoons Dijon mustard

- Place all sauce ingredients in blender. Cover and blend well. Makes 1½ cups. (Keeps for 2 months in refrigerator.)

Batter:

1½ cups flour
1 tablespoon baking powder
1 teaspoon paprika
1 teaspoon salt
½ cup salad oil
1 cup cold water
1 quart salad oil for deep-fat cooking

- Combine flour, baking powder, paprika, and salt in a large bowl. Gradually add oil, stirring with a wooden spoon until mixture leaves sides of bowl and forms ball. Gradually add water and stir. Batter is very thick.
- In deep-fat fryer or 3-quart saucepan, heat oil to 360°. Dip shrimp into batter. Cook a few at a time until golden brown, about 2-3 minutes. Remove with slotted spoon and drain on paper towels. Repeat with remaining shrimp. (This step may be prepared in advance to this point.)
- Place shrimp in a 200° oven on a large cookie sheet. May keep warm up to 2 hours.
- Serve sauce with shrimp.

Shrimp and Walnuts

Easy
6 Servings

       2   onions, chopped
1¼-1½   cups celery, chopped
       4   tablespoons butter
       4   tablespoons flour
       1   teaspoon salt
       2   cups milk
            Dash cayenne pepper
       4   tablespoons white wine
       1   cup sharp Cheddar cheese,
              grated
       1   pound shrimp, boiled
       1   cup chopped walnuts, toasted

- Sauté onion and celery in butter.
- Blend in flour and salt.
- Add milk and stir until thickened.
- Stir in cayenne, wine, and cheese and blend well.
- Add shrimp and walnuts and heat thoroughly.
- Serve over patty shells or waffles.

Shrimp Creole

Average
8-10 Servings

   1   pound shrimp
   4   slices bacon
   ½   cup celery, chopped
   ½   cup green pepper, chopped
   ½   cup onion, chopped
   1   clove garlic, finely chopped
   2   cups tomatoes, peeled and
         chopped
   ½   cup chili sauce
   1   teaspoon Worcestershire sauce
   ¼   teaspoon salt
   ¼   teaspoon black pepper
   4   shakes hot pepper sauce
   3   sprigs thyme
   1   bay leaf
   1   tablespoon parsley, chopped
   ½   tablespoon sugar
   1   tablespoon butter
        Fresh parsley, chopped

- Shell and devein shrimp. Refrigerate. This may be done one day ahead.
- Fry bacon in a skillet until crisp. Remove and drain on paper towels. Reserve one tablespoon bacon drippings. Crumble and reserve bacon.
- Sauté celery, green pepper, onion, and garlic in bacon drippings until wilted. Add tomatoes, chili sauce, and Worcestershire sauce. Season with salt, pepper, hot pepper sauce, thyme, bay leaf, parsley, and sugar. Cook slowly, stirring occasionally, for 20-30 minutes. (Sauce may be made one day in advance.)
- Melt butter in a sauté pan. Add shrimp and sauté until pink.
- Thirty minutes before serving add shrimp to sauce. Heat thoroughly and serve with crumbled bacon and chopped parsley on top.

Barbecued Shrimp

Easy
2 Servings

1¼-1½   pounds fresh shrimp, washed,
          peeled, and deveined
     3   stalks celery with leaves,
          coarsely chopped
     1   clove garlic, chopped
     2   lemons, cut in half
    ⅛   cup butter, cut into cubes
  1½   teaspoons salt
     2   tablespoons black pepper
     1   tablespoon Worcestershire sauce
    ½   teaspoon hot pepper sauce
          Lemon wedges

- Preheat broiler.
- Arrange shrimp in a large, shallow pan. Add celery and garlic. Squeeze the juice from two lemons over the top. Dot shrimp with butter and sprinkle the salt, pepper, Worcestershire sauce, and hot pepper sauce over all.
- Broil shrimp for 5 minutes or until they turn slightly pink, stirring often.
- Reduce heat to 350° and bake shrimp for 15-20 minutes, stirring often. Do not overcook.
- Garnish with lemon wedges.

Shrimp Pilau

Easy
6 Servings

     4   slices bacon, cooked crisp
     1   cup long-grain rice
    ½   cup celery, chopped
    ½   cup green pepper, chopped
     3   tablespoons butter or margarine
     1   teaspoon Worcestershire sauce
1½-2   pounds small shrimp, cooked
          Salt and pepper to taste

- Cook bacon and set aside.
- Cook rice according to package directions.
- Lightly sauté celery and green pepper in butter until vegetables are tender-crisp.
- Stir in Worcestershire sauce.
- Add cooked shrimp and heat until warm.
- Add cooked rice. Season with salt and pepper to taste.
- Add crumbled bacon, mix thoroughly, and serve.

Shrimp Curry

6	pounds shrimp
2	(12-ounce) cans beer
	Juice of one lemon
2	stalks celery
20	tablespoons butter
4	medium onions, chopped
4	tart apples, peeled and chopped
20	tablespoons flour
3	tablespoons curry powder
1	cup sherry
6	tomatoes, peeled, seeded, and diced
3	cups golden raisins
1½	teaspoons salt
⅛	teaspoon hot pepper sauce
2	teaspoons lemon pepper

- Boil shrimp in beer, lemon juice, celery, and water to cover until just pink. Drain shrimp and reserve strained cooking liquid in a large pot.
- Peel shrimp and place shells in the cooking liquid. Boil to reduce to 11 cups and strain.
- Melt butter in a large dutch oven. Add onions and apple and cook until softened. Add flour and curry and cook 3-5 minutes, blending well. Add hot liquid and sherry, stirring well. Add tomatoes and raisins. Season with salt, hot pepper sauce, and lemon pepper. Cook over low heat for 20 minutes. Add shrimp and heat thoroughly. Serve with rice and assorted condiments.
- Suggested condiments; chutney, nuts, chopped egg, banana, crumbled bacon.

Ocean Spray Shrimp

1	pound shrimp, cooked and peeled
	Salt and pepper to taste
½	pound fresh mushrooms, sliced
3	tablespoons butter
1	tablespoon flour
1	cup sour cream
1	tablespoon soy sauce
¼	cup Parmesan cheese, grated
1	teaspoon paprika
	Bread crumbs
2	tablespoons butter, softened

- Preheat oven to 400°.
- Place shrimp in a buttered, shallow baking dish just large enough for one layer. Sprinkle with salt and pepper.
- In a skillet, melt butter and sauté mushrooms until lightly browned. Remove mushrooms from skillet with a slotted spoon and put in a bowl.
- Toss mushrooms with flour. Stir in sour cream and soy sauce. Pour sauce over shrimp. Sprinkle with Parmesan cheese and paprika. Top with bread crumbs and dot with butter.
- Bake for 10 minutes. Serve over cooked rice.
- This dish may be prepared in individual shells and served as an appetizer.

Seafood Casserole Miami
Heritage of Hospitality

1½   pounds shrimp, shelled
        and deveined
1   bay leaf
2   cups king crabmeat, canned
            or
1   pound fresh crabmeat
1   (9-ounce) package frozen
        artichoke hearts
5   tablespoons butter or margarine
½   pound fresh mushrooms, sliced
1   clove garlic, crushed
2   tablespoons shallots, finely
        chopped
¼   cup flour
½   teaspoon pepper
1   tablespoon fresh dill weed,
        chopped
        or
1   teaspoon dried dill weed
¾   cup milk
1   (8-ounce) package sharp
        Cheddar cheese, grated
⅔   cup dry white wine
2   tablespoons seasoned corn
        flake crumbs

- Preheat oven to 375°.
- Cook shrimp in salted boiling water with bay leaf for 3 minutes. Drain and set aside.
- If using canned crabmeat, drain, remove cartilage, and flake. If using fresh crabmeat, leave in lumps.
- Cook artichoke hearts according to package directions and drain well.
- Sauté mushrooms for 5 minutes in 2 tablespoons of butter in a skillet. Set aside.
- Sauté garlic and shallots for 5 minutes in 2 tablespoons of the butter in a saucepan. (Do not allow shallots to brown.) Remove from heat.
- Stir in flour, pepper, dill weed, and milk. Bring mixture to a boil and stir until thickened. Remove from heat.
- Add half the cheese and stir until melted. Stir in wine.
- In a 2-quart casserole, combine shrimp, crabmeat, artichoke hearts, mushrooms, sauce, and remaining cheese. Mix lightly and sprinkle with corn flake crumbs. Dot with remaining butter.
- Bake, uncovered, for 30 minutes or until bubbly.
- This can be made ahead and refrigerated.

Use 2 tablespoons pickling spices in water when boiling shrimp. Reduces smell in house and adds a wonderful flavor (mild) to shrimp. Cook shrimp only 3 minutes after they begin to boil. Rinse shrimp after cooking.

Wild Rice and Shrimp Casserole

Easy
8-10 Servings

2 (6-ounce) packages wild rice
4 tablespoons butter or margarine
1 small yellow onion, chopped
1 pound fresh mushrooms, sliced
2 tablespoons flour
1¼ cup chicken stock
2 tablespoons fresh lemon juice
½ cup dry white wine
2 tablespoons fresh parsley, chopped
¼ teaspoon tarragon
3 tablespoons fresh Parmesan cheese, grated
2½ pounds medium shrimp, peeled and deveined

- Preheat oven to 350°.
- Cook rice according to package directions.
- In large saucepan, melt butter and sauté onion until tender.
- Add mushrooms and sauté 1 minute.
- Add flour and stir.
- Add chicken stock, lemon juice, and wine. Stir slowly until mixture thickens.
- Add parsley, tarragon, cheese and stir.
- Combine cooked rice, shrimp, and sauce.
- Spoon into 2-quart casserole and bake, uncovered, for 45 minutes.

Seafood Dump

Easy
1 Serving

Per person:
½ pound Polish sausage
1 medium onion
1 ear corn, cut in half
½ pound shrimp
Butter
Cocktail sauce

- Cut sausage into ½-inch slices. Place in stock pot and cover with water. Cover with lid and cook for 20 minutes.
- Add onion and cook, covered, for 5 minutes.
- Add corn and cook, covered, for 25 minutes.
- Remove sausage, onion, and corn. Bring cooking liquid to a boil and cook shrimp for 2-3 minutes.
- Drain water and dump all food on a table covered with plastic and aluminum foil.
- Place several sticks of butter, as desired, and cocktail sauce along the table on aluminum foil.
- When finished, fold up everything and throw away!

Great meal for a crowd at the beach or in the backyard. This is easily adjusted to serve any number of people.

Seafood Gumbo

1   pound okra, sliced
4   tablespoons butter
4   tablespoons bacon drippings
1   cup onion, chopped
½   cup green pepper, chopped
½   cup celery, chopped
2   tablespoons flour
1   quart chicken stock
1   (6-ounce) can tomato paste
2   cups canned tomatoes, chopped
3   bay leaves and one handful fresh
        parsley, tied together
        (Bouquet Garni)
½   teaspoon thyme
2   teaspoons salt
      Pinch cayenne pepper
½   teaspoon hot pepper sauce
1   pound shrimp, peeled
1   pound scallops
1   pint oysters
1   tablespoon Worcestershire sauce

- Sauté okra in butter for 3 minutes in a skillet.
- Heat bacon drippings in a large pot. Sauté onion, pepper, and celery in drippings.
- Stir in flour and blend. Slowly add stock, stirring well.
- Add okra, tomato paste, tomatoes, Bouquet Garni, thyme, salt, cayenne pepper, and hot pepper sauce. Bring to a boil, stirring well. Reduce heat and simmer 30 minutes.
- Add shrimp and scallops and simmer 5 minutes. Add oysters with liquid and simmer until oysters curl around the edges.
- Add Worcestershire sauce and remove Bouquet Garni.
- Serve over rice.

Angler's Crab Imperial
Heritage of Hospitality

1   cup mayonnaise
1   egg, well beaten
½   teaspoon dry mustard
½   green pepper, chopped
1   pound fresh lump crabmeat
1   cup cracker crumbs

- Preheat oven to 350°, or if deep frying, heat oil to 350°.
- Combine first five ingredients and mix thoroughly.
- For deep frying, form into large cakes and coat with cracker crumbs. Fry for 5 minutes.
- For baking, put crab mixture into a buttered baking dish and top with cracker crumbs. Dot with butter and bake for 30 minutes.

Crab Cakes with Basil Tartar Sauce

Average
8 Servings

Crab Cakes:

1	egg plus 1 egg yolk, beaten
4½	teaspoons heavy cream
1	teaspoon lemon juice
½	teaspoon red pepper
½	teaspoon dry mustard
¼	teaspoon Worcestershire sauce
¼	teaspoon black pepper
2	tablespoons green onion, chopped
2	tablespoons fresh parsley, chopped
2	tablespoons cracker crumbs
1	pound lump crabmeat
¼	cup bread crumbs
2	tablespoons butter, melted

- Blend first nine ingredients. Add cracker crumbs and crabmeat. Mix well. (Mixture will be crumbly.)
- Divide into eight equal portions and shape into patties. Sprinkle all sides with bread crumbs and place on a greased cookie sheet. Drizzle with butter, cover, and refrigerate until ready to cook.
- Before serving, preheat oven to 475° with rack on highest position. Bake 10 minutes or until lightly browned.
- Serve with Basil Tartar Sauce.

Basil Tartar Sauce:

½	cup packed fresh basil leaves
½	cup mayonnaise
1	tablespoon sour cream
1	teaspoon lemon juice
½	teaspoon minced garlic (optional)
⅛	teaspoon salt
	Dash red pepper and red pepper sauce

- Rinse basil leaves in very hot water and pat dry. Place all ingredients in blender or food processor until well blended.
- Refrigerate until ready to serve.

Baked Crabmeat with Sherry

1	pound fresh crabmeat
½	cup sherry
3	slices white bread, cubed
½	cup half and half
7	tablespoons butter, melted
1½	tablespoons lemon juice
½	cup mayonnaise
1	teaspoon Worcestershire sauce
	Salt and pepper to taste
⅓	cup bread crumbs
3	tablespoons butter

- Marinate crabmeat in sherry for 1 hour.
- Preheat oven to 350°.
- Place bread in a mixing bowl. Add half and half and 4 tablespoons of the melted butter. Add lemon juice, mayonnaise, Worcestershire sauce, salt, and pepper. Mix well.
- Add crabmeat and sherry to mixing bowl and blend. Pour into a buttered 2-quart casserole.
- Combine remaining 3 tablespoons melted butter and bread crumbs and sprinkle on top of casserole.
- Bake 20-30 minutes, until bubbly.

Deviled Crab

4	tablespoons butter
2	tablespoons flour
1	cup milk or half and half
1	tablespoon parsley, chopped
1	teaspoon Dijon mustard
½	teaspoon salt
½	teaspoon horseradish
2	tablespoons fresh lemon juice
2	cups fresh lump crabmeat
2	hard-boiled eggs, riced or sieved
	Mushrooms, chopped (optional)
6	tablespoons bread crumbs

- Preheat oven to 400°.
- Melt butter in a saucepan.
- Stir in flour and cook over low heat for 3-5 minutes, stirring constantly.
- Slowly whisk in half and half and continue cooking over low heat, stirring until the sauce thickens. Remove from heat.
- Add the parsley, mustard, salt, horseradish, and lemon juice to the sauce. Blend well.
- Add crab, egg, and mushrooms (if desired) to the sauce.
- Spoon mixture into individual ramekins or shells. Sprinkle bread crumbs lightly on top.
- Bake for 15 minutes.
- Can be prepared twelve hours in advance or frozen for one month.

Crabmeat-Vegetable Pie

Easy
4-6 Servings

   6 ounces crabmeat, fresh or frozen
  ½ cup water chestnuts, chopped
   8 ounces fresh snow peas,
        blanched
   1 tablespoon soy sauce
  1½ cups milk
  ¾ cup prepared biscuit mix
   3 eggs
  ½ teaspoon pepper

- Preheat oven to 400°. Lightly grease a 10-inch pie pan.
- Combine first four ingredients in pie pan.
- Beat remaining ingredients until smooth and pour over crabmeat.
- Bake 35 minutes or until golden brown.
- Let stand 5 minutes before cutting.

Can also be made in 2-quart casserole.

Crab Cakes

Easy
6 Servings

   1 pound crabmeat
   2 eggs, beaten
  ½ cup cracker crumbs
   3 tablespoons mayonnaise
   1 tablespoon mustard
  ½ teaspoon Worcestershire sauce
        Salt and pepper to taste
        Garlic powder to taste
  ½ green pepper, chopped
        Cracker crumbs to roll cakes
   3 tablespoons vegetable oil
   3 tablespoons butter

- Mix all ingredients, except cracker crumbs for rolling, oil, and butter.
- Form six patties.
- Roll each patty in cracker crumbs.
- Heat oil and butter in frying pan, 300°-350°.
- Fry approximately 5 minutes on each side or until brown. Do not overcook.

Devilish Crab

½ cup onion, chopped
½ cup green pepper, chopped
¼ cup butter or margarine, melted
¾ pound fresh lump crabmeat, drained
¾ cup fresh bread crumbs
¼ cup milk
1½ tablespoons Dijon mustard
1½ teaspoons Worcestershire sauce
½ teaspoon salt
½ teaspoon white pepper
¼ teaspoon cayenne pepper
¼ cup fresh bread crumbs
Paprika to sprinkle

- Sauté onion and green pepper in butter until tender.
- Remove from heat; add next eight ingredients; mix well.
- Spoon mixture into 6, six-ounce, lightly greased individual baking shells or dishes.
- Sprinkle each with fresh bread crumbs and paprika.
- Bake at 400° for 15 minutes.
- Garnish with parsley, pimiento, lemon, and green pepper if desired.

Baked Scallops

1½ pounds scallops
⅓ cup shallots, minced
6 tablespoons butter
Salt and pepper to taste
Juice of ½ lemon
⅓ cup white wine or dry vermouth
⅔ cup fine bread crumbs
3 tablespoons fresh parsley, chopped

- Preheat oven to 375°.
- Wash and dry scallops. If they are large, cut in half. Place scallops in shallow baking dish or individual shells.
- Sauté shallots in butter until soft. Sprinkle over scallops.
- Season scallops with salt, pepper, and lemon juice. Sprinkle with wine and top with bread crumbs.
- Bake for 12 minutes or until scallops are no longer translucent.
- Top with fresh parsley and serve immediately.
- Two pounds shrimp may be substituted for scallops.

Light and tasty served as an appetizer or as an entrée.

vegetables

Midnight Breakfast
Champagne Marinated Fruit
Butternut Squash and Apple Bake
served over Canadian Bacon Slices
Garlic Cheese Grits
Bran Muffins

Reynolda House Museum of American Art, Inc., designed by noted architect, Charles Barton Keen

Some of the finest examples of eighteenth, nineteenth, and twentieth-century American art can be found at Reynolda House Museum of American Art. The extensive collection is displayed in the gracious country home built in 1914-17 by Richard Joshua Reynolds, founder of R.J. Reynolds Tobacco Company. Of particular note are the landscape paintings of the Hudson River School which includes "The Andes of Equador" by Frederic E. Church.

Visitors to the museum are encouraged to take advantage of the relaxed atmosphere and explore the architecture, furnishings, period clothing, recreational facilities, gardens, and grounds.

Photo by Smith/Weiler/Smith

Asparagus Mimosa

1 pound fresh asparagus, trimmed
4 tablespoons butter
¼ cup fresh bread crumbs
2 eggs, hard boiled, finely chopped
2 tablespoons fresh parsley, finely minced

- Steam asparagus 5-8 minutes or until crisp tender.
- In a medium skillet, melt butter. Add bread crumbs and cook until lightly browned.
- Arrange hot asparagus on a large platter. Sprinkle with eggs and parsley. Top with bread crumb mixture.
- Serve immediately.

Asparagus Chantilly

2 pounds fresh asparagus
6 quarts water
3 tablespoons salt

- Cut off the tough ends of the stems. Use a vegetable peeler to scrape off the tough outer skin and any scales below the tip.
- In a large bowl of cold water, wash asparagus thoroughly.
- Divide the asparagus into four bunches with nine to twelve spears in each. Tie each bundle with cotton string near the tips and the ends.
- In a large pot, bring water and salt to a rapid boil. Gently lower asparagus bundles into the water so that they lie flat. Let water come to a boil again and then reduce heat. Cook asparagus until crisp tender. Remove from water and drain on paper towels. Remove strings and serve with sauce.

Sauce:

⅔ cup heavy cream
⅓ cup sour cream
1 teaspoon dry mustard
1 teaspoon fresh lemon juice
1 teaspoon onion, grated
Salt and pepper to taste
Dash paprika (optional)

- Beat heavy cream until stiff peaks are formed. Fold in sour cream, mustard, lemon juice, and onion. Season with salt and pepper.
- Sprinkle with paprika.

For repairing curdled hollandaise sauce, put curdled sauce in a blender and turn on medium speed. Add one egg yolk and continue blending for about 30 seconds.

213

Flavored Butters for Vegetables

Maitre D'Hotel Butter:

½ cup butter, softened
2 teaspoons fresh lemon juice
2 teaspoons fresh parsley, chopped
¼ teaspoon salt
½ teaspoon fresh thyme, chopped
⅛ teaspoon pepper

- Combine all ingredients in the bowl of an electric mixer or food processor. Beat until fluffy. Chill.
- Serve with green beans, peas, or carrots.

Dijon Butter:

Maitre D'Hotel Butter ingredients minus thyme
2 tablespoons Dijon mustard

- Combine all ingredients in the bowl of an electric mixer or food processor. Beat until fluffy. Chill.
- Serve on zucchini, broccoli, or asparagus.

Fines Herbes Butter:

½ cup butter, softened
1 tablespoon fresh parsley, minced
1 tablespoon fresh chives, chopped
1 teaspoon fresh tarragon, chopped
1 teaspoon fresh chervil, chopped
¼ teaspoon salt
Pepper to taste

- Combine all ingredients in the bowl of an electric mixer or food processor. Beat until fluffy. Chill.
- Serve on any green vegetable or French bread.

Red Onion Butter:

10 tablespoons butter, softened
1 medium red onion, finely chopped
2 tablespoons dry red wine
¼ teaspoon salt

- In a skillet, heat 2 tablespoons of the butter and sauté the onion until soft. Add the red wine and cook until the liquid is evaporated. Let cool thoroughly.
- In the bowl of a mixer or food processor, combine the onion mixture with the remaining 8 tablespoons butter and salt. Beat until fluffy and chill.
- Serve with any green vegetable or fresh corn.

Basil Butter:

½ cup butter, softened
½ cup fresh basil leaves, chopped
2 tablespoons fresh parsley, minced
1 tablespoon fresh lemon juice
¼ cup Parmesan cheese, grated

- In the bowl of an electric mixer or food processor, combine all ingredients and beat until fluffy. Chill.
- Serve with green beans, broiled tomato slices, or baked potatoes.

Orange Butter:

½ cup butter, softened
¼ cup fresh orange juice, strained
2 tablespoons orange rind, grated

- In the bowl of an electric mixer or food processor, combine the ingredients and beat until fluffy. Chill.
- Serve on fresh asparagus and garnish with orange slices.

Tips for cooking rice:
—1 cup raw rice = 3 cups cooked
—1 cup pre-cooked rice = 2 cups cooked
—White rice should be cooked in double the amount of liquid for approximately 17 minutes.
—Brown rice should be cooked in triple the amount of liquid for approximately 50 minutes.
—After cooking rice, fluff with fork. It is not necessary or desirable to rinse rice before or after cooking process. If done, valuable nutrients are lost.

Green Beans and Zucchini Bundles

Easy
8 Servings

1½ pounds green beans, stringed
2 zucchini squash, two inches in
  diameter
½ cup vegetable oil
¼ cup white wine vinegar
2 tablespoons Dijon mustard
2 tablespoons honey
2 cloves garlic, minced
2 teaspoons fresh basil

- Cook beans in salted water until crisp tender, about 7 minutes. Cool beans in ice water and drain. Set aside.
- Cut zucchini into eight 1½-inch slices. Carve out the centers so that you have rings with ¼-inch rims.
- Steam zucchini rings for 2-3 minutes until crisp tender. Immerse rings in ice water and drain well.
- Poke 8-12 beans through each zucchini ring. Arrange bundles in a 13x9-inch casserole dish.
- Combine the remaining ingredients in a blender and pour over the beans.
- Cover and refrigerate for 24 hours.

Fresh Green Bean and Zucchini Sauté

Easy
6 Servings

4 tablespoons butter
1 small onion, minced
2 medium zucchini, sliced ¼-inch
  thick diagonally
3 cups fresh green beans, sliced
  diagonally and blanched
  Salt and pepper to taste

- Melt butter in a large sauté pan over medium heat. Add onion and cook until wilted.
- Increase heat slightly. Add zucchini and stir-fry until crisp tender.
- Add green beans and toss, heating thoroughly. Season with salt and pepper. Serve immediately.

Green Bean and Carrot Sauté

Easy
4-6 Servings

2 tablespoons butter
⅓ pound green beans, washed and
  trimmed
2 large carrots, julienned
½ small red onion, thinly sliced
¼ teaspoon dried basil

- Melt butter in saucepan over medium low heat.
- Add beans, carrots, and onion, stirring to coat.
- Cover and cook 15 minutes or until vegetables are tender.
- Sprinkle on basil, mix gently, and serve.

Bean Pot

4	tablespoons oil
1	clove garlic, minced
3	onions, thinly sliced
1	can pork and beans with liquid
1	can red kidney beans with liquid
1	can small lima beans, drained
½	cup brown sugar
¼	cup vinegar
½	cup ketchup
1	teaspoon prepared mustard
1	teaspoon salt
½	teaspoon pepper

- Preheat oven to 350°.
- Heat oil in a medium skillet and sauté garlic and onion.
- In a large bowl, mix all of the ingredients together and pour into a 2-quart baking dish.
- Cook, uncovered, for 1 hour to 1 hour and 15 minutes. Stir twice during the first 10 minutes of cooking.

Glazed Broccoli with Almonds

2	pounds fresh broccoli
½	teaspoon salt
1	beef bouillon cube
¾	cup hot water
1	cup half and half
¼	cup margarine
¼	cup flour
2	tablespoons sherry
2	tablespoons lemon juice
⅛	teaspoon pepper
1	teaspoon MSG (optional)
½	cup Cheddar cheese, grated
¼	cup slivered almonds

- Preheat oven to 375°.
- Trim tough ends of broccoli and separate into spears. Cook in salted water until crisp tender. Drain and place broccoli in a 12x8-inch baking dish.
- Dissolve beef bouillon in hot water. Stir in half and half. Set aside.
- Melt margarine in a saucepan. Blend in flour until smooth. Pour in bouillon mixture and stir until thickened.
- Add sherry, lemon juice, pepper, and MSG. Pour over broccoli.
- Sprinkle broccoli with cheese and almonds. Bake for 30 minutes.
- Serve hot.

Carrots Tarragon

Easy
2-3 Servings

½ pound carrots, peeled and sliced
1 tablespoon butter
¾ teaspoon lime juice
¼ teaspoon fresh tarragon,
    chopped
⅛ teaspoon salt
    Pepper to taste

- Steam carrots until crisp tender. Drain if necessary.
- In a medium skillet, melt the butter. Stir in the lime juice, tarragon, salt, pepper, and carrots. Stir over low heat until the carrots are warm.

Spiced Carrots

Easy
6-8 Servings

4 teaspoons butter, melted
2 tablespoons honey
1 pound carrots, peeled and sliced
    Salt and pepper to taste
    Freshly grated nutmeg

- In a small bowl, stir together the butter and honey. Set aside.
- Steam carrots until crisp tender, about 5-8 minutes. Drain carrots. Stir butter-honey mixture into the carrots. Season with salt, pepper, and nutmeg.
- Serve hot or cold.

Fresh Carrots Vinaigrette

Easy
6 Servings

8 medium carrots, peeled and
    julienned
2 tablespoons tarragon vinegar
2 tablespoons vegetable oil
1 teaspoon salt
⅛ teaspoon pepper
1 teaspoon sugar
½ teaspoon fresh dill weed,
    chopped
½ teaspoon fresh lemon juice
2 tablespoons scallions, chopped

- Place carrots in a saucepan and cover with water. Cook over medium high heat until tender. Drain and immerse in ice water to cool. Remove from water and arrange in a 2-quart casserole dish.
- Whisk together the remaining ingredients and pour over the carrots. Refrigerate overnight, stirring occasionally. Serve chilled.

Sesame Broccoli

1   large bunch broccoli, trimmed
2   tablespoons vegetable oil
2   tablespoons vinegar
2   tablespoons soy sauce
1   teaspoon sugar
2   tablespoons sesame seeds, toasted

- Steam broccoli to crisp tender.
- Combine oil, vinegar, soy sauce, sugar, and sesame seeds. Bring to a boil.
- Pour hot sauce over warm broccoli and serve.

Corn Soufflé

2   eggs, slightly beaten
1   (8½-ounce) corn muffin mix
1   (8-ounce) can creamed corn
1   (8-ounce) can whole kernel corn, slightly drained
1   cup sour cream
½   cup butter, melted

- Preheat oven to 350°.
- Combine all ingredients in a mixing bowl.
- Spread into a greased 2-quart soufflé dish.
- Bake for 45 minutes or until a knife inserted in center comes out clean.

Mexicali Creamed Corn

4   tablespoons butter
1   medium onion, finely chopped
1   clove garlic, minced
8   ears fresh corn, kernels scraped from the cob
1   (4-ounce) can chopped green chilies
½   teaspoon salt
¾   cup Swiss cheese, diced
    Sour cream

- In a large skillet, melt butter and sauté onion and garlic until lightly browned. Add corn, chilies, and salt.
- Carefully drape a tea towel over the skillet. (Skillet should be larger than the burner.) Cook over low heat about 30 minutes, stirring occasionally.
- Add cheese and blend with corn mixture until melted.
- Serve immediately and garnish with a dollop of sour cream.

Miss Lottie's Corn Pudding

1	cup milk
3	eggs
2	tablespoons butter, melted
½	teaspoon salt
3	tablespoons sugar
3	cups white shoepeg corn
2	tablespoons butter

- Preheat oven to 350°.
- Mix milk, eggs, butter, salt, and sugar in a large mixing bowl.
- Add corn and blend well.
- Pour corn mixture into a lightly buttered 10-inch baking dish. Dot with butter. Bake, uncovered, for 30 minutes or until set.

Cooking corn-on-the-cob: Place corn in a steamer over cold water. Bring to a rolling boil. Cover and remove from heat. Let sit at least 10 minutes. May sit indefinitely without getting water-soaked.

Eggplant With Cheese

2	medium eggplants, cut in half lengthwise
6	cups water
1	teaspoon salt
1	cup fresh Parmesan cheese, grated
1	egg
½	cup plus 2 tablespoons butter, softened
3	tablespoons cracker crumbs (4 saltine crackers)

- Preheat oven to 375°.
- Place eggplant in a large saucepan with water and salt.
- Bring to a boil. Cover pan and cook rapidly for 30 minutes.
- Remove eggplant from pan. Peel it and mash with a fork in a large bowl.
- Add cheese, egg, and ½ cup butter.
- Mix well and place in a greased 1-quart casserole.
- Sprinkle with cracker crumbs and dot with 2 tablespoons butter.
- Bake for 30 minutes.

Légumes Fricassés
Stocked Pot and Company

1   large onion, sliced julienne style
1   tablespoon oil
½   pound carrots, peeled and cut julienne style
1   pound small potatoes, peeled and quartered
1   sprig fresh thyme
1   package frozen French cut string beans
    Pinch salt
¼   cup fresh parsley, chopped

- In a large covered pan, sauté onions in oil until transparent.
- Add carrots and potatoes. Cover and cook on medium heat until potatoes are done.
- Add thyme, string beans, and salt. Continue cooking, uncovered, until vegetables reach serving temperature.
- Place in a casserole dish and sprinkle parsley on top. Serve.

Add sautéed shrimp to make a delicious entrée.

More Than Mushroom Casserole

1   pound fresh mushrooms, sliced
4   tablespoons butter
½   cup celery, chopped
½   cup green pepper, chopped
½   cup onion, chopped
2   tablespoons parsley, chopped
¾   teaspoon salt
¼   teaspoon pepper
¼   teaspoon Accent (optional)
½   cup mayonnaise
6   slices white bread, cubed
3   eggs
2   cups milk

- Preheat oven to 325°.
- In a small skillet, sauté mushrooms in butter until tender. Remove from heat and place in a large bowl.
- Sauté celery, green pepper, and onion in remaining butter. Remove from heat and place with mushrooms.
- Add parsley, salt, pepper, and Accent to mushrooms. Mix well and let cool. Add mayonnaise and blend well.
- Line greased, 2½-quart casserole with half of the bread cubes. Spoon in mushroom mixture. Cover with remaining bread.
- Beat eggs and combine with milk. Pour over bread cubes.
- Cover and refrigerate overnight or for 6 hours.
- Bake, uncovered, for 50 minutes or until firm.

Fresh Mushroom Pie

- 2 pounds fresh mushrooms, dried and trimmed
- 2 shallots or green onions, minced
- 6 tablespoons butter
  Juice of ½ lemon
  Salt and freshly ground pepper to taste
- 4 tablespoons flour
- 1½ cups chicken stock
- ½ cup heavy cream, heated
- 1 stick pie crust mix
- 1 egg, beaten

- Preheat oven to 450°.
- In a large skillet, melt 4 tablespoons of butter. Add mushrooms, shallots, lemon juice, salt, and pepper. Cook 10 minutes, stirring occasionally.
- Remove mushrooms from skillet and place in center of 1-quart casserole.
- Add remaining butter to juices in skillet and stir in flour and stock. Cook, stirring constantly, until sauce is thickened. Add heated cream and adjust seasonings.
- Roll out pie crust to fit over casserole.
- Pour sauce over mushrooms and cover casserole with pie crust.
- Use sharp knife to cut out mushroom designs from leftover crust.
- Garnish crust with these and brush with beaten egg. Make several slits on top.
- Bake for 15 minutes. Lower temperature to 300° and bake for 10-15 minutes longer or until crust is nicely browned.

This is best made shortly before serving.

Spanish Onion Pie

- 2 pounds Spanish onions, thinly sliced
- 1 stick butter
- 3 eggs, well beaten
- 1 cup sour cream
- ¼ teaspoon salt
- ½ teaspoon white pepper
  Dash of hot pepper sauce
- 1 deep dish pastry shell, unbaked
- ½ cup Parmesan cheese, grated

- Preheat oven to 450°.
- In a large skillet, sauté onions in butter. Remove from heat.
- Combine eggs and sour cream. Add to sautéed onions. Season with salt, white pepper, and hot pepper sauce. Mix well.
- Pour into pie shell. Top with cheese.
- Bake for 20 minutes. Then bake at 325° for 20 minutes. Serve.

Delicious with a country style supper.

Vidalia Onions Stuffed with Nuts

Average
6 Servings

6   **large Vidalia onions**
2   **tablespoons butter**
1   **cup coarse dry bread crumbs,
    or cooked rice**
1¼ **cup pecans, coarsely chopped**
1   **egg, beaten**
¼   **teaspoon thyme**
    **Salt and freshly ground pepper
    to taste**
    Buttered bread crumbs

- Preheat oven to 375°.
- Peel onions without cutting off root ends. Cut a thick slice from the top of each. Reserve tops.
- In a large saucepan, boil onions and tops for 20-30 minutes or until just tender. Drain and cool.
- Scoop out the centers of each onion. Invert onion shells to drain. Chop onion centers and tops.
- In a medium skillet, melt butter. Add chopped onion, dry bread crumbs, pecans, egg, thyme, salt, and pepper. Mix well.
- Stuff onion shells. Top with buttered bread crumbs.
- Place onions in a shallow baking dish. Add water to cover bottom of pan.
- Bake for 25 minutes.

Serve as is or with a cheese, mushroom, or tomato sauce.

French Epicurean Peas

Easy
8 Servings

2   **(10-ounce) packages frozen
    green peas**
4   **slices bacon, chopped**
1   **tablespoon onion, chopped**
1   **tablespoon flour**
1   **cup half and half**
1   **cup fresh mushrooms, sliced
    and sautéed**
2   **tablespoons butter**
½   **teaspoon salt**

- Cook peas according to package directions. Reserve cooking liquid.
- In a large skillet, fry the bacon until crisp. Remove the bacon.
- Sauté onion in the bacon drippings until translucent. Stir in the flour. Add the liquid from the peas and the half and half. Cook over medium heat until thickened, stirring occasionally. Stir in peas and mushrooms and season with butter and salt.

Company Potatoes

Easy
12 Servings

1   (2-pound) package frozen hash
    browns
1   pint sour cream
1   can cream of chicken soup
2   cups Cheddar cheese, shredded
½   cup onion, chopped
8   tablespoons margarine
2   cups corn flakes, crushed

• Preheat oven to 350°.
• Thaw hash browns for about 30 minutes.
• In a large bowl, mix hash browns with sour cream, soup, cheese, onions, and 4 tablespoons margarine.
• Melt remaining 4 tablespoons margarine and combine with corn flakes.
• Pour hash brown mixture into a 3-quart casserole dish. Top with corn flakes.
• Bake for 45 minutes.

A busy woman's recipe—quick, delicious, and serves a crowd!

Washing onions in cold water before peeling them helps reduce tears. Leaving the root end on during slicing also works.

Potato and Sour Cream Casserole

Easy
6-8 Servings

6   medium potatoes
1   (8-ounce) package cream
    cheese
1   cup sour cream
1   teaspoon salt
⅛   teaspoon pepper
½   cup chives, chopped
1   tablespoon margarine
½   teaspoon paprika

• Preheat oven to 350°.
• Boil potatoes until tender. Peel and beat in a mixing bowl until smooth.
• Add cream cheese, sour cream, salt and pepper. Beat until smooth and stir in chives.
• Grease a 10-cup casserole dish with the margarine and spoon potatoes into dish.
• Sprinkle with paprika.
• Bake for 30 minutes. Serve immediately.

Casserole may be made several hours ahead and refrigerated until ready to bake.

Rosemary Potatoes

1½ teaspoons (or more) rosemary
    leaves, preferably fresh
½ cup olive oil
1½ teaspoons salt
3 pounds baking potatoes

- Preheat oven to 350°.
- Gently crush the rosemary with a mortar and pestle.
- In a large bowl, combine the oil, salt, and rosemary.
- Scrub potatoes. Slice very thin.
- Toss slices in the oil mixture until completely coated. Remove with a slotted spoon.
- Place potatoes into one or two large, shallow baking dishes.
- Bake uncovered for approximately 1 hour and 15 minutes.
- Potatoes should be golden, crispy but tender.

Garnish with whole rosemary. Great with grilled meats.

Potato Pancakes

16 small new potatoes, peeled
2 tablespoons flour
4 tablespoons heavy cream
¼ cup shallots (or onions), minced
   Salt and pepper to taste
   Butter
   Sour cream
   Chopped chives
   Black and/or red caviar

- Drop potatoes into boiling water to cover. Cook, covered, until tender, approximately 20 minutes.
- Remove from heat and drain.
- Chop potatoes finely and combine them with flour, cream, shallots, salt, and pepper in a large mixing bowl.
- Shape potato mixture into four thin pancakes, each about 5-6-inches in diameter.
- Melt 1-2 tablespoons of butter at medium high heat in a large skillet.
- Place pancakes in skillet and lower heat. Cook until they have a good, brown crust. Turn carefully and cook on the other side.
- Serve topped with sour cream, caviar, and chives.

This recipe is a delicious first course. For a breakfast version, make one large pancake. Cut into wedges. Serve with sour cream and salsa.

Wild Rice and Almond Casserole

Easy
8-10 Servings

½ cup butter
½ pound mushrooms, sliced
1 clove garlic, minced
2 tablespoons green onions, chopped
2 tablespoons blanched, slivered almonds
1 cup wild rice
3 cups chicken broth
   Salt and pepper to taste

- Preheat oven to 325°.
- In a heavy skillet, heat the butter over medium heat. Stir in the mushrooms, garlic, green onions, almonds, and rice. Cook, stirring constantly, until the rice begins to turn yellow. This will take about 5 minutes.
- Stir in the chicken broth and season with salt and pepper. Transfer to a 2-quart buttered casserole. Cover tightly and bake for 1 hour or until the liquid is absorbed.
- One-half cup raisins may be substituted for the mushrooms.

Fresh mushrooms: Choose ones with caps tightly closed at the bottom.

Wild Rice Mélange

Easy
8 Servings

1 cup wild rice, washed and soaked overnight
1 cup Cheddar cheese, grated
1 cup whole pitted ripe olives, halved
1 cup canned tomatoes, undrained, coarsely chopped
1 cup fresh mushrooms, sliced
½ cup onion, chopped
½ cup olive oil
1 cup hot water
   Salt and pepper to taste

- Preheat oven to 350°.
- Drain rice.
- Combine all ingredients in an ovenproof casserole. Stir to combine. Cover and bake 1 hour or until rice is tender.
- Bring to room temperature before baking. This dish may be assembled one day in advance.

Rice Primavera

Marinade:

½ cup olive oil
¼ cup red wine vinegar
½ teaspoon salt
  Freshly ground pepper to taste
1 teaspoon lemon pepper
1 tablespoon fresh chives,
    chopped
2 tablespoons fresh parsley,
    chopped

4 cups rice, cooked
2 tablespoons spring onion,
    chopped
2 tablespoons green pepper,
    minced
¼ cup green olives, sliced
1½ cups combination of: broccoli
    florets, blanched carrots,
    blanched peas

- Combine marinade ingredients and stir into warm rice. Stir in onion, peppers, olives, and vegetables.
- Cover and refrigerate.
- May be served hot or cold. To reheat, place rice in a colander over a pan of simmering water. Heat thoroughly and fluff with a fork.

Armenian Rice

1 cup rice
2 cups chicken broth
8 tablespoons butter
4 cloves garlic, minced
1 cup vermicelli, broken into small
    pieces
1 (4-ounce) can sliced
    mushrooms, drained
1 (2-ounce) can ripe olives,
    chopped
1 (8-ounce) can water chestnuts,
    sliced

- Preheat oven to 350°.
- Rinse rice and drain. Place in a 2-quart casserole with the chicken broth.
- In a skillet, melt butter and sauté garlic. Add vermicelli and brown. Stir into rice. Add the mushrooms, olives, and water chestnuts to the rice-vermicelli mixture.
- Cover and bake for 40 minutes. Serve.

Summer Wild Rice

4 ounces wild rice
1 cup lemon vinaigrette
  (recipe below)
¼ cup red onion or scallion,
  chopped
1 tablespoon orange zest, finely
  chopped
⅓ cup currants, soaked in ⅓ cup
  orange juice
½ cup cucumber, peeled, seeded,
  and sliced
  Freshly ground pepper to taste
¼ cup parsley, chopped
1 avocado
½ cup walnuts or pecans, chopped
  (optional)
¼ cup fresh mint, chopped
  (optional)

- Cook rice according to package directions. Drain and toss with ⅓ cup lemon vinaigrette while rice is warm. Cool to room temperature.
- Add onion, orange zest, currants, cucumber, pepper, and parsley.
- Toss with enough remaining vinaigrette to moisten. (May be made several hours in advance to this point and refrigerated.)
- Just before serving, chop avocado and add. Add nuts and mint if desired.
- Serve at room temperature. Delicious with grilled chicken for a summer buffet.

Lemon Vinaigrette:

⅓ cup fresh lemon juice
1 teaspoon salt
¼ teaspoon pepper
½ teaspoon sugar
⅔ cup olive oil (or ⅓ cup olive oil
  and ⅓ cup vegetable oil)

- Place lemon juice, salt, pepper, and sugar in the bowl of a food processor. Blend.
- With machine running, add oil in a steady stream.

During vegetable season, slice garden fresh tomatoes, cucumbers, and onions. Sprinkle with a little salt, pepper, and sugar and set aside until meal time. The salt brings out the juices so that the vegetables are served in a "natural dressing."

Curried Rice with Pineapple

2½   cups uncooked rice
½   cup butter, melted
1   medium onion, chopped
2   (10½-ounce) cans consommé
2   (10½-ounce) cans beef broth
½   teaspoon garlic salt
2   (13¼-ounce) cans pineapple
      chunks, drained
2   teaspoons curry powder

- Preheat oven to 350°.
- In a large heavy skillet, brown the rice, stirring constantly. Transfer the rice to a 2½-quart casserole.
- In a skillet, heat 2 tablespoons butter and sauté the onion until translucent.
- Stir the onions, consommé, beef broth, garlic salt, and 2 tablespoons of the melted butter into the rice.
- Bake for 1 hour.
- In a bowl, combine the pineapple chunks with the remaining butter and curry powder. Stir the pineapple into the rice and bake for an additional 15-20 minutes. Serve.

A wonderful accompaniment to grilled chicken, pork, or beef.

Herbed Wild Rice

1   cup wild rice, uncooked
1   teaspoon salt
2   tablespoons butter
4   tablespoons onion, minced
2   green peppers, chopped
1   (4-ounce) can mushrooms,
      sliced
1   (10-ounce) can cream of
      mushroom soup
¾   cup half and half
¼   teaspoon marjoram
⅛   teaspoon basil
⅛   teaspoon tarragon
½   teaspoon curry
½   teaspoon salt
¼   teaspoon pepper

- Preheat oven to 350°.
- Rinse rice three to four times in cold water.
- Bring 3 cups water to a boil. Add rice and 1 teaspoon salt and simmer, covered, for 30 minutes.
- In a saucepan, melt butter. Add onion, green pepper, mushrooms, and sauté. Add to cooked rice.
- In a saucepan, combine remaining ingredients. Heat for 10 minutes. Add to rice mixture.
- Pour rice into a 2-quart casserole and bake 30 minutes or until hot. Serve.

Butternut Squash and Apple Bake

Easy
6 Servings

2 pounds butternut squash, peeled, halved, and cut into ½-inch cubes
3 medium apples, peeled, cored, and cut into ½-inch slices
¼ cup brown sugar
2 tablespoons butter or margarine, melted
½ tablespoon flour
   Salt to taste

- Preheat oven to 350°.
- In a medium-sized casserole dish, layer squash and apples.
- Combine next four ingredients and blend well. Sprinkle over squash and apple mixture.
- Cover dish with foil and bake 45-60 minutes or until tender.

How to skin peaches or tomatoes: Dip them into boiling water for 30 seconds; cool slightly. The skins should easily slip off the fruit.

Butternut Squash Soufflé

Average
8-10 Servings

1 (3-pound) butternut squash, peeled, seeded, and cut into 2-inch squares
1⅛ teaspoon salt
⅓ cup 100% pure maple syrup
3 tablespoons brown sugar, packed
4 tablespoons cornstarch
4 eggs, separated
1½ sticks butter, melted and cooled
1 cup heavy cream
½ cup pecans, chopped

- Preheat oven to 350°.
- Put squash in a medium saucepan and cover with water. Cook over medium heat until fork tender.
- Drain squash. Purée squash and put 2½ cups into a large mixing bowl.
- Stir in 1 teaspoon salt, maple syrup, brown sugar, cornstarch, egg yolks, and butter. Beat until fluffy.
- Stir in heavy cream.
- In another bowl, beat the egg whites and ⅛ teaspoon salt until stiff peaks are formed.
- Fold egg whites into squash mixture. Pour into a buttered 2-quart soufflé dish. Sprinkle pecans on top.
- Bake for 55 minutes.

Squash-Zucchini Stir-Fry

Easy
4-6 Servings

1 tablespoon oil
2-3 small yellow squash,
    thinly sliced
2-3 small zucchini squash,
    thinly sliced
1 small onion, halved and
    thinly sliced
1-2 tablespoons fresh basil, chopped
½ teaspoon pepper

- Heat oil in a skillet or wok.
- Add the vegetables, onion, and seasoning. Stir constantly until the vegetables are crisp tender.

Italian Zucchini Pie

Easy
6 Servings

4 cups unpared zucchini,
    thinly sliced
6 tablespoons butter
1 cup onion, chopped
2 tablespoons fresh parsley,
    chopped
    Salt and pepper to taste
¼ teaspoon garlic powder
¼ teaspoon basil
¼ teaspoon oregano
2 eggs, lightly beaten
2 cups mozzarella cheese, grated
1 (8-ounce) can crescent rolls
2 teaspoons Dijon mustard

- Preheat oven to 375°.
- Lightly salt zucchini and place in a colander. Weight down top with a plate. Allow to drain for 30 minutes. Pat dry with a paper towel.
- Melt butter in a sauté pan. Add zucchini and onion. Sauté until tender. Season with parsley, salt, pepper, garlic powder, basil, and oregano. Remove from heat.
- In a large mixing bowl, combine eggs and cheese. Stir in zucchini mixture.
- Separate crescent rolls into eight triangles. Press on the bottom and sides of a 9x2-inch quiche dish to form a crust. Brush with mustard.
- Pour zucchini mixture over crust. Bake for 25-30 minutes. Cover loosely with foil if crust becomes too brown during baking. Let pie stand for 10 minutes before slicing.
- This pie may be baked ahead. To reheat, cover loosely and heat at 375° for 15 minutes.

One-half pound cooked, drained sausage may be added to make this a delicious main course.

231

Baked Zucchini

3 tablespoons olive oil
1 medium yellow onion, diced
4 medium zucchini, unpeeled,
    diced into ¼-inch pieces
⅔-1 cup cooked rice
½ cup Swiss cheese, grated
½ cup parsley, chopped
1 large egg, beaten
    Salt and pepper to taste
2 tablespoons bread crumbs
1 tablespoon olive oil

- Preheat oven to 375°.
- In a large skillet, heat oil over low heat. Add onion and sauté until soft.
- Add zucchini to skillet stirring to coat. Cook, covered, 8-10 minutes. Let cool slightly.
- In a large bowl, combine rice, cheese, parsley, egg, salt, and pepper. Add zucchini mixture and mix well.
- Place in a greased 1½-quart casserole dish. Sprinkle with bread crumbs and olive oil.
- Bake, uncovered, 20-25 minutes. Serve.

Shredded Zucchini

7 zucchini squash, shredded
    or grated
    Salt to taste
¾ cup onion, chopped
2 tablespoons butter
2 tablespoons sour cream
    Pepper to taste

- Sprinkle zucchini generously with salt. Let it stand for 15 minutes then rinse in cold water and drain.
- Press zucchini with paper towels to remove as much moisture as possible.
- Melt butter in a large skillet and sauté onion until tender. Add zucchini and cook over high heat, stirring constantly, until most of the moisture is absorbed. Stir in sour cream and season with pepper.
- Serve immediately.

Especially nice with the addition of fresh chopped dill.

Sauerkraut with Champagne and Pineapple

Easy
8 Servings

4 slices bacon, chopped
1 medium onion, chopped
1 (28-ounce) can sauerkraut in wine, undrained
1 bay leaf
1 (20-ounce) can pineapple tidbits in juice, undrained
¼-½ teaspoon freshly ground pepper
12 ounces champagne or dry white wine

- Sauté bacon until lightly browned.
- Add onion and sauté until transparent.
- Add remaining ingredients and cook on low heat for 40 minutes, stirring occasionally.
- Remove bay leaf and serve.

Spinach and Artichoke Casserole

Easy
8 Servings

1 stick butter
1 medium onion, chopped
1 (8-ounce) package cream cheese
3 (10-ounce) packages frozen chopped spinach, cooked and drained well
Salt and pepper to taste
1 (8½-ounce) can artichoke hearts, drained and quartered
1 cup buttered bread crumbs

- Preheat oven to 350°.
- Melt butter in a sauté pan. Sauté onions in butter. Add cream cheese and stir until it melts and blends in.
- Add spinach to the mixture. Season with salt and pepper as desired.
- Layer spinach mixture and artichoke hearts alternately in a greased 2-quart baking dish. Top with bread crumbs.
- Bake for 30 minutes until heated through.

Steamed Spaghetti Squash with Fresh Tomatoes

Easy
8 Servings

1   (4-pound) spaghetti squash
4   large tomatoes, seeded and
      chopped
2   cloves garlic, minced
3-4   green onions, chopped
½   cup Niçoise olives
¼   cup fresh basil, julienned
2   tablespoons red wine vinegar
5   tablespoons olive oil
      Pepper to taste
1-1½   cups mozzarella cheese,
      shredded

- Steam spaghetti squash until tender, about 50 minutes.
- While steaming squash, mix remaining ingredients, except cheese, together. Let sit at room temperature for 1 hour.
- Cut cooked squash in half and let cool 5 minutes. Scoop out seeds and then with a fork, pull out strands of squash.
- In a large bowl, mix squash and tomato mixture together, tossing well.
- Serve with cheese.

Scalloped Tomatoes and Artichoke Hearts

Easy
6 Servings

1   (2-pound, 3-ounce) can whole
      tomatoes
1   (14-ounce) can artichoke hearts
4   tablespoons butter
½   cup onion, finely chopped
2   tablespoons shallots, finely
      chopped
½   teaspoon basil
1   tablespoon sugar
      Salt and pepper to taste

- Preheat oven to 325°.
- Butter a 9x13-inch casserole dish.
- Drain tomatoes and coarsely chop. Rinse, drain, and quarter artichoke hearts.
- Melt butter in a sauté pan. Add onions and shallots and cook until tender.
- Add tomatoes, artichoke hearts, and basil to onion mixture.
- Season with sugar, salt, and pepper.
- Pour into baking dish and cook for 10-15 minutes. Serve.

A nice light "winter" accompaniment to fowl, beef, or pork! Fresh tomatoes may certainly be used in season!

Broccoli Stuffed Tomatoes

Easy
6 Servings

6   medium tomatoes
    Salt and pepper to taste
1   (10-ounce) package frozen
    chopped broccoli
1   cup Swiss cheese, shredded
1   cup soft bread crumbs
½   cup mayonnaise
2   tablespoons onion, chopped
2   tablespoons Parmesan cheese,
    grated

- Wash tomatoes thoroughly. Cut tops off and scoop out pulp, leaving shell intact.
- Sprinkle cavities of tomatoes with salt and pepper, invert, and drain on a wire rack for 30 minutes.
- Preheat oven to 350°.
- Cook broccoli according to package directions, omitting salt. Drain well.
- Combine broccoli with the cheese, bread crumbs, mayonnaise, and onion. Blend well.
- Spoon broccoli mixture into the tomato shells and sprinkle with Parmesan cheese.
- Bake for 30 minutes and serve hot.

Tomatoes are much better if kept at room temperature.

Fresh Tomato Pie

Easy
6 Servings

1   (9-inch) pie shell, baked and
    cooled
2-3 large tomatoes, peeled and
    sliced
2-3 green onions, chopped
    Salt and pepper to taste
1   tablespoon fresh basil, chopped
1   tablespoon fresh chives,
    chopped
1   cup mayonnaise
1   cup sharp Cheddar cheese,
    grated

- Preheat oven to 350°.
- Sprinkle tomatoes lightly with salt and drain on a cooling rack for 15-20 minutes.
- Layer tomatoes, onions, salt, pepper, basil, and chives in pie shell.
- Blend mayonnaise and cheese together in a mixing bowl. Spread over top of pie.
- Bake for 30 minutes or until top is lightly browned.

A delicious accompaniment to grilled seafood.

235

Tangy Baked Tomatoes

4 large or 8 medium tomatoes
2 tablespoons green pepper, chopped
2 tablespoons water chestnuts, chopped
1 tablespoon onion, chopped
1 tablespoon Dijon mustard
¼ teaspoon salt
2 tablespoons margarine or butter, melted
⅔ cup soft bread crumbs

- Preheat oven to 350°.
- Cut large tomatoes in half crosswise or cut off tops of medium tomatoes. Scoop out pulp, leaving shells intact.
- Chop tomato pulp and combine with green pepper, water chestnuts, onion, mustard and salt. Stir well.
- Spoon mixture into tomato shells and place in a 13x9x2-inch baking dish.
- Toss bread crumbs in melted butter and sprinkle over tomatoes.
- Bake for 25-30 minutes and serve immediately.

Tomatoes Provencal

4 slices bacon, diced
1 clove garlic, minced
1 medium onion, thinly sliced
¼ pound fresh mushrooms, sliced
1 tablespoon flour
½ teaspoon seasoned salt
10 tomatoes, peeled
¼ cup plus 2 tablespoons Parmesan cheese, grated
1 tablespoon butter

- Preheat oven to 350°.
- Cook bacon in medium skillet until crisp. Set aside bacon to drain, reserving drippings in skillet.
- In the drippings, sauté the garlic, onion, and mushrooms until tender. Stir in bacon, flour, and seasoned salt.
- Cut tomatoes in ½-inch slices and place half of the slices in a lightly greased 10x6x2-inch baking dish.
- Spoon half of the bacon mixture over the tomatoes and sprinkle with Parmesan cheese.
- Repeat layers with remaining tomatoes, bacon mixture, and Parmesan cheese. Dot with butter.
- Bake for 25 minutes and serve immediately.

Brown Rice and Vegetable Casserole

Easy
5-6 as main dish—6-8 as side dish

2 tablespoons butter
½ cup carrots, thinly sliced
½ cup broccoli, thinly sliced
½ cup cauliflower, thinly sliced
½ cup yellow squash, sliced
½ cup zucchini, sliced
½ cup mushrooms, sliced
½ cup red cabbage, chopped
⅓ cup white wine
⅓ cup water
2 tablespoons soy sauce
6 cups brown rice, cooked
1 cup sour cream
1 cup sharp Cheddar cheese, grated
¾ cup cashews

- Preheat oven to 450°.
- In a large skillet, sauté vegetables in butter to coat them. Stir in white wine, water, and soy sauce. Toss until vegetables are softened.
- Layer a 9x15-inch casserole pan with the cooked rice, cooked vegetables, sour cream, cheese, and cashews.
- Bake until everything is hot and cheese is melted.

Absolutely delicious!

Vegetable-Cheese Casserole

Easy
6 Servings

3 tablespoons olive oil
1 large onion, chopped
2 cloves garlic, minced
1 cup fresh bread crumbs
¼ cup Parmesan cheese, grated
¼ cup fresh parsley, chopped
2 tablespoons fresh basil, chopped
1 pound medium zucchini, sliced
1 pound medium yellow squash, sliced
1 (8-ounce) package mozzarella cheese, grated
2 tomatoes, peeled and sliced
Salt and pepper to taste

- Preheat oven to 350°.
- Heat 2 tablespoons of the olive oil in a large skillet. Sauté onion and garlic until translucent. Set aside.
- In a bowl, combine the bread crumbs. Parmesan cheese, parsley, and basil. Set aside.
- Oil a 2½-quart casserole dish with the remaining 1 tablespoon of olive oil. Layer zucchini, yellow squash, mozzarella cheese, tomatoes, onions, salt, pepper, and bread crumb mixture. Repeat layers and end with mozzarella cheese.
- Cover with foil and bake for 20 minutes. Remove foil and bake an additional 20 minutes.

Baked Apricots

2 (17-ounce) cans apricot halves
3 tablespoons brown sugar
½ teaspoon cinnamon
½ teaspoon ginger
3 tablespoons butter
7 Ritz crackers

- Preheat oven to 375°.
- Butter a round 1½-quart casserole dish.
- Drain apricots and reserve ⅓ of the total liquid. Remove seeds, if any.
- Combine sugar, cinnamon, and ginger.
- Arrange a layer of apricots, then spice/sugar mixture and finish with remaining apricots.
- Top with the 1½ tablespoons butter.
- Pour reserved liquid over apricots.
- Crumble crackers over top and dot with remaining butter.
- Bake, uncovered, for 40-45 minutes.

Champagne-Marinated Fruit

Easy

Reynolda House, Museum of American Art

- In a large glass bowl, arrange a selection of cut up fruit (oranges, grapefruit, pineapple, grapes, melon, etc.). Cover with champagne; then cover with plastic wrap and chill overnight. Add any fresh berries just before serving.
- Serve the fruit and its champagne in champagne glasses for both sipping and eating.

desserts

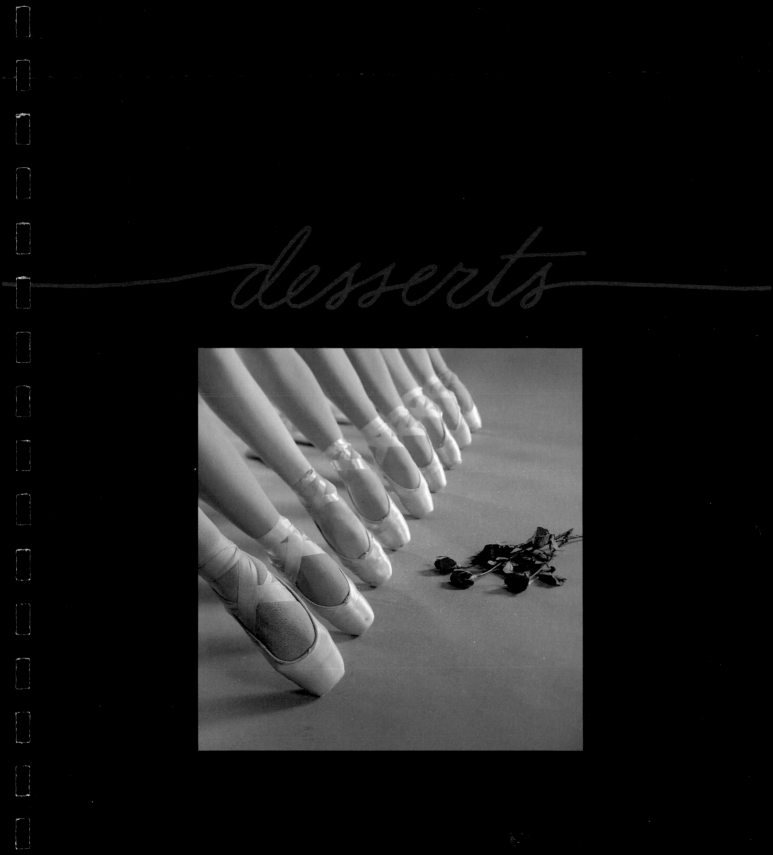

Nutcracker Tea

Fresh Vegetable Mold
Smoked Oyster Spread
Cheese Straws
Scones
Ginger Roll Chantilly with Brandied Walnut Sauce
Million Dollar Pound Cake
Fruit Jewels
Summit Lemon Squares
Sherry
Hot Tea

Dancers from the North Carolina School of the Arts

Internationally renowned alumni from the North Carolina School of the Arts have been thrilling audiences throughout the United States and Europe for nearly two decades. One of the 16 constituent institutions of The University of North Carolina, the North Carolina School of the Arts trains exceptionally talented high school and college students for professional careers in the performing arts.

Founded in 1965, the school combines professional instruction in dance, design and production, drama, and music with a liberal arts curriculum. The more than 700 students who attend the North Carolina School of the Arts come from virtually every state in the nation and more than a dozen foreign countries.

Photo by Smith/Weiler/Smith

Fourteen Carat Cake

2   cups flour
2   teaspoons baking powder
1½ teaspoons baking soda
1   teaspoon salt
2   teaspoons cinnamon
4   eggs
2   cups sugar
1½ cups vegetable oil
2   cups raw carrots, grated
1   (8½-ounce) can crushed pineapple, drained
½   cup chopped nuts

Vanilla Cream Cheese Frosting:

½   cup butter or margarine, softened
1   (8-ounce) package cream cheese, softened
1   teaspoon vanilla extract
1   pound confectioners sugar

- Preheat oven to 350°.
- Sift together first five ingredients.
- In a separate bowl, beat eggs with wire whisk. Add sugar and beat until dissolved.
- Add remaining ingredients. Mix well.
- Turn into three greased and floured 9-inch cake pans. Bake 34-40 minutes, until done.
- Cool in pans 10 minutes. Invert onto racks to cool completely.
- Frost with Vanilla Cream Cheese Frosting between layers, on top, and sides.

- Combine butter, cream cheese, and vanilla in mixing bowl and blend until smooth.
- Add sugar gradually until well incorporated.

*"This is a book about **real** food. The fabulous moist 14 Carat Cake recipe alone is worth double the price!" [Charles Kuralt, CBS News]*

Mom's Chocolate Cake

Cake:

1   stick butter, softened
1   cup sugar
4   eggs
1   teaspoon vanilla extract
1   (12-ounce) can chocolate syrup
1   cup self-rising flour

- Preheat oven to 350°.
- Cream butter and sugar together in the bowl of an electric mixer.
- Add eggs one at a time.
- Add vanilla.
- Add chocolate syrup and flour alternately. Beat only until ingredients are just blended.
- Pour batter into two well greased and floured 8 inch cake pans. (A circle of waxed paper, also greased and floured, cut to fit cake pans will help prevent sticking.)
- Bake 25 minutes or until cakes test done. Cool slightly and unmold layers on a rack. Cool completely before icing.

Icing:

1   stick butter
½   cup heavy cream
1   (6-ounce) package semi-sweet
      chocolate morsels
1½ cups confectioners sugar, sifted

- Melt butter, cream, and chocolate together in a double boiler or heavy bottomed saucepan. Cool.
- Whisk in sifted confectioners sugar until you have a desirable spreading consistency (approximately 1½ cups).

Warm cake slices in the microwave before serving. Heaven!

Cake-baking tips: Have ingredients at room temperature (butter, eggs, milk) to give the cake a higher volume and better texture. The smoother the batter, the better the cake, so mix well between each step. Presift flour, measure, add it to other dry ingredients, and sift again.

Chocolate Bourbon Cake With Raisins

Average
10 Servings

Cake:

½	cup	raisins
½	cup	bourbon
1	cup	whole hazelnuts
4	ounces	semi-sweet chocolate
8	ounces	bittersweet chocolate
3	sticks	unsalted butter
⅓	cup	sugar
2	tablespoons	cornstarch
6		eggs

Bourbon Crème Chantilly:

1	cup	heavy cream
1	tablespoon	bourbon
2	tablespoons	powdered sugar

Caramel Hazelnuts:

3	tablespoons	sugar
3	tablespoons	water
		Reserved nuts

Garnish:

Powdered sugar
Fresh mint

- Soak raisins in bourbon overnight.
- Place hazelnuts on a cookie sheet and bake at 400° for 12-14 minutes. Let cool and remove skins by rubbing with a cloth towel. Reserve ten toasted hazelnuts for decoration and coarsely chop the remaining hazelnuts.
- Line a 12-inch cake pan with buttered parchment.
- Reduce oven temperature to 350°.
- Drain bourbon from the raisins, reserving raisins and bourbon.
- Combine the chocolate, butter, and sugar in a double boiler and heat until smooth. Remove from heat.
- Combine bourbon and cornstarch.
- Combine the eggs, raisins, bourbon/cornstarch mixture, and chopped hazelnuts and add to chocolate mixture.
- Pour into prepared cake pan.
- Bake for 18-20 minutes.
- Remove cake from oven and cool to lukewarm.
- Prepare Bourbon Crème Chantilly by beating the heavy cream until stiff peaks form and fold in bourbon and powdered sugar.
- Prepare Caramel Hazelnuts by placing the sugar and water in a small heavy saucepan and cook over medium high heat about 7-8 minutes or until the sugar turns to a light brown caramel color.
- With spoon, dip reserved nuts into caramel. Place on lightly oiled cookie sheet. Let cool.
- Sprinkle cake lightly with powdered sugar.
- Place coated hazelnuts along outer edge of cake for 10 servings.
- Serve portions with a generous dollop of Bourbon Crème Chantilly.
- Garnish with mint.
- Note: The caramel-coated hazelnuts must be served within 2 hours or they will soften.

Chocolate Upside Down Cake

Easy
6-8 Servings

1 cup flour
1½ cups sugar
3 teaspoons baking powder
½ teaspoon salt
1 (1-ounce) square unsweetened chocolate
2 tablespoons butter
½ cup milk
1 teaspoon vanilla
½ cup nuts, chopped
½ cup brown sugar, packed
4 tablespoons cocoa
1 cup boiling water

- Preheat oven to 350°.
- Sift together the flour, ¾ cup of the sugar, baking powder, and salt. Set aside.
- Melt chocolate and butter in double boiler or microwave.
- Add milk, vanilla, and nuts to chocolate mixture.
- Add dry ingredients to chocolate mixture. Mix well.
- Pour mixture into a buttered 9-inch pan.
- Sprinkle the remaining ½ cup sugar, brown sugar, and 4 tablespoons cocoa over the chocolate mixture. Pour boiling water over all.
- Bake for 45 minutes. Serve warm with ice cream.

Showhouse Lemon Cake

Easy
16 Servings

Cake:

3 cups sifted flour
2 teaspoons baking powder (double acting)
½ teaspoon salt
2 sticks unsalted butter, softened
2 cups sugar
4 eggs
1 cup milk
Rind of 2 lemons, finely grated (2 tablespoons)

Glaze:

⅓ cup fresh lemon juice
¾ cup sugar

- Preheat oven to 350°.
- Sift together flour, baking powder, and salt. Set aside.
- In mixer, cream butter. Add sugar and beat for 2-3 minutes.
- Add eggs, beating after each addition.
- Add sifted dry ingredients alternately with milk, beating after each addition.
- Stir in lemon rind.
- Pour batter into greased and floured 9-inch tube or Bundt pan.
- Bake for 50 minutes until done.
- Allow cake to cool for 5 minutes in pan. Invert on cooling rack.
- Mix together glaze ingredients. Using pastry brush, brush glaze over cake. (Do not pour over cake or glaze will run off.)
- Wait several hours before slicing. Serve with sweetened whipped cream and fresh berries if desired.

Chocolate Torte Caramela

4 ounces semi-sweet chocolate
½ cup butter, softened
½ cup powdered sugar
2 egg yolks
1 teaspoon vanilla
1 5x9-inch loaf pound cake, frozen
⅓ cup granulated sugar
½ cup sweetened whipped cream

- Melt chocolate in the top of a double boiler. Let cool to room temperature.
- Cream butter until fluffy. Gradually add powdered sugar. Add egg yolks one at a time. Beat until smooth. Beat in vanilla and cooled chocolate.
- Slice the top crust from a lightly frozen pound cake and discard.
- Slice remaining loaf horizontally into six or seven thin layers. Reserve one layer. Spread chocolate icing between cake layers and restack into a loaf. Reserve ½ to ¾ cup of icing for sides of cake.
- Place reserved layer on a piece of aluminum foil.
- Heat sugar in a heavy-bottomed saucepan until melted and amber, not too dark. Pour sugar quickly over reserved layer to coat evenly. Place on top of cake.
- Heat a knife blade over gas or electric burner and mark serving slices in caramel.
- Ice the sides of cake with reserved frosting. Pipe top edge and bottom edge with whipped cream. Chill before serving.
- Almond Brandy Sour Cream Pound Cake, page 249 is delicious paried with this recipe.

A quick, impressive dessert if using a purchased pound cake!

3 tablespoons cocoa + 1 tablespoon oil = 1 square of unsweetened baking chocolate.

Caramel Cake
Heritage Of Hospitality

Cake:

- 2 sticks butter or margarine, softened
- 2 cups sugar
- 4 eggs, separated
- 3 cups flour, sifted
- 2 teaspoons baking powder
- Pinch of salt
- 1 cup milk
- 1 teaspoon vanilla

- Preheat oven to 350°.
- In a mixer, cream butter and sugar. Add egg yolks and blend well.
- In a bowl, mix together flour, baking powder, and salt.
- Add dry ingredients alternately with milk to the batter. Add vanilla.
- Fold in well beaten egg whites.
- Pour batter into three well greased 9-inch cake pans.
- Bake for 20 minutes until light brown and firm in the middle.

Icing:

- 1½ (1-pound) boxes light brown sugar
- 1½ cups light cream or milk
- 1½ sticks butter or margarine

- Place brown sugar and milk in saucepan. Boil on medium high until medium ball forms if dropped into a cup of cold water, or 240° on a candy thermometer.
- Add butter and beat by hand until it cools and begins to thicken.
- Spread icing between cake layers and on top and sides. (If icing is too hard, add a little milk. If icing is too soft, cook a little longer.)

Place 2 or 3 marbles in the bottom of a double boiler or teapot. They will sound the alarm if the water gets too low by banging loudly.

Coffee Almond Torte
Stars Restaurant

⅓ cup dry bread crumbs
¾ cup egg whites, room
temperature
1 cup fine granulated sugar
3 tablespoons instant coffee
2 cups blanched almonds, grated
¼ cup strong brewed coffee
¾ stick unsalted butter, softened
4 egg yolks
1½ cups confectioners sugar
1½ cups heavy cream, whipped
1 cup sliced blanched almonds,
lightly toasted

- Preheat oven to 350°.
- Butter two 8-inch cake pans. Line each with parchment or waxed paper. Butter the paper and sprinkle each with 1 tablespoon of the bread crumbs.
- Beat egg whites until frothy. Add ½ cup of the sugar, slowly. Beat until stiff. Fold in remaining sugar, remaining bread crumbs, 2 tablespoons of the instant coffee and 1¾ cups of the grated almonds.
- Divide the mixture between two pans. Smooth gently and bake 20 minutes.
- Turn out onto a rack, peel off paper and sprinkle each round, while hot, with the brewed coffee. Let cool completely.
- Beat butter, egg yolks and confectioners sugar until well blended. Fold in remaining grated almonds, remaining instant coffee and whipped cream. Use to fill and frost the torte. Chill.
- When close to serving, decorate the top and sides with toasted almonds. Serve.

Add 1 teaspoon instant vanilla pudding mix to 1 cup whipped cream; it will not separate.

245

Four Seasons Cake

1   package angel food cake mix
3   cups fresh fruit
1   envelope unflavored gelatin
¼   cup cold water
6   egg yolks, beaten
    Dash salt
½   cup sugar
½   teaspoon grated lemon, lime, or
    orange peel
½   cup lemon, lime, or orange juice
6   egg whites
½   cup sugar
1   cup heavy cream, whipped
    and sweetened
¾   cup fresh fruit, well-drained
    Mint leaves

- Prepare angel food cake according to package directions and bake in a 10-inch tube pan.
- When cake is baked, cool, remove from pan, and set aside. Wash pan.
- Prepare selected fruits, peeling and slicing as needed. Drain well on paper towels.
- Soften gelatin in cold water. Set aside.
- Combine egg yolks, salt, ½ cup sugar, fruit peel, and juice in the top of a double boiler. Beat constantly over hot water until mixture coats a spoon. Whisk in gelatin. Set aside to cool, stirring occasionally.
- Beat egg whites until soft peaks form. Gradually beat in ½ cup sugar and beat until glossy.
- Fold whites into slightly cooled custard.
- Slice cake into four horizontal layers. Return bottom slice to tube pan. Spoon one-third of custard over cake layer. Spread 1 cup of fruit over custard and place second layer on top. Repeat procedures and finish with the fourth layer. Cover pan with foil and refrigerate overnight.
- When ready to serve, unmold cake onto a serving platter. Ice or garnish cake with whipped cream and mint leaves.
- Four seasons fruits:
  Fall-Winter: grapes, pears, melons, pineapple, oranges, papaya
  Spring: strawberries, papaya, melons, grapes, pineapple
  Summer: strawberries, peaches, blueberries, cherries, blackberries, raspberries

Apple Dapple Cake

Cake:

 3 eggs
 2 cups sugar
1⅓ cups vegetable oil
 1 teaspoon vanilla
 3 cups flour
 1 teaspoon soda
 1 teaspoon salt
 3 cups tart cooking apples,
     peeled and chopped
 1 cup nuts, chopped

- Preheat oven to 350°.
- In a mixer, beat eggs and sugar. Add oil and vanilla and mix.
- Fold in flour, soda, and salt. Mix well.
- Stir in apples and nuts.
- Pour batter into a greased and floured tube pan.
- Bake for 1 hour and 15 minutes, or until done.

Glaze:

 1 cup light brown sugar
 1 stick margarine
 ¼ cup evaporated milk

- In a saucepan, bring all glaze ingredients to a boil. Boil 2½ minutes and pour over warm cake. Leave in pan 2 hours. Turn cake out upright and serve.

A wonderful breakfast cake!

Million Dollar Pound Cake

 3 cups sugar
 1 pound butter, softened
 6 eggs, room temperature
 4 cups flour
 ¾ cup milk
 1 teaspoon almond extract
 1 teaspoon vanilla extract

- Preheat oven to 350°
- In a mixer, combine sugar and butter. Cream until light and fluffy.
- Add eggs one at a time, beating well after each addition.
- Add flour and milk alternately, beating well after each addition.
- Stir in flavorings.
- Pour batter into a well-greased and floured 10-inch tube pan.
- Bake 1 hour and 40 minutes or until cake tests done.

247

Orange Blossom Pound Cake

1 cup blanched almonds
1 cup sugar
2 sticks unsalted butter, softened
4 eggs
1 tablespoon freshly grated
    orange rind
1 cup flour
1 teaspoon baking powder
¼ teaspoon salt
¼ cup fresh orange juice

Glaze:
¼ cup fresh orange juice
2 cups confectioners sugar

Candied Orange Slices:
1 thin-skinned orange, sliced thinly
¾ cup sugar

- Preheat oven to 350°.
- Place almonds and sugar in the bowl of a food processor and grind until almonds are very fine.
- In the bowl of an electric mixer, cream butter. Add almond mixture and beat until light.
- Add eggs, one at a time, and orange rind.
- Sift flour, baking powder, and salt together. Add to butter mixture alternately with orange juice. Blend well after each addition.
- Pour batter into a buttered and floured 8-inch round pan, 2 inches deep.
- Bake for 50 minutes or until cake tests done. Remove and cool on a rack before glazing.
- Prepare glaze by pouring orange juice in a mixing bowl. Sift sugar into bowl and whisk until smooth.
- Pour glaze over top of cake and smooth with a spatula. Allow some of the glaze to drip down the sides. Allow glaze to harden before serving.
- Garnish cake and platter with fresh or candied orange slices.

- Combine orange slices in a saucepan with cold water to cover. Bring to a boil. Drain and repeat.
- Combine ½ cup water and sugar in a saucepan. Simmer, covered, until sugar dissolves.
- Add orange slices and simmer, partially covered, for 45 minutes, or until syrup is thick and rind is translucent.

Lemon juice removes the brown stain from your fingers after you've peeled a lot of apples.

Eggnog Pound Cake

Easy
16 Servings

2 sticks butter, softened
½ cup vegetable shortening
3 cups sugar
5 eggs, room temperature
3 cups flour
1 teaspoon baking powder
1 cup milk
1 teaspoon each of the following
   extracts: brandy, rum, vanilla,
   lemon, almond
1 teaspoon sherry

- Preheat oven to 325°.
- In a mixer, cream butter, shortening, and sugar until fluffy.
- Add eggs, one at a time, beating well after each addition.
- Combine flour and baking powder. Add these dry ingredients and milk to batter alternately, beginning and ending with flour. Mix well.
- Add extracts and sherry. Mix well.
- Turn into greased and floured tube pan.
- Bake 1½ hours or until cake tests done.

A light pound cake with a delicious golden crust.

Almond Brandy Sour Cream Pound Cake

Easy
1 10-inch Bundt or tube pan
plus 1 (5x9x3-inch) loaf pan
or 3 loaf pans

1½ cups butter, softened
3 cups sugar
6 eggs, room temperature
1 cup sour cream
3 cups flour
½ teaspoon baking soda
   Dash salt
1 teaspoon vanilla extract
1 teaspoon almond extract
2-3 tablespoons brandy

- Preheat oven to 325°.
- Grease and flour pans.
- In a large mixing bowl, cream butter and sugar until fluffy.
- Add eggs, one at a time, beating well after each addition.
- Stir in sour cream.
- In a separate bowl, sift flour, soda, and salt together. Add gradually to butter mixture, mixing well.
- Add vanilla, almond, and brandy and mix well.
- Pour into prepared pans. Bake bundt pan for 1 hour and loaf pans for 45-50 minutes.
- Cool in pans 10 minutes; then remove and cool on a rack.
- Rum may be substituted for brandy.

This cake is good served with fresh peaches or strawberries and cream or ice cream.

Blueberry Pound Cake

1   pint blueberries, washed
       and drained
3   cups flour
1   teaspoon baking powder
½   teaspoon salt
2   sticks butter, softened
2   cups sugar
4   eggs, room temperature
1½   teaspoons vanilla

- Preheat oven to 325°.
- Toss berries with ¼ cup of the flour. Set aside.
- Sift remaining flour with baking powder and salt. Set aside.
- In a mixer, cream butter and sugar.
- Add eggs, one at a time, beating well after each addition.
- Add vanilla and beat until fluffy.
- Fold dry ingredients into batter until well blended.
- Gently stir in berries.
- Turn into a greased and floured 10-inch tube pan.
- Bake 1 hour and 15 minutes, until cake tests done.
- Cool cake in pan for 10 minutes before removing.

Chocolate Pound Cake

3   cups flour
1   teaspoon baking powder
½   teaspoon salt
6   tablespoons cocoa
2   sticks butter, softened
½   cup vegetable shortening
3   cups sugar
5   eggs, room temperature
1   cup milk
1   tablespoon vanilla

- Preheat oven to 325°.
- Sift together first four ingredients. Set aside.
- In a mixer, cream butter and shortening. Add sugar. Cream until fluffy.
- Add 4 of the eggs, one at a time, beating after each addition.
- Add dry ingredients and milk alternately, beating after each addition.
- Add vanilla and remaining egg. Mix well.
- Turn batter into greased and floured Bundt pan.
- Bake 1½ hours until cake tests done.

St. Timothy's Coffee Cake
Heritage of Hospitality

2   sticks butter or margarine
2   cups sugar
½   teaspoon vanilla
2   eggs
2   cups flour, unsifted
1   teaspoon baking powder
¼   teaspoon salt
1   teaspoon cinnamon
1   cup nuts, chopped
½   cup golden raisins
1   cup sour cream
    Cinnamon sugar

- Preheat oven to 350°. Grease and flour Bundt pan.
- Cream butter until light and fluffy, add sugar gradually, and continue to cream.
- Blend in vanilla; add eggs one at a time, beating well after each addition.
- Sift together flour, baking powder, salt, and cinnamon. Add nuts and raisins; coat well.
- Add dry ingredients and sour cream alternately. Blend well.
- Turn into Bundt pan and sprinkle with cinnamon sugar.
- Bake for 1 hour.
- Leave in pan for 1 hour before turning out. Turn out and sprinkle with more cinnamon sugar. Serve.

This recipe is named for St. Timothy's Episcopal Church and is a local favorite.

Blueberry Sugar Cake

½ cup butter, softened
1 cup sugar
3 eggs, beaten
1 teaspoon baking powder
¼ teaspoon soda
½ teaspoon salt
2 cups plus 1 tablespoon flour
1 cup sour cream
2 cups blueberries, fresh or frozen

Topping:
1 cup brown sugar
¼ cup butter, softened
¼ cup flour

- Preheat oven to 350°.
- In a medium mixing bowl, cream together butter and sugar. Add eggs.
- In another bowl, sift together baking powder, soda, salt, and 2 cups flour.
- Add flour mixture and sour cream alternately to butter/sugar mixture.
- Toss blueberries with 1 tablespoon flour to keep them from sinking to the bottom or bleeding into the cake. Fold blueberries into batter.
- Pour batter into a greased 9x13-inch pan.
- Mix topping ingredients and sprinkle on top.
- Bake for 30 minutes.

Black Walnut Coffee Cake

1 cup butter or margarine
1 cup buttermilk, warm
2 cups brown sugar
2 eggs, beaten
2 cups self-rising flour
1 teaspoon baking soda
2 tablespoons cola
1 teaspoon vanilla extract

Topping:
1¼ cups butter
1 cup brown sugar
6 tablespoons evaporated milk
1 cup walnuts, chopped

- Preheat oven to 350°.
- Melt 1 cup butter.
- Stir in buttermilk, brown sugar, and eggs.
- Combine flour and soda and add to buttermilk mixture; mix well.
- Add cola and vanilla.
- Bake in greased 9x13-inch baking dish for 25 minutes.

- Melt butter.
- Add remaining ingredients; mix well.
- Spread on hot cake and broil until bubbly.
- Serve warm.

Ginger Roll Chantilly With Brandied Walnut Sauce

Difficult
10 Servings

Ginger Roll:

3 eggs
½ cup sugar
¼ teaspoon salt
⅔ cup cake flour
2 teaspoons baking powder
1 teaspoon cinnamon
1 teaspoon ginger
1 teaspoon allspice
¼ cup molasses

- Preheat oven to 375°.
- Oil a 10x14-inch jelly roll pan and line with waxed paper. Allow at least a 1-inch overhang at the ends.
- In the bowl of an electric mixer, beat eggs, sugar, and salt until very light and fluffy, about 5-7 minutes.
- Sift together flour, baking powder, cinnamon, ginger, and allspice.
- Fold flour mixture into egg/sugar mixture. Fold in molasses.
- Pour batter into a prepared jelly roll pan. Place in oven and bake 12-14 minutes or until cake tests done.
- Remove cake from oven. Dust with granulated sugar. Turn cake upside down onto a piece of waxed paper. Remove paper from cake. Roll cake into a jelly roll widthwise. Cool.
- When cake is completely cooled, unroll and spread with Chantilly Cream. Re-roll and refrigerate, covered, until time to serve.

Chantilly Cream:

1 cup heavy cream
½ teaspoon vanilla
2 tablespoons powdered sugar

- Combine cream, vanilla, and sugar in the bowl of an electric mixer. Beat until firm peaks form.

Brandied Walnut Sauce:

1 cup brown sugar
4 tablespoons butter
¼ cup heavy cream
2 tablespoons light corn syrup
¼ cup brandy
½ cup toasted walnuts, chopped

- In a small saucepan, combine brown sugar, butter, cream, and corn syrup. Bring mixture to a boil, stirring constantly. Reduce heat and cook 5 minutes. Add brandy and nuts.

To serve:
- Arrange cake on a serving platter. Serve warm sauce on the side.

A delicious fall cake. Use colorful leaves for a garnish.

253

Pecan Roll With Caramel Nut Sauce

¾ cup flour
½ cup ground pecans
1 teaspoon baking powder
¼ teaspoon salt
3 eggs
1 cup sugar
⅓ cup water
1 teaspoon vanilla
2 tablespoons powdered sugar
½ gallon butter pecan ice cream

Caramel Nut Sauce:

½ cup brown sugar
½ cup light corn syrup
2 tablespoons butter
⅛ teaspoon salt
¾ cup chopped pecans, toasted
¼ cup heavy cream
1 teaspoon vanilla

- Preheat oven to 375°
- Grease a jelly roll pan, line with waxed paper, grease again, and flour. Set aside.
- Combine flour, nuts, baking powder, and salt.
- In a large bowl, using electric mixer, beat eggs and sugar on medium speed for 5 minutes. At low speed, add water and vanilla. Gradually beat in flour mixture.
- Pour batter into pan and bake 20-25 minutes. Watch carefully!
- Sprinkle powdered sugar on a linen dish towel. Turn cake out onto dish towel and peel off waxed paper. Roll towel and cake up lengthwise. Cool on a rack.
- When cool, spread softened ice cream over cake roll and carefully roll up again. Fill ends of cake roll with ice cream as well. (Not all of the ice cream will be used.) Freeze overnight or up to several days ahead.
- Prepare Caramel Nut Sauce. Combine sugar, syrup, butter, and salt. Stir over medium heat just until sugar dissolves. Remove from heat and stir in cream, nuts, and vanilla. Can be refrigerated at this point for several days.
- To serve, reheat sauce. Remove cake from freezer and trim ends diagonally. Slice on the diagonal and serve cake with sauce spooned over it.

Mocha Mousse

4½ ounces semi-sweet chocolate
¾ cup sugar
⅓ cup water
4 egg yolks
2 tablespoons coffee liqueur
1 cup heavy cream
    Additional whipped cream
    Mandarin orange sections

- Melt chocolate in a small saucepan over low heat. Cool.
- Place sugar and water in another small, heavy saucepan. Cook over medium high heat until mixture comes to a boil. Cover saucepan with a piece of aluminum foil and cook for 5 minutes exactly. Do not stir.
- While syrup is cooking, scrape cooled chocolate into bowl of food processor.
- With food processor running, pour syrup into the chocolate mixture.
- With food processor running, add egg yolks one at a time.
- Blend in coffee liqueur.
- Whip the cream until soft peaks form.
- Fold the chocolate mixture into the whipped cream, carefully but thoroughly. Pour into individual serving dishes and chill 6-8 hours.
- To serve, top each mousse with a dollop of whipped cream and a mandarin orange segment.

Chocolate Orange Mousse

2 eggs
3 egg yolks
½ cup sugar
1 tablespoon Grand Marnier
6 ounces semi-sweet chocolate
    Juice of 1 orange
1 package unflavored gelatin
1 cup heavy cream, softly whipped

Garnish (optional):
1 cup sweetened whipped cream
    Mint leaves
    Candied violets

- Combine eggs, yolks, and sugar in a medium bowl. Beat together until pale yellow. Stir in Grand Marnier.
- In a small saucepan, melt chocolate with 2 ounces of water over low heat.
- In a small saucepan, place orange juice. Sprinkle gelatin over top to soften (about 2 minutes). Melt over low heat. Add to egg and sugar mixture.
- Fold chocolate into eggs. Add cream. Blend well.
- Pour into 1½-quart serving bowl. Refrigerate for several hours or until chilled.
- Garnish with whipped cream rosettes and mint leaves or candied violets.

The better the quality of chocolate you use, the better your mousse will be!

255

Chocolate Mousse Pie

Crust:
  3   cups chocolate wafer crumbs
  ½   cup unsalted butter, melted

- In a bowl, combine the chocolate wafer crumbs and butter.
- Press into the bottom and up the sides of a 10-inch springform pan. Refrigerate for 30 minutes.

Filling:
  16   ounces semi-sweet chocolate
  2   eggs
  2   egg yolks
  2   cups heavy cream
  6   tablespoons confectioners sugar
  4   egg whites, room temperature

- In top of double boiler, soften chocolate over simmering water. Remove from heat and cool to lukewarm. Whisk in whole eggs and then egg yolks.
- In the bowl of a mixer, beat the cream and confectioners sugar until soft peaks form.
- In another bowl of a mixer, beat the egg whites until stiff, but not dry.
- Stir a small amount of the whipped cream and egg whites into the chocolate mixture to lighten it. Gently fold in the remaining whipped cream and egg whites, alternating, until completely mixed.
- Pour filling into the crust and refrigerate for at least 6 hours or overnight.

Chocolate Leaves:
  8   ounces semi-sweet chocolate
  1   tablespoon vegetable shortening
      Holly leaves or other waxy leaves

- In the top of a double boiler, melt the chocolate and shortening.
- Generously coat the back of the leaves with chocolate with a spoon.
- Chill or freeze until chocolate has hardened. Starting at the stem, gently peel the leaf away from the chocolate.

Garnish:
  2   cups heavy cream
      Confectioners sugar to sweeten

- In the bowl of a mixer, whip the cream and sugar until it is very stiff.
- Loosen crust of pie on all sides using a sharp knife and remove it from the springform pan.
- Spread all but ½ cup of the whipped cream over the top of the mousse. Decorate with leaves in a circular pattern in the middle of the pie.
- Using a pastry bag and fluted tube, pipe the remaining whipped cream into rosettes in the center and around the outer edges of the pie.

New York City Chocolate Cheesecake

Easy
12-16 Servings

Crust:

8	ounces chocolate wafers
6	tablespoons unsalted butter

Filling:

12	ounces semi-sweet chocolate
24	ounces cream cheese, softened
1	teaspoon vanilla
⅛	teaspoon salt
1	cup sugar
3	eggs
1	cup sour cream
	Whipped cream for garnish

- Preheat oven to 375°.
- Butter only the sides of a 9-inch springform pan.
- Process cookies in food processor until fine crumbs. Add melted butter and mix thoroughly.
- Place ⅔ of the crumb/butter mixture in the springform pan and press a layer onto the sides of the pan to within ¾-inch of the top edge.
- Place the remaining crumbs in the bottom of the springform pan making a compact layer. Set aside.
- Melt chocolate in a double boiler. Remove from heat and stir until smooth. Cool slightly.
- In a large bowl, beat the cream cheese until smooth. Add vanilla, salt, and sugar. Beat well. Add chocolate and beat well. Add eggs one at a time and beat until blended after each. Add sour cream and beat until smooth.
- Pour filling into crust. Rotate briskly in one direction and then in the other to smooth top.
- Bake for 1 hour.
- Cool completely on rack.
- Chill completely. Loosen sides with a sharp knife prior to removing from springform pan.
- To serve, garnish with sweetened whipped cream.

Put whole lemon in microwave for 40-50 seconds on high. This will result in twice as much juice.

White Chocolate Cheesecake

Crust:
1½   cups chocolate cookie crumbs
½   cup sifted powdered sugar
4   ounces butter, melted

Filling:
½   pound white chocolate
2   eggs
½   cup sugar
¾   pound cream cheese, softened
½   teaspoon vanilla extract
1   ounce semi-sweet chocolate
   Strawberries
   Mint leaves

- Preheat oven to 375°.
- To make the crust, grind cookies in a food processor until fine, or roll cookies between two sheets of waxed paper with a rolling pin.
- Place crumbs in a bowl and stir in sugar and melted butter. Mix until well blended.
- Pat crust into an 8-Inch springform pan, bringing crust up on sides to top of pan.
- Bake crust for 6-8 minutes. Chill well.
- In a double boiler, melt white chocolate over medium high heat.
- Meanwhile, cream the eggs and sugar with electric mixer or in food processor.
- Gradually add cream cheese to egg mixture until well incorporated. Beat until light and fluffy, about 3 minutes.
- Slowly beat in the melted white chocolate and add the vanilla extract.
- Pour the filling into the chilled crust and bake for 30 minutes. Cheesecake should be firm and toothpick inserted into center should come out clean.
- Let cake cool at room temperature.
- To garnish the cake, melt the semi-sweet chocolate over very low heat. Drizzle the chocolate with a spoon over the cake, using a back and forth motion to create a web effect. Garnish with strawberries and mint leaves.
- Store in refrigerator.
- May be made a day ahead.

This cake is rich and delicious and fairly easy to prepare. The block white chocolate can be obtained at larger grocery stores or specialty food shops.

Fudge Almond Cheesecake

Average
12 Servings

1½ **cups ginger snap cookie crumbs**
¼ **cup butter, melted**
24 **ounces cream cheese**
1 **cup sugar**
3 **eggs**
2 **teaspoons vanilla**
2 **teaspoons almond extract**
6 **ounces semi-sweet chocolate chips**
3 **tablespoons butter**

- Preheat oven to 350°.
- Crumble ginger snaps in food processor.
- Add melted butter; process a few seconds more.
- Press crumbs into 9-inch springform pan.
- In clean bowl of food processor, add cream cheese. Process until smooth.
- Add sugar, eggs, and extracts; process until well blended.
- Pour into pan and bake for 45 minutes.
- Turn off oven and allow cake to cool in oven with door open.
- Remove from pan.
- In double boiler, melt chocolate and butter.
- With teaspoon, swirl chocolate mixture over top of cake.

Absolutely delicious!

Praline Cheesecake

Average
14-16 Servings

Crust:
1 **cup graham cracker crumbs**
3 **tablespoons sugar**
3 **tablespoons butter, melted**

- Preheat oven to 350°.
- Combine crumbs, sugar, and butter.
- Press into a 10-inch springform pan. Bake for 10 minutes. Cool.

Filling:
3 **(8-ounce) packages cream cheese**
1¼ **cups dark brown sugar**
2 **tablespoons flour**
3 **eggs**
1½ **teaspoons vanilla**
½ **cup pecans, chopped**

- In the bowl of an electric mixer, combine cream cheese, brown sugar, and flour. Blend well.
- Add eggs one at a time blending well after each addition.
- Add vanilla and chopped pecans.
- Pour filling into prepared crust and bake at 350° for 50-55 minutes.
- Remove from oven and cool slightly. Remove sides of springform pan.

Garnish:
1 **tablespoon light corn syrup**
Whole pecans

- Brush top of cake with corn syrup and garnish with pecan halves. Chill completely before serving.

Pumpkin Cheesecake

Crust:
1½   cups graham cracker crumbs
⅓   cup almonds, ground
½   teaspoon ginger
½   teaspoon cinnamon
⅓   cup butter, melted

- Preheat oven to 425°.
- Combine ingredients and press into pan. Bake for 10 minutes.
- Remove from oven and reduce oven temperature to 325°.

Filling:
32   ounces cream cheese, softened
1¼   cups sugar
3   tablespoons maple syrup
3   tablespoons cognac
1   teaspoon ginger
1   teaspoon cinnamon
½   teaspoon nutmeg
4   eggs, room temperature
¼   cup heavy cream
1   cup canned pumpkin

- Beat cream cheese with mixer until smooth.
- Gradually add sugar. Add maple syrup, cognac, ginger, cinnamon, and nutmeg. Beat well.
- Add eggs one at a time, beating well after each egg.
- Add cream and pumpkin; blend well.
- Pour into prepared crust. Bake for 45 minutes.
- Turn off oven. Leave cake in oven and do not open oven door for 1 hour.

Topping:
2   cups sour cream
¼   cup sugar
1   tablespoon maple syrup
1   tablespoon cognac

- Preheat oven to 425°.
- Blend all ingredients.
- Spread over cake and bake for 10 minutes.
- Allow cake to cool at room temperature, about 1 hour.
- Chill about 3 hours before removing from pan.
- If desired, garnish with ¼ cup almonds sautéed in 1 tablespoon butter.

Fabulous fall dessert.

Amaretto-Amaretti Chocolate Cheesecake

Easy
20 Servings

Crust:

5	tablespoons unsalted butter
1	ounce semi-sweet chocolate
1½	cups amaretti cookies, finely ground (18 packages of 2 cookies)
2	tablespoons sugar

- Preheat oven to 300°.
- Butter a 10-inch springform pan.
- Melt butter and chocolate over low heat.
- Remove from heat and add ground amaretti cookies and sugar.
- Press into the bottom of springform pan.

Filling:

7	ounces semi-sweet chocolate
3½	ounces almond paste
⅓	cup amaretto liqueur
32	ounces cream cheese, softened
4	eggs
½	cup heavy cream
½	cup sugar
½	cup amaretti cookies, finely ground (6 packages of 2 cookies)

- Melt chocolate over low heat. Remove from heat and reserve.
- Chop almond paste into small pieces and place in bowl of electric mixer.
- Add amaretto liqueur and beat on low speed until smooth.
- Add cream cheese and beat until blended.
- Add eggs one at a time and beat after each addition, until blended.
- Add chocolate, cream, and sugar and beat until blended.
- Stir in ground amaretti cookies. Pour filling into prepared crust.
- Bake for 60 minutes in the preheated 300° oven.
- Turn off oven and allow cheesecake to remain in oven for 30 minutes.
- Remove cheesecake from oven.
- Cool 5 minutes; remove springform ring.
- Chill thoroughly before cutting.
- Garnish with a dollop of sweetened whipped cream and a chocolate coffee bean.

Garnish:

Sweetened whipped cream
Chocolate coffee beans

261

Rum Raisin Cheesecake with Myers's Rum Sauce
Just Desserts

Average
12-16 Servings

Crust:
- 1 cup graham cracker crumbs
- ¼ cup ground almonds
- 4 tablespoons melted butter

Filling:
- ⅓ cup Myers's Rum
- 1 cup seedless raisins
- 3 pounds cream cheese, room temperature
- 2 cups sugar
- 2 eggs, room temperature
- 1 teaspoon vanilla extract

Rum Sauce:
- 1 cup brown sugar
- 2 ounces butter
- ½ cup Karo syrup
- ½ cup cream
- ¼ cup Myers's Rum
- ½ teaspoon vanilla

Crust:
- Combine ingredients and press into the bottom of a 10-inch springform pan. Refrigerate.

Filling:
- Preheat oven to 300°.
- In a small saucepan, bring rum to a boil. Remove from heat. Put raisins in the rum, cover and steep for at least 10 minutes.
- In a mixer, beat cream cheese and sugar until smooth. Scrape down sides of bowl and add eggs one at a time, beating after each addition.
- Add vanilla and rum-raisin mixture and stir to combine.
- Carefully place mixture into crust (so as not to make a hole in crust). Bake for 1 hour. (The top of the cheesecake should be golden, but it will still be loose. Cake may seem to go over edges of pan, but it won't.)
- Cool at room temperature for 1 hour and then refrigerate overnight. Run a hot knife around the edge of the pan to remove the cheesecake.

Rum Sauce:
- In a saucepan, combine first 4 ingredients and stir over medium heat until boiling.
- Remove from heat and stir in rum and vanilla. Serve warm over cheesecake.

262

Danish Raspberry Shortcake

Pastry:

1	cup flour
6	tablespoons butter, softened
6	tablespoons powdered sugar
1	egg yolk
½	teaspoon vanilla

Glaze:

1	cup red currant jelly or seedless raspberry jam, melted
1	pint fresh raspberries
	Sweetened whipped cream

Pastry:

- Place flour, sugar, and butter in a food processor. Blend with a steel blade until the texture of coarse meal. Add yolk and vanilla. Blend until pastry forms a ball.
- Place pastry between two layers of waxed paper or plastic wrap. Press into a circle 8 inches in diameter and ¼-inch thick. Chill until firm, about 30 minutes.
- Transfer pastry to a cookie sheet and bake at 375° for 15-20 minutes. Pastry will be deep cream-colored, not brown. Cool.

To Assemble:

- Brush pastry generously with the glaze. Arrange raspberries on top and brush with remaining glaze. Chill.
- Before serving, garnish edges with whipped cream rosettes.

Fruit Pizza

1	(15-ounce) box sugar cookie mix
1	egg
1	tablespoon water
1	(8-ounce) package cream cheese, room temperature
⅓	cup sugar
1	teaspoon vanilla or almond extract
	Fresh strawberries, blueberries, bananas, kiwi, peaches

Glaze:

1	cup fresh orange juice
½	cup sugar
2	tablespoons cornstarch

- Preheat oven to 375°.
- In a bowl, combine contents of both sugar cookie mix packets with egg and water. Mix with a spoon. Do not roll out the dough.
- Place the dough in the center of a greased 11-inch pizza pan. Use your fingers to press the dough to the edge of the pan. Bake for about 15 minutes, or until doneness of a sugar cookie. Let cool completely.
- In a bowl, mix together the cream cheese, sugar, and vanilla. Spread on top of the cookie crust.
- Slice fresh fruit and arrange over the crust.

- In a saucepan, combine all ingredients. Cook over medium heat until thickened, stirring occasionally. Spoon glaze over "pizza."

Basic Food Processor Pastry

3 cups flour, sifted
½ teaspoon salt
4½ tablespoons chilled vegetable
    shortening
12 tablespoons butter, cut into
    cubes
5-7 tablespoons cold water

- Place flour, salt, vegetable shortening, and butter in the bowl of a food processor fitted with a steel blade.
- Blend ingredients using "on and off," or pulsing speeds, until mixture resembles coarse meal.
- With processor running, add 5-7 tablespoons of cold water, 1 tablespoon at a time. When dough forms a ball, stop the processor.
- Divide dough in half. Shape each half into a ball and then flatten. Wrap and refrigerate for 30-45 minutes.
- Roll pastry into a rough circle and fit into tart or pie tin.
- For recipes requiring a pre-baked shell: bake pastry covered with foil and weighted with dried beans in a preheated 450° oven for 10-15 minutes. Remove foil and continue to bake until pastry appears dry, but not brown.
- This pastry may also be made by blending ingredients with a pastry blender. Add water by tablespoons and blend with a fork. Gather dough into a ball by hand and proceed as directed in food processor recipe.
- Pastry freezes well.

Clean the inside of copper bowl by rubbing it with salt on a lemon half.

Almond Tart
Newmarket Grille

Pastry:
1 cup plus 1 tablespoon flour
1 tablespoon plus 1 teaspoon sugar
1 stick butter
¼ teaspoon vanilla
¼ teaspoon almond extract
1 tablespoon water

- Preheat oven to 375°.
- In a large bowl, mix all ingredients. Manipulate into pliable dough ball with no lumps.
- Flatten out three-fourths of the dough and press into bottom of an 8-inch springform pan. Smooth evenly covering the bottom. With remaining dough, smooth evenly ½-inch on the sides.
- Bake 10-15 minutes or until light brown.

Filling:
1 cup blanched almonds, sliced
1 cup heavy cream
Pinch of salt
¾ cup sugar
1 tablespoon Grand Marnier
1 tablespoon Kirsch or sherry brandy (optional)

- Preheat oven to 350°.
- In a saucepan, combine all ingredients and heat until silky smooth.
- Pour into baked pastry and bake for 25-30 minutes. Rotate last 15 minutes. Cool.
- Chill before serving.

Fresh Blueberry Tart

1 (9-inch) tart shell
1 (3-ounce) package cream cheese, softened
4 cups fresh blueberries
¼ cup water
¾ cup sugar
2 tablespoons cornstarch
2 tablespoons lemon juice
½ pint heavy cream whipped with 2 tablespoons sugar

- Spread the cream cheese in the bottom of a cooked, cooled tart shell.
- Fill the tart with 3 cups of the blueberries and set aside.
- In a saucepan, combine the remaining cup of blueberries with the water and bring to just a boil. Reduce heat and simmer for 2 minutes. Strain and reserve the juice.
- In a saucepan, combine sugar and cornstarch. Gradually add ½ cup of the reserved juice. Cook, stirring constantly, until the mixture is thick and clear. Cool slightly. Stir in lemon juice. Pour over berries in the tart shell and chill.
- Top with sweetened whipped cream before serving.

Mile High Strawberry Pie

Average
10-12 Servings

½ pint heavy cream
1 (10-ounce) package frozen
   strawberries
1 cup sugar
2 egg whites
1 tablespoon fresh lemon juice
⅛ teaspoon salt
1 teaspoon vanilla
1 9-inch deep dish pie shell, baked
   and cooled

- Whip cream and refrigerate.
- Defrost strawberries partially.
- In the large bowl of a mixer, combine the strawberries, sugar, egg whites, lemon juice, and salt. Beat at medium speed for 10 minutes or until the mixture is stiff and holds its shape. Add vanilla and then fold in the whipped cream quickly.
- Lightly pile the strawberry mixture into the pie shell. Freeze immediately.
- Two cups of coarsely mashed and sweetened fresh strawberries may be substituted.

Fruit Jewels

Average
24 Tartlets

Crust:
½ cup butter, softened
½ cup sugar
1 egg yolk
1 tablespoon orange juice
1 tablespoon orange peel, grated
1 teaspoon vanilla
1¾ cups flour

- Preheat oven to 350°.
- In the bowl of a mixer, beat butter until fluffy and gradually mix in sugar. Beat in egg yolk, orange juice, peel, and vanilla. Mix in flour.
- Press dough into 24 (2- to 3-inch) metal tartlet molds.
- Bake 15-20 minutes until brown. Let cool in molds for 10 minutes. Flip crust shells out and cool completely on a rack. Shells may be frozen.

Glaze:
½ cup sugar
1½ tablespoons cornstarch
   Dash of salt
1 cup orange juice
2 teaspoons orange peel, grated
1 tablespoon orange liqueur
3-4 cups fresh fruit (orange sections,
   sliced strawberries, kiwi,
   fresh pineapple, blueberries,
   seedless grapes, halved, or
   whatever is in season)

- In a saucepan, combine sugar, cornstarch, and salt. Gradually stir in orange juice. Heat to boiling, stirring constantly. Let boil for 2 minutes.
- Add orange peel. Cover and let cool. Stir in orange liqueur.

To Assemble:
- Fill shells with fruit, using one type of fruit per tart.
- Carefully spoon glaze over the top, covering fruit completely. Chill.
- Assemble no more than six hours in advance.

Frozen Lemon Pie

Average
6-8 Servings

Crust:
1   cup graham cracker crumbs
3   tablespoons butter, melted
3   tablespoons sugar

- Preheat oven to 350°.
- In a bowl, combine crumbs, butter, and sugar.
- Coat a 9-inch pie pan with non-stick cooking spray. Pour in crumb mixture and press on bottom and up sides of pan. Bake for 8-10 minutes. Let cool before filling.

Filling:
3   eggs, separated
½   cup plus 1 teaspoon sugar
    Juice and grated zest of
       1 large lemon
1   cup heavy cream

- In the bowl of a mixer, beat egg yolks and ½ cup of sugar until light. Blend in the lemon juice and zest.
- In another bowl of a mixer, beat the egg whites with the remaining teaspoon of sugar until stiff, but not dry. Fold the whites into the egg yolk mixture.
- In a bowl, quickly whip the cream. Fold the whipped cream into the egg mixture.
- Pour filling into the crust and freeze for at least 5 hours.
- Garnish with a sprinkling of graham cracker crumbs.

Coffee Ice Cream Pie

Easy
8 Servings

½   cup butter, melted
1   (7-ounce) can flaked coconut
2   tablespoons flour
½   cup pecans, chopped
½   gallon coffee ice cream, softened
1   cup heavy cream
¼   cup powdered sugar
    Sweet chocolate curls
½-⅔ cup coffee liqueur

- Preheat oven to 375°.
- Combine butter, coconut, flour, and pecans. Mix well and press on bottom and sides of a 10-inch pie pan. Bake for 10-12 minutes until lightly browned. Let cool.
- Spoon softened ice cream into pie shell and freeze until firm.
- Beat heavy cream until foamy. Gradually add powdered sugar, beating until soft peaks form. Spread over pie and top with grated chocolate curls.
- Pour 1 tablespoon coffee liqueur over each slice.

Granny's Pumpkin Pie

⅔ cup brown sugar
⅓ cup white sugar
3 eggs, beaten
1 cup milk
2 rounded tablespoons flour
2 cups fresh pumpkin, cooked
1 teaspoon cinnamon
¼ teaspoon ginger
½ teaspoon nutmeg
¼ teaspoon ground cloves
⅓ teaspoon salt
1 9-inch deep dish pie shell

- Preheat oven to 400°.
- Beat sugars and eggs together.
- Add all other ingredients and mix well.
- Place all ingredients in unbaked pie shell.
- Bake for 15 minutes, reduce heat to 325°, and continue baking until set, approximately 45 minutes.

The best ever!

Southern Fudge Pecan Pie

2 ounces unsweetened chocolate
¼ cup butter
½ cup packed brown sugar
½ cup sugar
3 eggs, lightly beaten
¼ teaspoon salt
½ cup milk
¼ cup corn syrup
½ teaspoon vanilla
1 cup pecan pieces, lightly toasted
1 9-inch pie shell, unbaked

- Preheat oven to 350°.
- In the top of a double boiler, melt the chocolate and butter over medium heat. Stir to blend. Remove from heat.
- Whisk sugars into chocolate until smooth. Whisk in eggs, salt, milk, corn syrup, and vanilla. Stir in the pecans.
- Pour filling into an unbaked pie shell. Bake for 50 minutes or until set.
- Serve warm with ice cream or whipped cream.

Tipsy Trifle

⅓	cup dry sherry
1	(1-pound) sponge cake, cubed or
1	(9x5-inch) loaf pound cake, cubed
2	cups raspberries or strawberries, mashed
2-3	cups fresh peaches, peeled and sliced
2	tablespoons sugar
10-12	almond macaroons
1	cup whole raspberries or strawberries
2	cups heavy cream
2	tablespoons sugar
	Nutmeg

- Pour ⅓ cup sherry over sponge cake pieces to moisten.
- Line bottom of glass bowl (10-inch diameter and 5-6 inches deep) with sponge cake.
- Spread mashed raspberries or strawberries over moistened cake.
- Sweeten peaches with 2 tablespoons sugar and layer on top of berries.
- Next layer almond macaroons.
- Top with 1 cup of whole raspberries or strawberries. Set aside glass bowl.
- Prepare Crème Anglaise.
- Pour Crème Anglaise over layer of whole raspberries in glass bowl.
- In a small bowl, whip cream and sweeten with 2 tablespoons sugar. Top trifle with layer of whipped cream. Sprinkle with nutmeg.
- Chill at least 8 hours. Scoop into small bowls to serve.

Crème Anglaise:

7	egg yolks
½	cup sugar
1	tablespoon flour
2	cups heavy cream
1	cup half and half
1½	teaspoons vanilla
4	tablespoons rum

- In top of a double boiler, beat egg yolks until thick.
- Mix together sugar and flour. Beat into yolks.
- Add heavy cream, half and half, vanilla, and rum. Stirring gently, mix well.
- Cook over hot water until mixture becomes thick and coats metal spoon.
- Makes about 2 cups.

A very authentic version of this delicious English dessert.

English Upside Down Gingerbread Pudding

Topping:

- 2 ounces butter
- 1 cup brown sugar
- 1 (29-ounce) can pear halves, drained
- 8-12 walnut halves

Pudding:

- 1 cup flour
- ½ teaspoon baking soda
- ¼ teaspoon salt
- 2 teaspoons cinnamon
- 1 teaspoon ginger
- ¼ teaspoon nutmeg
- ⅛ teaspoon ground cloves
- 1 egg, beaten
- ¾ cup brown sugar
- 3 ounces molasses
- 4 ounces buttermilk
- ¼ cup vegetable oil

Soured Cream Sauce:

- 1 cup heavy cream
- 1 cup plain yogurt or sour cream

- Preheat oven to 350°.
- Melt the butter over low heat and stir in the brown sugar. Cook for 1-2 minutes.
- Pour mixture into a 9-inch cake pan. Arrange pears with the flat side down and place the walnuts between the pear halves.
- In a mixing bowl, sift together the flour, soda, salt, and spices.
- In a separate bowl, mix together the egg, sugar, molasses, buttermilk, and oil. Stir into the flour mixture and beat hard for 1 minute until smooth.
- Pour the batter over the fruit. Bake for 40-50 minutes.
- Meanwhile, make the soured cream. Whip the cream until very soft peaks form. Stir in the yogurt or sour cream.
- To serve, invert cake onto serving plate. Serve warm with Soured Cream Sauce. This cake is also good cold.

Try tossing cut up bananas, peaches, apples, or pears with water and any type of citrus juice to keep them from turning brown.

Gingerbread
Old Salem Tavern

⅔ cup sugar
⅓ pound butter, softened
⅓ cup honey
⅓ cup molasses
⅔ cup milk
2 eggs
Grated rind of one orange
2 tablespoons ginger
1 teaspoon cinnamon
2 cups flour
½ teaspoon potassium carbonate
2 teaspoons white vinegar

- Preheat oven to 350°.
- Cream together sugar and butter in the bowl of a mixer. Add honey and molasses. Mix until smooth. Add milk, eggs and grated orange rind.
- Sift spices with flour and add to the batter. Mix until smooth.
- In a small bowl stir potassium carbonate into vinegar for just a second. It will begin to fizz. Add immediately to the batter. Mix batter on low speed for two minutes. Pour into a buttered loaf pan.
- Bake at 350° until browned. Turn heat down to 200° and continue to bake 1-1½ hours until a toothpick comes out clean.

At the Tavern this gingerbread is served warm with lemon ice cream.

Blueberry Gingerbread

½ cup vegetable oil
1 cup sugar
½ teaspoon salt
3 tablespoons molasses
1 egg
2 cups flour
½ teaspoon ginger
1 teaspoon cinnamon
½ teaspoon nutmeg
1 teaspoon baking soda
1 cup blueberries
1 cup buttermilk
2 tablespoons sugar

- Preheat oven to 350°.
- Grease and flour 8x12-inch baking dish.
- Beat first four ingredients with an electric mixer; then beat in egg.
- In a bowl, combine flour, ginger, cinnamon, nutmeg, and baking soda.
- Dredge blueberries in 2 tablespoons of the flour mixture.
- Add remaining flour mixture, alternating with buttermilk, to molasses mixture, beating well.
- Stir in blueberries.
- Pour into baking dish and sprinkle top with sugar.
- Bake about 35 minutes or until done.
- Serve warm and top with lemon sauce or whipped cream.
- Can be reheated in microwave.

Bread Pudding with Whiskey Sauce

Easy
8-10 Servings

Pudding:

1   cup raisins
1   cup dark rum
1   loaf stale French bread, torn into
      small pieces (6-8 cups)
4   cups milk
2   cups sugar
1   cup fresh coconut, shredded
3   tablespoons butter, melted
2   tablespoons vanilla
3   eggs, beaten

- Soak raisins overnight or for several hours in rum.
- Combine remaining ingredients in a large bowl. Mix well. Pour into a 9x13-inch lightly greased baking dish.
- Bake in a preheated 375° oven for 1 hour and 15 minutes.

Whiskey Sauce:

½   cup butter
1   cup confectioners sugar
1   egg yolk
2   cups whiskey (dark rum or
      bourbon)

- Cream butter and sugar in a saucepan over low heat.
- Blend in egg yolk.
- Pour in whiskey gradually, stirring constantly.
- Serve warm with pudding.
- This dish can be baked ahead of time for 45-50 minutes. Then just before serving, cover and heat for 15 minutes or until very warm.

Peach and Blackberry Cobbler

Easy
6 Servings

1   cup fresh peaches, sliced
1   cup fresh blackberries
1½   cups sugar
¾   cup flour
2   teaspoons baking powder
¾   cup milk
½   cup butter, melted

- Preheat oven to 350°.
- In a bowl, combine peaches, blackberries, and ½ cup sugar.
- In another bowl, stir together the remaining 1 cup of sugar, flour, baking powder, and milk.
- Pour melted butter into a 1½-quart casserole dish. Pour in milk mixture, but do not stir. Add fruit. Bake for 1 hour.
- Serve hot with ice cream.

Chilled Fruit Pudding with Caramel Crumb Topping

Easy
8 Servings

1 cup sugar
3 tablespoons cornstarch
¼ teaspoon salt
1¼ cups water or fruit juice
1 egg, beaten
⅓ cup lemon juice
½ teaspoon grated lemon zest
2 tablespoons butter
1 cup seedless grapes
1 cup fresh strawberries, washed, capped, and sliced
1 cup fresh peaches, peeled and sliced

Caramel Crumbs:
⅓ cup brown sugar
½ cup flour
¼ teaspoon salt
2 tablespoons butter, softened

Lovely, light summertime dessert.

- In a medium saucepan, combine first four ingredients.
- Bring to a boil over medium heat and cook until mixture is thickened.
- Remove from heat and stir in egg.
- Return to heat and cook 1 minute.
- Add lemon juice, zest, and butter. Stir to combine and cool.
- Layer fruit in a 9x12-inch glass dish.
- Pour cooled sauce over fruit. Chill.
- Prepare topping by combining all Caramel Crumb ingredients in a small bowl until crumbly.
- Place on a jelly roll pan in a thin layer.
- Bake at 375° for 10 minutes or until crisp and golden.
- Sprinkle prepared crumbs over chilled fruit pudding just prior to serving.
- May also garnish with sweetened whipped cream.

For a good meringue: Wire whisks make better meringues than electric beaters. Beat egg whites until stiff peaks form that are stiff enough not to fall out when bowl is inverted. Then add sugar.

Crème Brûlée with Fresh Raspberry Sauce

Brûlée:

4½ cups heavy cream
9 tablespoons sugar
9 egg yolks
3 teaspoons vanilla
¾ cup light brown sugar, sifted

- Preheat oven to 300°.
- In a double boiler, heat cream over boiling water. Stir in the sugar.
- Beat egg yolks in a large bowl until very light. Gradually pour hot cream over them, blending well. Stir in vanilla.
- Strain the mixture into a 2-quart shallow baking dish. Place dish in a pan with 1-1½ inches very hot water in bottom.
- Bake for 1-1½ hours, or until a knife inserted in the center comes out clean. Be careful not to overbake. Remove from oven.
- While still warm, cover surface with brown sugar. Broil for about 2 minutes, being careful not to burn.
- Chill well. Serve on individual plates or bowls.

Raspberry Sauce:

2 cups fresh raspberries
    or
1 (10-ounce) package frozen raspberries, thawed
1 tablespoon (or to taste) fresh lemon juice
1-3 tablespoons sugar

- Purée and sieve seeds from 1 cup of raspberries. Reserve the other cup of raspberries.
- Add lemon juice and sugar to purée. Blend well.
- Pour purée on top of brûlée. Garnish with fresh raspberries.

Ripening bananas won't waste if you slice them and freeze them for children's snacks (the same with seedless grapes).

Raspberries 'n Cream

Cream:

1 tablespoon lemon juice
2 tablespoons water
1 envelope unflavored gelatin
2 cups heavy cream
1 cup sugar
2 cups sour cream
1 teaspoon vanilla extract
1 teaspoon almond extract

- Combine lemon juice, water, and gelatin in a small bowl. Set aside.
- Heat cream over medium heat until lukewarm. Add gelatin mixture and stir well. Continue heating and stirring slowly until cream mixture comes just to a boil.
- Remove from heat and add sugar. Stir in sour cream and extracts.
- Pour into 8 individual serving dishes. Refrigerate for 4-6 hours or until set.

Raspberry Topping:

1 pint fresh raspberries
   or
1 (10-ounce) package frozen raspberries, thawed
2 tablespoons Crème de Cassis (optional)

- Purée and sieve seeds from half of raspberries. Reserve remaining half of raspberries.
- Add Crème de Cassis to purée. Stir.
- After cream is set, spoon 1-2 tablespoons of purée over each serving. Garnish with remaining raspberries.

Individual Chocolate Soufflés

1 (6-ounce) package semi-sweet chocolate bits
1 egg
1 teaspoon vanilla extract
2½ teaspoons sugar
   Pinch of salt
¾ cup hot milk
4 teaspoons Kahlua liqueur, approximately
   Whipped cream

- Put first six ingredients in blender in order listed. Mix on low for 1 minute.
- Pour into small, individual soufflé dishes. Cover with plastic wrap and chill for several hours or overnight.
- Before serving, top each with 1 teaspoon Kahlua liqueur and whipped cream.

Very rich, very elegant, and very easy!

Strawberries Romanoff

Easy
6-8 Servings

4 cups fresh strawberries, washed, capped, and sliced
6 tablespoons powdered sugar
2 tablespoons vodka
2 tablespoons rum
2 tablespoons triple sec

- Place prepared berries in a bowl with powdered sugar. Toss until sugar is dissolved.
- Add vodka, rum, and triple sec. Toss to combine.
- Chill well prior to serving.
- Serving suggestions: delicious served in a meringue shell or over ice cream; can be served alone topped with sour cream or Crème Fraiche.

Crème Fraiche:

1 cup sour cream
1 cup heavy cream

- In a medium bowl, mix both creams together well.
- Cover with plastic wrap and let stand overnight.
- The next day, stir well, re-cover with the plastic wrap, and chill until serving.
- Can be made several days in advance. Will keep up to one week.

Peaches and Cream

Easy
6 Servings

3 large peaches
1 envelope unflavored gelatin
¾ cup sugar
1 teaspoon vanilla or rum extract
or
½ teaspoon almond extract
2 egg whites
½ pint heavy cream

- Purée peaches in a blender (will make about 1¾ cups).
- In a medium saucepan, stir together gelatin and sugar. Add purée and mix well. Heat until gelatin dissolves and mixture reaches a boil.
- Remove from heat and stir in flavoring. Set pan in ice water or refrigerator until beginning to set.
- In separate small bowls, beat egg whites until stiff and whip cream until peaks form.
- Stir cream into gelatin mixture. Fold in egg whites.
- Pour into 1½-quart mold and chill for 4 hours.
- Unmold and serve.

This dish is pretty garnished with fresh peaches and mint leaves.

Summertime Marinated Fruit

Easy
10-12 Servings

1   (6-ounce) can frozen lemonade,
      undiluted
¼   cup orange marmalade
2   tablespoons triple sec
3   cups melon (cantaloupe,
      honeydew, watermelon),
      cut up
1   cup fresh strawberries, halved
1½   cups fresh pineapple
1   (11-ounce) can mandarin
      oranges, drained

- Mix lemonade, marmalade, and triple sec together.
- In a large bowl, combine fruits. Pour lemonade mixture over fruit, stirring gently.
- Cover and chill for at least 2 hours.

Swedish Pancake

Easy
6-8 Servings

4   tablespoons butter
3   eggs, room temperature
1½   cups milk, room temperature
6   tablespoons sugar
¾   cup flour
¼   teaspoon salt

Garnish:

3   cups sliced strawberries or
      peaches
1   cup brown sugar
1   cup sour cream or sweetened
      whipped cream

- Preheat oven to 425°.
- Place butter in a 9-inch round cake pan. Heat in oven until butter is very bubbly.
- While butter is melting, beat eggs, milk, sugar, flour, and salt until smooth.
- Pour batter quickly into hot butter. Bake 30 minutes.
- Remove from oven and serve immediately. Cut pancake into pie wedges. Spoon fruit over and sprinkle with brown sugar. Top with sour cream or whipped cream.

A great last minute dessert!

Lemon Hearts

1 cup butter, softened
1 cup sugar
1 egg yolk
  Grated zest of 2 lemons
2 cups unsifted flour
½ cup blanched almonds,
    finely chopped
  Granulated sugar
20 glacé cherries

- Preheat oven to 325°.
- Cream together softened butter and sugar.
- Beat in egg yolks and lemon peel.
- Stir in flour and almonds.
- Form dough into a ball and refrigerate for 30 minutes.
- When dough is firm but not hard, place it on a lightly floured board. Roll out dough to ¼-inch thickness. Cut with a heart-shaped cutter and transfer to a greased cookie sheet.
- Re-roll scraps and repeat until all dough is cut.
- Sprinkle cookies with sugar. Put half of a glacé cherry in the middle of each one.
- Bake for 15-20 minutes, until golden around edges.
- Cool cookies on a rack. Store in an airtight tin for several days.

Summit Lemon Squares
Heritage of Hospitality

2 sticks butter, softened
2 cups flour
½ cup powdered sugar
4 eggs, beaten slightly
2 cups sugar
6 tablespoons lemon juice
1 tablespoon flour
½ teaspoon baking powder
1 cup pecans (optional)

- Preheat oven to 325°.
- Mix first three ingredients and press into a 10x14-inch pan. Bake for 15 minutes.
- Mix together remaining ingredients and pour on top of pastry. Bake at 325° for 40-50 minutes.
- Sprinkle with additional powdered sugar.

Winkler Sugar Cookies
Winkler Bakery—Old Salem

¾ pound butter
4½ cups sugar
5 eggs
5 cups flour
1 teaspoon cream of tartar
½ teaspoon salt
½ teaspoon baking soda
½ teaspoon nutmeg
1 teaspoon vanilla extract
1 teaspoon lemon extract
½ teaspoon almond extract

- Cream butter and sugar in a large mixing bowl.
- Add eggs one at a time.
- In a separate bowl, combine flour, cream of tartar, salt, soda, and nutmeg.
- Beat extracts into butter mixture and gradually incorporate flour mixture, blending thoroughly.
- Place dough in a greased bowl and refrigerate overnight.
- Before baking, preheat oven to 350°.
- Roll dough out on floured pastry cloth. Cut with cookie cutters and bake on greased cookie sheets for 10-15 minutes, until golden brown.

The World's Best Cookie

1 cup butter, room temperature
1 cup brown sugar
1 cup white sugar
1 egg
1 cup vegetable oil
1 teaspoon vanilla
1 cup rolled oats
1 cup crushed corn flakes
1 cup coconut, shredded (optional)
½ cup chopped nuts
3½ cups flour, sifted
1 teaspoon baking soda
1 teaspoon salt

- Preheat oven to 325°.
- In a large bowl, cream butter and sugars until fluffy. Add egg and mix well. Add oil and vanilla, blending well. Add oats, corn flakes, coconut, and nuts, stirring well.
- Combine flour, baking soda, and salt. Add to mixture. Mix well.
- Drop by teaspoonfuls onto ungreased cookie sheet. Flatten with fork dipped in water.
- Bake for 12 minutes. Remove from oven.
- Cool on cookie sheet for a few minutes before removing.

These cookies stay moist and keep beautifully.

Harvest Bars

⅔ cup pumpkin
1 cup brown sugar
¼ cup oil
1 teaspoon cinnamon
¼ teaspoon nutmeg
¼ teaspoon cloves
½ teaspoon vanilla
½ teaspoon ginger
1 cup flour
½ teaspoon baking soda
½ teaspoon salt
½ cup raisins
½ cup dates, chopped
½ cup nuts, chopped

- Preheat oven to 350°.
- In a large mixing bowl, blend ingredients one at a time, mixing well after each.
- Pour into greased and floured 9x13-inch pan.
- Bake for 25 minutes.
- Remove from oven and spread on frosting.

Frosting:

½ cup confectioners sugar
½ cup brown sugar
2 tablespoons butter, melted
1 teaspoon vanilla
1 teaspoon milk

- Cream together all ingredients. Spread on bars and cut into squares.

Wonderful fall treat!

Chocolate Mint Delights

20-30 Oreo cookies, cream center removed and crushed
1 stick margarine
3 squares unsweetened chocolate
3 eggs
2 cups confectioners sugar
½ gallon vanilla ice cream
¼ cup Crème de Menthe
Crushed Oreos (cream centers removed) for garnish

- Line a 9x13-inch pan with crushed cookies.
- In a saucepan, melt butter and chocolate.
- In a separate bowl, beat eggs. Add to chocolate and stir until thickened. Stir in sugar. Spread over cookies and freeze at least 1 hour.
- Soften ice cream. Stir in Crème de Menthe and spread over cookie mixture.
- Top with crushed Oreos. Freeze overnight.

Chocolate Chess Squares

Base:

1 cup flour, sifted
⅓ cup powdered sugar
½ cup butter, softened

Filling:

1½ cups sugar
3 tablespoons cocoa
¼ cup butter, melted
2 eggs, beaten
⅛ teaspoon salt
1 (5.3-ounce) can evaporated milk
1 teaspoon vanilla
½-¾ cup chopped pecans (optional)

- Preheat oven to 350°.
- In a bowl, combine the first two ingredients.
- Cut ½ cup butter into this mixture until it is crumbly. Pat mixture in the bottom of an 8-inch square pan.
- Bake for 12-15 minutes or until slightly browned.
- In a mixing bowl, beat together the sugar, cocoa, and butter. Add eggs and beat for 2½ minutes. Add salt, milk, and vanilla. Beat to combine. Stir in pecans if desired.
- Pour filling over prepared base and bake for 35-45 minutes or until set.
- Cut into 1-inch squares while still warm.

Mincemeat Squares

¼ cup butter
1 cup brown sugar
1 egg
1 teaspoon vanilla
½ cup mincemeat
1 cup flour
¼ teaspoon salt
1 teaspoon baking powder
Powdered Sugar

- Preheat oven to 350°.
- Place butter in a medium saucepan and melt; cool slightly.
- Add sugar, egg, and vanilla. Mix well.
- Stir in mincemeat.
- Sift together flour, salt, and baking powder. Fold into mincemeat mixture.
- Pour into a greased 8-inch square pan and bake for 40 minutes.
- Cool and cut into squares.
- Roll in powdered sugar.
- May be served as a cookie or cut into larger squares and topped with vanilla ice cream.

Very nutritious snack.

Cheesecake Squares

Crust:
5	tablespoons butter, softened
½	cup brown sugar
1	cup flour
¼	cup chopped walnuts

- Preheat oven to 350°.
- In a mixing bowl, cream butter and sugar.
- Add flour and walnuts. Mix well. Reserve ½ cup of this mixture for topping.
- Press remaining mixture into an 8-inch square pan and bake for 12-15 minutes.

Filling:
½	cup sugar
8	ounces cream cheese, softened
1	egg
2	tablespoons milk
1	tablespoon lemon juice
1	teaspoon vanilla

- Reduce oven temperature to 325°.
- Blend sugar and cream cheese. Then add egg, milk, lemon juice, and vanilla. Beat well.
- Pour into baked crust and sprinkle with reserved topping.
- Place cheesecake in oven and bake for 25 minutes.
- Cool and cut into 25 squares.

Double Chocolate Crinkles

4	ounces unsweetened chocolate
½	cup shortening
2	cups sugar
2	teaspoons vanilla
4	eggs
2	cups flour
2	teaspoons baking powder
½	teaspoon salt
6	ounces chocolate chips
1	cup confectioners sugar, sifted

- In a double boiler, melt chocolate and shortening. When melted, stir in sugar.
- Place mixture in a medium bowl. Cool. Beat until well blended. Add vanilla. Beat in eggs one at a time, mixing well after each addition.
- In another medium bowl, sift flour, baking powder, and salt together.
- Stir flour mixture into chocolate mixture. Stir in chocolate chips.
- Refrigerate dough several hours or overnight.
- Break off small pieces of chilled dough and form into 1-inch balls. Roll balls in powdered sugar, covering completely.
- Place balls 2-inches apart on lightly greased baking sheets.
- Bake in a preheated 375° oven for 10 minutes.

Great for chocolate lovers!

Windy City Brownies

1	tablespoon butter
8	ounces unsweetened chocolate
1	cup unsalted butter
5	eggs
3¾	cups sugar
1	teaspoon almond extract
1	tablespoon vanilla
¼	teaspoon salt
3	tablespoons coffee liqueur
1⅔	cups sifted flour
2	cups walnut halves

- Preheat oven to 400°.
- Invert a 9x13x2-inch baking pan. Cover completely with a large sheet of aluminum foil and shape the foil to the pan. Turn pan right side up and insert shaped foil into pan. Melt 1 tablespoon butter and brush foil well.
- In a double boiler, melt the chocolate and butter. Cool to lukewarm and reserve.
- Place eggs in a mixing bowl and beat until light lemon-colored and thickened. Slowly add the sugar ½ cup at a time. Continue to beat until mixture is very thick and drizzles slowly back into the bowl.
- Add almond, vanilla, salt, and coffee liqueur.
- Beat the reserved and cooled chocolate/butter into egg mixture at low speed until just mixed.
- Fold in flour and walnuts.
- Pour mixture into prepared pan and smooth.
- Bake for 30-35 minutes and remove.
- Cool in pan for 20 minutes. Invert on cake rack and remove from pan and foil.
- Turn brownies right side up for final cooling. Cool completely prior to cutting. Cuts best if refrigerated until cold.
- Refrigerate and serve cold. Beautiful served with ice cream or topped with some sweetened whipped cream.

Frosted Brownies

Easy
3-4 Dozen

1 cup butter
4 (1-ounce) squares unsweetened chocolate
4 eggs, beaten
2 cups sugar
1 cup flour
¼ teaspoon salt
½ teaspoon vanilla
1 cup pecans, chopped

- Preheat oven to 350°.
- In a medium saucepan, melt butter and chocolate over low heat.
- Add remaining ingredients and stir until well blended.
- Pour brownie mixture into a lightly greased 9x13-inch pan.
- Bake for 25 minutes. Allow brownies to cool before spreading with frosting.

Frosting #1:

4 tablespoons butter, softened
2 cups confectioners sugar
2 tablespoons milk
1 teaspoon vanilla

- In a small bowl, blend ingredients. Spread evenly over brownie layer. Refrigerate until chilled.

Frosting #2:

1½ (4-ounce) bars German chocolate
6 tablespoons butter

- In a small saucepan, melt together ingredients. Cool slightly. Pour evenly on top of brownies. Let harden.
- Cut into small squares or bars.

Molasses Sugar Cookies

Easy
4-5 Dozen

¾ cup shortening
1 cup sugar
1 egg
¼ cup molasses
2 cups flour
2 teaspoons baking soda
1 teaspoon cinnamon
½ teaspoon salt
½ teaspoon ground ginger
½ teaspoon ground cloves
Sugar

- Preheat oven to 375°.
- In a large bowl, cream shortening and sugar, beating well until light and fluffy. Add egg and molasses. Mix well.
- In a separate bowl, combine flour, baking soda, cinnamon, salt, ginger, and cloves. Add to shortening mixture. Blend well. Chill 1 hour.
- Break off small pieces of chilled dough and form into 1-inch balls. Roll in sugar.
- Place balls 2 inches apart on ungreased cookie sheets.
- Bake for 10 minutes.

Brown Sugar Chews

Easy
20 Squares

4 ounces butter, softened
2 cups brown sugar
2 eggs
1 heaping cup flour
  Pinch of salt
2 teaspoons vanilla extract
1 cup pecans or walnuts, chopped

- Preheat oven to 350°. Grease and flour an 11x7-inch pan.
- Cream butter and sugar in a mixing bowl.
- Add eggs, one at a time, beating well after each addition.
- Add flour and salt, mixing well.
- Add vanilla. Stir in nuts.
- Pour into prepared pan. Bake for 40-45 minutes.
- Let cool and cut into squares.

Congo Squares

Easy
24 Servings

⅔ cup margarine, melted
1 box light brown sugar
3 eggs
2½ cups flour
2½ teaspoons baking powder
½ teaspoon salt
1 cup nuts, chopped
1 (6-ounce) package chocolate chips

- Preheat oven to 350°.
- In a mixing bowl, combine margarine and sugar. Add eggs one at a time.
- In a separate bowl, sift dry ingredients together. Add to butter mixture.
- Blend in nuts and chocolate chips.
- Pour into a greased 9x13-inch pan and bake for 25 minutes.

Just Peachy Ice Cream

Easy
1 Quart

2 cups heavy cream
2 cups half and half
1 cup sugar
1½ teaspoons vanilla
⅛ teaspoon salt
6 peaches, mashed (about
    1-1½ cups)
¼ cup sugar

- In a 2-quart bowl, add first five ingredients and mix until sugar dissolves.
- Mix peaches with sugar and add to above ingredients.
- Pour into a 1-quart ice cream freezer and freeze according to manufacturer's instructions.

Strawberries or bananas may be substituted for peaches.

Lemon Velvet Ice Cream

Easy
1 Gallon

8 lemons
1 tablespoon lemon zest
5½ cups heavy cream
5½ cups milk
4 cups sugar
2 teaspoons lemon extract
Yellow food coloring (optional)

- Juice lemons.
- Blend all ingredients thoroughly.
- Add a few drops of yellow food coloring if desired.
- Place in ice cream freezer and process according to manufacturer's directions.

Refreshing after a heavy meal with shortbread cookies or as a summer luncheon dessert.

Lotus Ice Cream

Easy
2 Quarts

1 cup almonds, chopped
2 quarts half and half
3 cups plus 3 tablespoons sugar
Grated zest of 5 lemons
1 cup fresh lemon juice
1 teaspoon vanilla
½ teaspoon almond extract

- Toast almonds and let cool.
- In a large bowl, combine remaining ingredients and mix well.
- Pour into an ice cream freezer and freeze according to freezer directions.

Sin

Easy
12 Servings

Crust:

1¼   cups chocolate wafer crumbs
¼   cup butter, melted

Filling:

6   chocolate toffee candy bars,
       chilled
½   gallon vanilla ice cream, softened
4   ounces butter
2   teaspoons vanilla
1   (12-ounce) package semi-sweet
       chocolate chips
2   cups powdered sugar
1   (15-ounce) can evaporated milk

- Mix crumbs and melted butter. Press into bottom of 13x8-inch pan. Chill until firm.
- Crush chilled candy bars and mix together with ice cream. Spread over chilled crust. Cover and freeze overnight.
- Melt remaining butter with chocolate chips over low heat. Add sugar, vanilla, and milk. Cook about 8 minutes or until thickened. This may be prepared ahead and reheated.
- To serve, cut into serving pieces and spoon warm sauce over each piece.

Cinnamon Ice Cream

Easy
2 Quarts

1   pint half and half
½   pint heavy cream
1   cup milk
¾   cup sugar
1   teaspoon vanilla
2   teaspoons cinnamon
4   egg yolks

- In a medium saucepan over medium heat, combine half and half, cream, milk, sugar, vanilla, and cinnamon until sugar dissolves.
- In a mixing bowl, whisk yolks together. Add 1 cup cream mixture to yolks.
- Over medium heat, slowly incorporate all yolk mixture into remaining cream mixture and cook until thickened, stirring constantly. Remove from heat and chill.
- Freeze in ice cream machine according to manufacturer's directions.
- This ice cream is great on top of apple pie!

Raspberry Buttermilk Sherbet

Easy
8 Servings

2 pints fresh raspberries
   or
1 (10-ounce) package frozen
   raspberries
2 cups sugar (for fresh berries,
   1 cup for frozen)
2 cups buttermilk
1 teaspoon grated lemon zest
½ teaspoon vanilla

- In a blender or food processor, purée raspberries.
- Add remaining ingredients and blend well.
- Pour mixture into an ice cream freezer and freeze according to freezer directions.
- Mixture may also be put in a bowl and put in the freezer. Just before mixture freezes, take out and beat with an electric mixer. Return to freezer and freeze until set.

Fresh Fruit Sorbet

Easy
3 Quarts

4 pints fresh fruit, either
   strawberries, raspberries,
   or blueberries
1 cup superfine sugar
¼ cup liqueur (Grand Marnier for
   strawberries, and Crème de
   Cassis for raspberries and
   blueberries)
½ cup orange juice
4 egg whites
⅛ teaspoon salt

- Purée berries and then sieve to remove seeds and/or skins.
- Add sugar, liqueur, and orange juice to puréed and sieved berries.
- Beat egg whites with salt until stiff peaks form.
- Fold beaten egg whites into berry mixture carefully but thoroughly.
- Pour the sorbet mixture into an ice cream freezer and proceed according to manufacturer's directions or pour into freezer container and freeze for 2-3 hours, until it has begun to set.
- If manually freezing sorbet, remove from freezer and beat vigorously with a mixer and then freeze again for an hour, then turn into final container.
- If using an ice cream freezer, when sorbet is set, remove to final container.
- To serve, garnish with fresh mint and serve with a delicious butter cookie.
- For special occasions, serve sorbet in meringue shells or swans.

May process regular sugar in food processor for 1 minute with steel blade to make superfine sugar.

Frozen Pineapple Yogurt with Raspberries

Easy
4 Servings

1 (20-ounce) can unsweetened
    pineapple chunks, drained
½ cup plain low-fat yogurt
2½ tablespoons sifted powdered
    sugar
1 tablespoon lemon juice
1 cup fresh raspberries
    Mint leaves

- Freeze pineapple on baking sheet for 2 hours or more.
- Combine yogurt, sugar, and lemon juice in food processor until well combined.
- Add pineapple and process until smooth.
- Divide mixture between four sherbet glasses. Garnish with raspberries and mint leaves. Serve immediately.
- This recipe can be frozen, but it will lose its smooth consistency after being frozen.

Chocolate Truffles

Easy
26-30

7 ounces bittersweet Swiss
    chocolate, cut into 1-inch
    pieces
½ cup heavy cream
2 tablespoons butter
¾ cup powdered sugar, measured,
    then sifted
2 egg yolks
2 tablespoons Grand Marnier, or
    other liqueur to taste
    Unsweetened cocoa

- In top of a double boiler, over simmering water, combine chocolate, cream, and butter.
- Add sugar and yolks to chocolate mixture; whisk until smooth.
- Remove from heat and add liqueur.
- Place in flat glass dish and chill until malleable, about 2 hours in refrigerator.
- Shape into balls, toss in cocoa, place in paper or foil candy cups, and refrigerate until serving time.

Truffles could also be tossed in powdered sugar or chopped nuts.

Incredible Toffee

Average
1½ Pounds

2 cups almonds, sliced
1 pound butter
1 box light brown sugar
1 6-bar package Hershey's milk
   chocolate bars, unwrapped

- Grease a 10½x15x1-inch cookie sheet.
- Spread 1 cup almonds evenly on cookie sheet.
- Melt butter and sugar in a heavy saucepan. Stir constantly with a wooden spoon until candy thermometer reaches 290°. Remove from heat immediately.
- Pour toffee back and forth evenly over cookie sheet.
- Put chocolate bars on hot toffee; spread evenly over mixture.
- Sprinkle with remaining almonds.

Britton Brittle

Easy

1¼ cups sugar
¼ teaspoon salt
¼ cup water
½ cup butter
½ cup pecans, chopped
¼ teaspoon soda
1 cup pecans, chopped

- Preheat oven to 400°.
- Heat 15x10x1-inch jelly roll pan in oven.
- Mix first five ingredients in large saucepan.
- Using a candy thermometer and stirring constantly, heat mixture to 285°.
- Add soda and 1 cup pecans. Stir rapidly to mix well.
- Spread quickly on heated jelly roll pan.
- Allow to cool, break into pieces, and store in airtight containers.

Packaged in small plastic bags and tied with red and green ribbon, this makes a wonderful small Christmas gift.

Patricia Inn Fudge Sauce

Easy
Approximately 9 Cups

5 cups sugar
3 (13-ounce) cans evaporated
   milk
2 teaspoons vanilla
2 (8-ounce) packages
   unsweetened chocolate
2 sticks butter

- In a double boiler, combine first three ingredients.
- Add remaining ingredients.
- Cook for 45 minutes. Stir five times while cooking.
- Serve over yellow cake or pound cake with ice cream.

A favorite from the Patricia Inn, Myrtle Beach, South Carolina, now closed after 50 years of operation.

Strawberry Topping

Easy
6-8 Servings

1 quart strawberries, cleaned,
   hulled, quartered or sliced
½-¾ cup sugar (depending upon
   sweetness of berries)
2 ounces butter, sliced

- Place strawberries in a medium saucepan.
- Add sugar and butter and heat over medium high heat until butter is melted and berries are softened, about 5 minutes.
- Remove from heat, cover, and let cool.
- Will keep in refrigerator for 7-10 days. Great over ice cream!

Mocha Hot Fudge Sauce

Easy
6-10 Servings

1 cup sugar
¾ cup unsweetened cocoa
    powder, sifted
1 teaspoon instant coffee powder
1 cup heavy cream
¼ cup butter

- Combine sugar, cocoa, and coffee powder in a medium saucepan.
- Add ½ cup heavy cream and blend to a smooth paste.
- Add remaining cream, blending well.
- Cook over medium heat, stirring constantly until sugar is completely dissolved.
- Add butter and cook until mixture is smooth and thickened, about 5-8 minutes.
- Cover and refrigerate up to one week.
- Warm over low heat to serve.
- Serve over ice cream with raspberry sauce, made by puréeing a 10-ounce package frozen raspberries.

Gingerbread Topping

Easy
Topping for 8-inch or 9-inch square pan

½ cup brown sugar
2 tablespoons cinnamon
¼ cup flour
¼ cup butter, softened
½-1 cup pecans, chopped

- Combine brown sugar, cinnamon, flour, and butter until crumbly.
- Stir in pecans.
- Spread over gingerbread during last 10 minutes of baking.

Praline Sauce

Easy
2½ Cups

1½ cups light corn syrup
½ cup heavy cream
2 tablespoons butter
2 cups toasted pecan halves
2 teaspoons vanilla

- In a 2-quart saucepan, combine first three ingredients until well blended. Stir constantly and bring to a boil. Cook over medium heat for 3 minutes. Remove from heat.
- Stir in pecans and vanilla. Cool.
- Refrigerate in tightly covered container. Serve hot or cold. May be reheated in microwave.

Christmas Candy House

1	cardboard house form
42	nougat blocks
24	peppermint sticks
58	gum drops
2	candied gum rings
6	candied "orange" slices, red and green
26	peppermint rounds
10	pieces Christmas hard candy
30	coconut wafer cookies
3	cups Royal Icing (made with Wilton's Meringue Powder)

To construct house form:

- Cut pieces of cardboard according to dimensions specified.
- Using a 1½-2-inch wide package tape, tape sides to front and back house pieces.
- Tape two roof pieces together and attach to house.
- Construct chimney from two notched and two unnotched pieces. (Do not attach to house at this time.)
- Tape door slightly ajar where desired.
- Cut squares of black construction paper and tape to house to form windows and door.
- Cut a baseboard 12x15 inches and cover with foil.
- Set house form on base.

To decorate house:

- Use meringue as "glue" for candy. Your imagination is the best guide. Nougat blocks are "bricks" of house. "Orange" slices are window shutters. Coconut wafers are roof shingles.
- When house and chimney are completely covered with candy, fill a pastry bag fitted with a small star tip with remaining Royal Icing. Place chimney on roof. Pipe "gingerbreading" on the house and chimney. Sift powdered sugar on top for snow.
- House may be saved up to three years by storing in a large plastic bag in a cool, dry location.

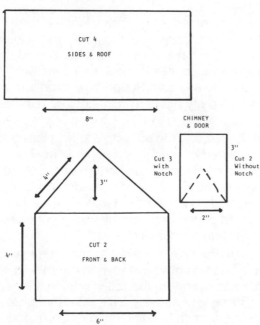

CANDY HOUSE PATTERN

CUT 4
SIDES & ROOF

4"

8"

CHIMNEY & DOOR

Cut 3 with Notch

4"

3"

Cut 2 Without Notch

3"

2"

CUT 2
FRONT & BACK

4"

6"

* CUT ONE BASE BOARD 12" x 15"

293

Bûche de Noël

8   ounces semi-sweet chocolate
⅓   cup water
8   egg yolks, room temperature
¾   cup sugar
8   egg whites, room temperature
⅛   teaspoon cream of tartar
7   tablespoons sugar
½   cup cocoa
¼   cup powdered sugar

Crème Chantilly (pg. 295)
Chocolate Icing (pg. 295)
Meringue Mushrooms (pg. 296)

- Oil an 11x17-inch jelly roll pan. Line with waxed paper, leaving a 3-inch overhang. Oil waxed paper as well.

- Melt chocolate and water in the top of a double boiler over simmering water. Cool to tepid.

- In mixing bowl of an electric mixer, whip egg yolks with ¾ sugar, adding it gradually. Whip the egg mixture until the mixture becomes light and fluffy and "forms a ribbon." Blend in the chocolate mixture. Reserve until whites have been beaten.

- In a clean bowl, whip the whites with cream of tartar, and gradually add 7 tablespoons sugar. Whip until fairly stiff peaks are formed. Fold ⅓ of the whites into the chocolate/egg mixture, blending well. Combine this mixture into the remaining egg whites and fold well, but gently, to thoroughly incorporate.

- Pour into a prepared jelly roll pan. Place in the middle of an oven, preheated to 350°, and bake for 17 minutes. The cake will lose its shine and rise to a chalky-looking souffléed sheet. Remove from oven and place two damp paper towels on top. Cover with two dry paper towels. Cool 20 minutes. Remove towels.

- Loosen the sides of the roll with a knife. Place two sheets of waxed or parchment paper in front of you, the top overlapping the bottom one. Sprinkle with some of the sieved cocoa/powdered sugar combination. Bravely flip the souffléed sheet onto the prepared paper. Remove the waxed paper and cover with Crème Chantilly.

- Starting with the side nearest you, roll cake toward middle. When you have just passed the middle, flip the other end over onto the rolled portion. Place on platter. Trim edges and decorate with Chocolate Icing, red and green candied cherries, Meringue Mushrooms, and sieved cocoa. Holly greens add a special touch during the Christmas season.

Continued

Crème Chantilly:

- 1 cup heavy cream
- 3 tablespoons powdered sugar
- 1 teaspoon vanilla

- Whip cream to firm peaks, flavoring with sugar and vanilla.

Chocolate Icing:

- 7 squares semi-sweet chocolate
- 1 square bittersweet chocolate
- ¾ cup sour cream
- 11 tablespoons butter, softened
- 2 cups powdered sugar
- 1 egg yolk
- 1 teaspoon vanilla

- Melt chocolates in a double boiler over simmering water. Stir in sour cream.
- Place butter, powdered sugar, and egg yolk in the bowl of a food processor fitted with a steel blade. Process until smooth. Add melted chocolate mixture and vanilla and process until well-blended. Chill to piping consistency.
- Place icing in a pastry bag fitted with the "Bûche" tip and ice Bûche de Noël, simulating tree bark and knots. (If not using a pastry bag, ice cake and run fork tines over surface.)
- Chocolate Icing may also be used to form the "gills" of Meringue Mushrooms.

Continued

Meringue Mushrooms:

    4   egg whites
        Pinch cream of tartar
    1   cup sugar
        Cocoa for sprinkling
        Chocolate icing for forming
            "gills"

- Place egg whites in the bowl of an electric mixer. Beat on low speed until frothy. Add cream of tartar. Beat on high until soft peaks form.
- Add sugar slowly, ¼ cup at a time. Continue beating until meringue is glossy and smooth.
- Place meringue in a pastry bag fitted with a ¾-inch plain tip and pipe out mounds about 1-inch in diameter onto cookie sheet lined with parchment paper. Sift cocoa onto each mound. Pipe out equal number of "stems" onto another prepared cookie sheet. Bake at 150-200 degrees for 1 hour. Remove from oven and push in the undersides of little caps. Return to the oven to dry out for about 30 minutes. Turn off heat and keep in oven overnight to completely dry out if desired.
- To form mushrooms: place about 1 cup of chocolate icing into pastry bag fitted with a small star tip. Pipe icing onto undersides of mushroom caps to simulate gills. Push cone into each cap. Chill until icing is firm. Store in refrigerator until ready to use.

acknowledgements

The Junior League of Winston-Salem, Inc. wishes to thank every person who volunteered to help create *"Stirring Performances."* With the generous contributions of time, talent, and money from these people, we were able to produce a community cookbook with a special blend of recipes.

We would also like to thank the many contributors whose recipes we were unable to include due to space limitations or duplication.

Testers and Donors

Beth Ritchie Alm
Jean Enderle Alsup
Nancy Jones Armstrong
Elizabeth Shaw Avant
Merry Swanson Barber
Molly Yelton Barber
Mary Brush Bass
Molly Bass
Louise Avett Bazemore
Frankie Drozak Bell
Lora Bellomy
Janice Bowman Bennett
Jody Swanson Bennett
Margaret Higgins Bennett
Carey Benton-Jewett
Susanne Hall Blanco
Dede Murphy Bloodworth
Jeanne Clement Booras
Cynthia Yeager Bouldin
Debbie Boyce
Rose Ellen Bowen
Mary Blake Brady
Lesa Williams Branch
Jane Dudley Bremer
Susan Franklin Brinkley
Libby Wilson Britton
Margaret Funch Brock
Dale Brock
Henri Dibrell Brown
Martha Brown
Patricia Tankard Brown
Sonia Brown
Julia Daniel Buchholz
Jenny Kimbrel Bunn
Brooke Fauth Burr

Anne Van Orden Butler
Ellon Craver Butler
Marsha Young Butler
Missy Ogburn Butler
Lynda Noffsinger Bynum
Nancy Irvine Campbell
Wanda Baxter Campbell
Susan Carson
Patricia Marshall Cavenaugh
Nilla Dudley Childs
Cindy Corey Christopher
Bernie Bazemore Clapp
Bonnie Herrmann Clark
Debbie Ross Clark
Ann Cline
Sally Remick Colacicco
Bonnie Riddle Colhoun
Dottie Kerr Cook
Elizabeth Combs
Joyce Call Comerford
Carol Conrad
Ann Phillips Copenhaver
Ellen Boyer Correll
Ellen Cox
Nancy Arnott Cramer
Cortlandt Preston Creech
Pat Criminger
Kathy Heavner Crowell
Ann Joyner Cross
Sara Nash Crowder
Elaine Dawkins Daves
Katherine Davey
Laura Dalton
Jan Dalton
Mary Ann Campbell Davis

Terrie Allen Davis
Martha Chevalier Deal
Margaret Decker
Annette Wampler Deleot
Rosena Ferrell Dillard
Beth Ansley Dixson
Polly Martin Donnelly
Janie Laffoon Douglas
Marian Millaway Douglas
Dolly Dudley
Lisa Spencer Dull
McChesney Scott Dunn
Kathryn Roberts Durity
Judy Sheperd Eddins
Amy Miller Egleston
Beth Johnson Einstein
Doris McMillan Eller
Amy Henderson Elliott
Sara Jane Witherow Elliott
Jeanine Jones Elster
Kathy Bacon Ely
Patti Berkey English
Katherine Albritton Eppert
Laura Ferguson Esleeck
Nancy Watkins Fagg
Ann Thompkins Faris
Arabelle Plonk Fedora
Nancy Edwards Fitzgerald
Elizabeth Lamb Fluharty
Jennifer Foster
Susan Dedmon Foushee
Lucia Freeman
Susan Berg Frenzel
Pat Fromen
Margaret Ward Gaddy

Christine Gray Gallaher
Jan Vickers Gallaher
Gay Dillard Gallins
Connie Belk Gant
Don R. Gatwood
Ellen Williams Gibb
Joyce Talton Gibson
Lucy Gidley
Emily Sowerby Glaze
Jean Pearce Glenn
Betty Allen Wyatt Graham
Carol Graham
Deede Dunn Grainger
Donna Clark Grainger
Anne Howell Gray
Joan Wilder Greason
Kitty Wilson Green
Jane Hutton Gregory
Cindy Nash Groce
Susan Bruggemann Groen
Mary Brooke Guernier
Bill Hanes
Lee Hanes
Nancy Hirsman Harper
Fran Brenegar Harrington
Martha Wilder Harrington
Partheria Harrington
Cathie Smith Hartness
Susan Richardson Hauser
Margaret Leinbach Hawkins
Jay Hedgpeth
D. D. Dippel Hellebush
Anne Courts Herman
Margaret Herman
Ann Waynick Hill

Linda Richmond Hill
Martha Hill
Joanne Wood Hinman
Wendy Dayton Hinman
Carol Baucom Holden
Sarah Wright Holland
Molly Holt
Carson Dowd Howard
Nancy Mehler Huber
Ann Lerian Humphrey
Vicki Powell Hunt
Patricia Hartrick Hunter
Laura Indorf
Anne Ingram
Dorothy Ingram
Roberta Weathers Irvin
Sally Anne Irvin
Ellen Parrish Jackson
Annie McLeod Jenkins
Gair Hartley Jewell
Diane Jobson
Kay Brewer Johnson
Mary Kay Warren Johnson
Molly Weeks Johnson
Lynn Jaquith Johnston
Joyce Jolly
Mary Jones
Jane Cottle Joyner
Mary Kearns
Jan Kelley
Louise Stokes Kinken
Susan Gordon King
Caroline Dixson Kinser
Debbie Hare Kimbrough
Barbara Clodfelter Kirby

Chris Skinner Kirkland
Mary Ellen Klinepeter
Nancy Jobe Koehler
Leigh Emerson Koman
Rhonda Hicks Kornegay
Penelope McCurry Krell
Bebe Aycock Krewson
Karen Pagie Kroncke
Gussie Kroustalis
Linda Stoess Kummer
Debby Lambert
Kaye Pass Lambert
Barbie Landers
Julie Dalton Laughter
Emelda Williams Lawing
Kathryn Lou McNair Leinbach
Margaret Worstell Lewallen
Nancy L. Lide
Meredith Tucker Lindel
Sara Coons Lindsay
Jayne Dolton Litzenburg
Meg McKeithan Lovett
Annette Perritt Lynch
Pearl Magovern
Corinna Dunn Mann
Mary Allen Mann Martin
Ann Morehead Mashburn
Kimberlee Lambe Masich
Linda Carroll Matthews
Julie McNair McBride
Melanie Indorf McCabe
Allison Towne McCall
Mary J. McDaniel
Anne Butler McDowell
Laura Turnage McNair

acknowledgements

Minta Aycock McNally
Skinner Anderson McGee
Barbara Dix McWhorter
Katherine Kerr Memory
Gayle Gilbert Meredith
Pat Michael
John E. Mickey
Susan Bingham Mickey
Kacy Ireland Mitchell
Caroline Cottingham Mitchell
Susan Scripture Mitchell
Cherri Mohler
Beverly Campbell Moore
Carolyn Moser
Martha Moser
Mary Nan Sweeney Moser
Isabelle Moss
Marti Hunter Mostellar
Mrs. Lewis M. Motycka
Lucy Hanes Mullen
Mary Jo Petree Murphy
Leigh Thurston Myers
Sheridan Townsend Newsome
Mary Walker Norfleet
Adrienne Warren Northington
Marianne DeHart Northington
Nancy Richardson Noell
Anita Hauser Ogburn
Ann Dozier Ogburn
Kate Pratt Ogburn
Candy Ludwick Palmer
Jeannette Anderson Parker
Ellen Carswell Parsley
Leigh Wood Pate
Maura Payne

Elizabeth Perkinson
Buff Cox Perry
Ann Peters
Lawrie Canale Peyton
Anne Bingham Philpott
Ben Philpott
Sandy Kidd Poehling
Dianne Milligan Pierce
Mary Jane Brown Pishko
Judith Morris Plonk
Louise Brock Pollard
Nancy Poole
Patti Powell
Nona Hanes Porter
Sallie Millis Pryor
Nancy Arzonico Pulliam
Anne Prescott Ramm
Mary Ann Wetherington Ratcliff
Anna Kathryn Reece
Bess McMullen Richardson
Betty Richardson
Beth Rickert
Beverly Riley
Martha Riggs
Doris Roach
Vicki Coppedge Robins
Kathy Linville Robinson
Becky Gantt Roediger
Amy Rogers
Kathryn Ryscavage
Kristen Russ
Rob Russ
Marcia Hale Russell
Martha Bowen Sarcone
Ruth Delapp Sartin

Becky Hutchinson Saunders
Liliane Schneider
Kathy Davis Schultz
Cathy Lewis Seaver
Patti McCollum Sellars
Garland Bagnal Shaffner
Sharon Amos Shealy
Karen Daniels Shearin
Julia Sherrill
Laurie Shore
Peggy Hart Shuping
Tillie Cordon Skoggard
Frances Brenner Sloan
Jane Pierce Slick
Sally Ward Slusher
Judy Odgers Smith
Leigh Taylor Smith
Jeannette Horton Smyth
Sharon Rowe Spangler
Mary Jo Wooten Spaugh
Nancy Meacham Spaugh
Susan Siewers Spence
Ann Spencer
Marty Brennan Spry
Amy Johnson Steele
Anna Ballentine Steele
Marianna Steele
Sandy Steele
Mary Lou Ford Stott
Jane Thomas Stokes
Janet Barden Stout
Anne Ford Strickland
Louise Strickland
Jean Olive Stubbs
Nancy Pulliam Sullivan

Meg Surratt
Cindy Robinson Sutton
Gwynne Stephens Taylor
Lawren Groce Thach
Ginny Gross Thomas
Tamra Wright Thomas
Kathryn Andrews Thompson
Jane Rankin Thompson
Hellena Huntley Tidwell
Sherry Smith Troop
Elizabeth Trulove
Jane Roscoe Tucker
JoAnna Durham Tudor
Evelyn Martin Turner
Helen Turner
Pink Willis Turner
Molly Ferrell Twine
Joy Bishop Van Zandt
Judy Montgomery Vogel

Joanne Achimon Voitus
Valerie O'Dea Von Isenburg
Gwyn Parker Wackerhagen
Margaret Patterson Wade
Susan Cutting Wade
Martha Little Wall
Janis Daddario Waltrip
Cacky Choate Ward
Katy W. Warren
Nancy Stone Watkins
Sarah Sloane Watts
Dannie Soenksen Weber
Jody Weber
Pollyann Elliott Weeks
Norma Wehner
Kathy Russell Welch
Terri Mattson Welfare
Anne Richmond Wessling
Margie West

Sandy Whaling
Heather Whitaker
Jane Robinson Whitaker
Shelly Braswell Whittington
Allison Copeland Williams
Beth Lewis Williams
Loren Bynum Williams
Janie Butler Wilson
Patty Speight Wilson
Candy Clark Witherow
Gail Barber Wold
Barbara Wood
LuAnne Chadwick Wood
Debbie Hartis Yancey
Mary Preston Yates
Nancy Smith Yates
Pat Gallins Young

Acorn Squash Bisque, 73
Admiral Parson's Barbecue Sauce, 153
Almond Brandy Sour Cream Pound
    Cake, 249
Almond Tart, 265
Amaretto-Amaretti Chocolate
    Cheesecake, 261
Angel Biscuits, 43
Angel Hair Pasta with Three Caviars, 121
Angels on Horseback, 143
Angler's Crab Imperial, 208
Ann's Canneloni, 126
APPETIZERS 9-32
  CHEESE
    Black-Eyed Susans, 16
    Cheese and Herbs Appetizer, 18
    Cheese Roll Ups with Mustard
        Sauce, 17
    Cheese Straws, 10
    Cheese Tart with Apples, 19
    Chutney Cheesecake, 20
    Danish Cheese Melt, 133
    Feta Tarts, 18
    Herbed Cheese Spread, 20
    Mushroom Bleu Cheese Spread, 19
    Pita Cheese Crisps, 9
    Rosa's Cheese Souffle
        Sandwiches, 30
    Tomato Cheese Spread, 21
  DIPS AND SAUCES
    Avocado and Tomato Dip, 24
    California Salsa, 31
    Curry Dip, 32
    Dill Dip, 32
    Sakowitz Remoulade Sauce, 31
    Scioto Dip, 32
    Shrimp Dip, 26
    Taco Dip, 22
    Tex-Mex Dip, 23
  MISCELLANEOUS
    Buffalo Hot Wings, 15
    Herb Pizza, 22
    Oyster Cracker Snacks, 10
    Party Lamb Pitas, 142
    Paté Hater's Delight, 21
    Pork Sates, 140
    Roasted Herbed Walnuts, 13
    Sesame Chicken Rolls, 14
    Spinach Wrapped Chicken with
        Dip, 15
    Sweet and Sour Chicken
        Drummettes, 14
    Tavern Nachos, 23
  SEAFOOD
    Angels on Horseback, 143
    Artichoke Clam Puffs, 29
    Charleston Marinated Shrimp, 25
    Crabmeat Spread, 28
    Crunchy Crab Puffs, 29
    Hot Crab Canapés, 27
    Marinated Shrimp, 25
    Oysters Orleans, 24
    Salmon Mousse, 30
    Smoked Oyster Spread, 24
    Special Crabmeat Appetizer, 28
    Tea Smoked Shrimp, 26
  VEGETABLES
    Artichoke Appetizers, 10

Avocado Pinwheel, 16
Cherry Tomatoes Stuffed with
    Pesto, 11
Cognac Mushrooms, 9
Fresh Vegetable Mold, 11
Marinated Broccoli and
    Cauliflower, 12
Mushroom Appetizers, 12
Mushroom Puffs, 13
APPLES
  Apple and Bacon Spinach Salad, 100
  Apple Dapple Cake, 247
  Apple Muffins, 39
  Butternut Squash and Apple Bake, 230
  Cheese Tart with Apples, 19
  Chicken Apple Curry Soup, 71
  Cranberry Apple Salad, 109
  Sautéed Chicken Livers with
      Apples and Onions, 190
Applesauce Muffins, 37
Apricot Nut Bread, 45
APRICOTS
  Baked Apricots, 238
  Roast Goose with Apricot Stuffing, 192
Armenian Rice, 227
Art of Grilling, 131
Artichoke Appetizers, 10
Artichoke Clam Puffs, 29
ARTICHOKES
  Artichoke Clam Puffs, 29
  Chicken-Artichoke Casserole, 175
  Curried Chicken and Artichoke
      Salad, 105
  Scalloped Tomatoes and Artichoke
      Hearts, 234
  Seafood Casserole Miami, 206
  Spinach and Artichoke Casserole, 233
ASPARAGUS
  Asparagus Chantilly, 213
  Asparagus Mimosa, 213
ASPIC
  Raspberry-Tomato Aspic with
      Horseradish Sauce, 108
  Tomato Aspic, 107
  Vegetable Aspic, 107
AVOCADO
  Avocado and Tomato Dip, 24
  Avocado Pinwheel, 16
  Avocado Zucchini Soup, 74
  San Francisco Crab Louis, 89
  Spinach and Avocado or Fruit
      Salad, 101

Baked Apricots, 238
Baked Crabmeat with Sherry, 210
Baked Goat Cheese Salad, 85
Baked Goose with Potato Stuffing, 192
Baked Grouper Provencal, 195
Baked Grouper with Pesto Tomatoes and
    Mushrooms, 194
Baked Italian Pork Chops with Tomato
    Sauce, 166
Baked Pasta with Chicken and Roasted
    Red Peppers, 122
Baked Salmon with Sour Cream
    Sauce, 198
Baked Scallops, 212

Baked Whole Red Snapper, 196
Baked Zucchini, 232
BARBECUE
  Admiral Parson's Barbecue Sauce, 153
  Barbecued Beef Brisket, 134
  Barbecued Chicken, 174
  Barbecued Shrimp, 204
  Individual Barbecued Beef Loaves, 161
  Lemon Barbecued Chicken, 138
  Memphis Outdoor Barbecued
      Chicken, 138
  Roast Lamb with Barbecue Sauce, 163
Barbecue Sauce, 161
Basic Food Processor Pastry, 264
Basil Tartar Sauce, 209
Basil Vinaigrette, 86
Basil-Lemon Dressing, 91
Batter-Fried Shrimp with Tangy
    Sauce, 202
BEANS
  Bean Pot, 217
  Fresh Green Bean and Zucchini
      Sauté, 216
  Green Bean and Carrot Sauté, 216
  Green Beans and Zucchini Bundles, 216
BEEF
  Barbecued Beef Brisket, 134
  Beef Strips Oriental, 160
  Beef Tenderloin with Vegetables, 158
  Chinese Casserole, 167
  Civet "Beef and Wine", 158
  Grilled Beef Brochettes, 137
  Grilled Flank Steak with Wine
      Sauce, 135
  Grilled London Broil, 136
  GROUND
    Ann's Canneloni, 126
    Cheesy Chili Casserole, 161
    Divine Italian Pie, 127
    Grilled Bleu Cheese Burgers, 133
    Individual Barbecued Beef
        Loaves, 161
    Mexican Meatball Soup, 61
    Mexichili, 61
    Taco Casserole, 162
    Taco Dip, 22
    Tavern Nachos, 23
  Herbert Smith's Grilled Beef
      Tenderloin, 134
  Lemon Grilled Chuck Steak, 135
  London Broil with Honey Ginger
      Marinade, 136
  Marinated Beef Brisket, 160
  Marinated Roast Tenderloin, 157
  Perfect Tenderloin, 157
  Rib Roast Perfection, 159
  Sauerkraut Stew, 159
  Sweet and Sour Beef Stew, 63
  Zesty Grilled Flank Steak, 134
Belgian Endive Salad with "Petite
    Marmite" Dressing, 87
Besciamellia Sauce, 126
Best Baked Ham Ever, 171
Best Baked Mustard Sauce, 171
BEVERAGES
  ALCOHOLIC
    Champagne Party Punch, 60
    Frozen Toasted Almond, 58

Mary's Dubonnet Fizz, 57
Pappa's Punch, 57
Peach Margarita, 58
Sangria, 57
Southern Plantation Eggnog, 59
Strawberry Margarita Sorbet, 58
NON-ALCOHOLIC
Children's Punch, 55
Fruit Punch, 55
Hot Percolator Punch, 56
Lovefeast Coffee, 59
Mint Tulips, 55
Minted Ice Tea, 60
Mulled Cider, 56
Salem College Iced Tea, 60
Selfridge's Tea Room Tomato
    Juice, 56
Black Walnut Coffee Cake, 252
Black-Eyed Susans, 16
Blackberry Pancakes, 34
Bleu Cheese Dressing, 114
Blossom Hill Chicken, 180
BLUEBERRIES
Blueberry Gingerbread, 271
Blueberry Pound Cake, 250
Blueberry Sugar Cake, 252
Fresh Blueberry Tart, 265
Blueberry Muffins, 40
Bob Neuman's Ham, 172
Bragg Bread, 53
Bran Muffins, 38
Brandied Walnut Sauce, 253
Bread Pudding with Whiskey Sauce, 272
BREADS
COFFEE CAKES
Black Walnut Coffee Cake, 252
Blueberry Sugar Cake, 252
Date Twists, 50
Julia Ross' Moravian Sugar Cake, 54
St. Timothy's Coffee Cake, 251
MUFFINS
Apple Muffins, 39
Applesauce Muffins, 37
Blueberry Muffins, 40
Bran Muffins, 38
Buttermilk Corn-Cheese Muffins, 38
Cranberry Muffins, 42
French Breakfast Muffins, 42
Morning Glorious Muffins, 41
Orange Raisin Muffins, 41
Squash Muffins, 39
Zucchini Raisin Muffins, 40
PANCAKES AND WAFFLES
Blackberry Pancakes, 34
Dot's Waffles, 35
Pancake Winx, 33
Wheat Germ Pancakes, 34
Wholewheat Oatmeal Hot Cakes, 35
QUICK
Angel Biscuits, 43
Apricot Nut Bread, 45
Bunker Hill Brown Bread, 43
Hatteras Corn Bread, 37
Jalapeño Corn Bread, 36
Poppy Seed Bread, 46
Rich Tea Scones, 33
Spinach Corn Bread, 36
Strawberry Nut Bread, 46
Zucchini Bread, 45

YEAST
Bragg Bread, 53
Carolina Cheese Bread, 51
Dilly Bread, 47
Fennel Bread Sticks, 50
French Bread, 52
Fresh Loaf Bread, 49
Pita Bread, 44
Whole Wheat Bread, 47
Whole Wheat Seed Bread, 48
BREADS AND BEVERAGES 33-60
Britton Brittle, 290
BROCCOLI
Broccoli and Cauliflower Salad, 97
Broccoli and Ham Soup, 67
Broccoli Salad, 97
Broccoli Stuffed Tomatoes, 235
Glazed Broccoli with Almonds, 217
Marinated Broccoli and Cauliflower, 12
Pasta Salad with Broccoli and Ham, 94
Sesame Broccoli, 219
Brown Rice and Vegetable Casserole, 237
Brown Sugar Cookies, 285
Brunch Casserole, 129
Brunswick Stew, 72
Bûche de Noël, 294
Buffalo Hot Wings, 15
Bunker Hill Brown Bread, 43
Buttermilk Corn-Cheese Muffins, 38
Butternut Squash and Apple Bake, 230
Butternut Squash Soufflé, 230

CABBAGE
Cabbage Soup, 81
Cole Slaw Salad, 103
German Cole Slaw, 102
Sweet 'n Sour Slaw, 101
Caesar Salad, 102
CAKES
Almond Brandy Sour Cream Pound
    Cake, 249
Apple Dapple Cake, 247
Blueberry Pound Cake, 250
Bûche de Noël, 294
Caramel Cake, 244
Chocolate Bourbon Cake with Raisins, 241
Chocolate Pound Cake, 250
Chocolate Torte Caramella, 243
Chocolate Upside Down Cake, 242
Coffee Almond Torte, 245
Eggnog Pound Cake, 249
Four Seasons Cake, 246
Fourteen Carat Cake, 239
Ginger Roll Chantilly with Brandied
    Walnut Sauce, 253
Million Dollar Pound Cake, 247
Mom's Chocolate Cake, 240
Orange Blossom Pound Cake, 248
Pecan Roll with Caramel Nut Sauce, 254
Showhouse Lemon Cake, 242
California Salsa, 31
Caramel Cake, 244
Caramel Icing, 244
Caramel Nut Sauce, 254
Carolina Cheese Bread, 51
Carrot Sauce, 125
CARROTS
Carrots Tarragon, 218

Fourteen Carat Cake, 239
Fresh Carrots Vinaigrette, 218
Green Bean and Carrot Sauté, 216
Spiced Carrots, 218
Cashew Chicken, 190
CASSEROLES
Ann's Canneloni, 126
Baked Crabmeat with Sherry, 210
Baked Pasta with Chicken and Roasted
    Red Peppers, 122
Brown Rice and Vegetable Casserole, 237
Brunch Casserole, 129
Cheesy Chili Casserole, 161
Chef's Choice Royale, 177
Chicken and Wild Rice Casserole, 175
Chicken-Artichoke Casserole, 175
Chinese Casserole, 167
Egg and Mushroom Casserole, 129
Fabulous Ham and Cheese Soufflé, 128
Lasagna with Fresh Spinach, 115
More than Mushroom Casserole, 221
Potato and Sour Cream Casserole, 224
Quick Vegetable Lasagna, 115
Seafood Casserole Miami, 206
SECCA Santa Spanakopeta, 128
Spinach and Artichoke Casserole, 233
Taco Casserole, 162
Vegetable-Cheese Casserole, 237
Wild Rice and Almond Casserole, 226
Wild Rice and Shrimp Casserole, 207
CAULIFLOWER
Broccoli and Cauliflower Salad, 97
Marinated Broccoli and Cauliflower, 12
Champagne Chicken, 186
Champagne Party Punch, 60
Champagne-Marinated Fruit, 238
Charleston Marinated Shrimp, 25
Cheddar Chowder, 75
CHEESE
Baked Goat Cheese Salad, 85
Black-Eyed Susans, 16
Brunch Casserole, 129
Buttermilk Corn-Cheese Muffins, 38
Carolina Cheese Bread, 51
Cheddar Chowder, 75
Cheese and Herbs Appetizer, 18
Cheese Dressing for Potatoes, 111
Cheese Roll Ups with Mustard Sauce, 17
Cheese Straws, 10
Cheese Tart with Apples, 19
Cheesy Broiled Flounder, 197
Cheesy Chili Casserole, 161
Chicken Alouette, 187
Chutney Cheesecake, 20
Danish Cheese Melt, 133
Eggplant with Cheese, 220
Fabulous Ham and Cheese Soufflé, 128
Feta Tarts, 18
Garlic Cheese Grits, 130
Grilled Bleu Cheese Burgers, 133
Herbed Cheese Spread, 20
Mushroom Bleu Cheese Spread, 19
Oriental Chicken on Golden Cheese
    Strata, 176
Pita Cheese Crisps, 9
Roasted Bell Pepper Salad or Sandwich
    with Prosciutto and Provolone, 86
Rosa's Cheese Souffle Sandwiches, 30
Sausage and Cheese Grits, 130

SECCA Santa Spanakopeta, 128
Tomato Cheese Spread, 21
Vegetable-Cheese Casserole, 237
Yogurt Parmesan Chicken, 184

CHEESECAKES
Amaretto-Amaretti Chocolate
Cheesecake, 261
Cheesecake Squares, 282
Fudge Almond Cheesecake, 259
New York City Chocolate Cheesecake, 257
Praline Cheesecake, 259
Pumpkin Cheesecake, 260
Rum Raisin Cheesecake with Myers's
Rum Sauce, 262
White Chocolate Cheesecake, 258
Cheesy Broiled Flounder, 197
Cheesy Chili Casserole, 161
Chef's Choice Royale, 177
Cherry Tomatoes Stuffed with Pesto, 11

CHICKEN
Baked Pasta with Chicken and Roasted
Red Peppers, 122
Barbecued Chicken, 174
Blossom Hill Chicken, 180
Brunswick Stew, 72
Buffalo Hot Wings, 15
Cashew Chicken, 190
Champagne Chicken, 186
Chef's Choice Royale, 177
Chicken Alouette, 187
Chicken and Wild Rice Casserole, 175
Chicken Apple Curry Soup, 71
Chicken Bombay, 183
Chicken Breasts with Vegetables, 186
Chicken Cacciatore à la Capocelli, 173
Chicken Kiev, 185
Chicken Parmesan with Herbed Tomato
Sauce, 183
Chicken Piccata, 179
Chicken Sauté with Variations, 181
Chicken Vegetable Soup, 70
Chicken Veronique, 184
Chicken Wellington, 182
Chicken-Artichoke Casserole, 175
Cobb Salad, 104
Cold Poached Tarragon Chicken with
Horseradish Cream, 180
Creamy Baked Chicken Breasts, 182
Crescent Chicken Squares, 177
Curried Chicken and Artichoke Salad, 105
Curried Chicken Salad, 106
Garden Chicken Pie, 178
Grilled Ginger Chicken Breasts, 139
Honey-Baked Chicken, 173
Hot Chicken Salad, 106
Japanese Chicken Salad, 104
Lemon Barbecued Chicken, 138
Marinated Chicken Sandwiches with Hot
Mustard Sauce, 137
Melt-in-Your-Mouth Chicken Pie, 178
Memphis Outdoor Barbecued Chicken, 138
Mom's Chicken Soup, 70
Oriental Chicken on Golden Cheese
Strata, 176
Pennsylvania Dutch Chicken Sauté, 185
Polynesian Luncheon Salad, 105
Sautéed Chicken Livers with Apples
and Onions, 190
Savory Chicken Pie, 179

Sesame Chicken Kebobs, 139
Sesame Chicken Rolls, 14
Sour Cream Chicken Breasts, 184
Spicy Oven Fried Chicken, 174
Spinach Wrapped Chicken with Sesame
Dip, 15
Sweet and Sour Chicken Drummettes, 14
Yogurt Parmesan Chicken, 184
Children's Punch, 55
Chilled Cucumber Soup with Fresh Dill, 75
Chilled Fruit Pudding with Caramel Crumb
Topping, 273
Chilled Shrimp and Cucumber Soup, 68
Chinese Casserole, 167

CHOCOLATE
Amaretto-Amaretti Chocolate
Cheesecake, 261
Bûche de Noël, 294
Chocolate Bourbon Cake with Raisins, 241
Chocolate Chess Squares, 281
Chocolate Icing, 240
Chocolate Mint Delights, 280
Chocolate Mousse Pie, 256
Chocolate Orange Mousse, 255
Chocolate Pound Cake, 250
Chocolate Torte Caramela, 243
Chocolate Truffles, 289
Chocolate Upside Down Cake, 242
Double Chocolate Crinkles, 282
Frosted Brownies, 284
Fudge Almond Cheesecake, 259
Individual Chocolate Soufflés, 275
Mocha Hot Fudge Sauce, 292
Mom's Chocolate Cake, 240
New York City Chocolate Cheesecake, 257
Patricia Inn Fudge Sauce, 291
Southern Fudge Pecan Pie, 268
White Chocolate Cheesecake, 258
Windy City Brownies, 283
Christmas Candy House, 293
Chutney Cheesecake, 20
Cilantro Sauce, 150
Cinnamon Ice Cream, 287
Civet "Beef and Wine", 158

CLAMS
Artichoke Clam Puffs, 29
Clam Bisque, 69
New England Clam Chowder, 67
Pasta with Clam Sauce for Two, 118
Vermicelli with Clam Sauce, 118
Cobb Salad, 104
Coffee Almond Torte, 245

COFFEE CAKES
Black Walnut Coffee Cake, 252
Blueberry Sugar Cake, 252
St. Timothy's Coffee Cake, 251
Coffee Ice Cream Pie, 267
Cognac Mushrooms, 9
Cold Poached Tarragon Chicken with
Horseradish Cream, 180
Cole Slaw Salad, 103
Company Potatoes, 224

CONFECTIONS
Britton Brittle, 290
Chocolate Truffles, 289
Christmas Candy House, 293
Incredible Toffee, 290
Congo Squares, 285

COOKIES

Double Chocolate Crinkles, 282
Lemon Hearts, 278
Molasses Sugar Cookies, 204
The World's Best Cookie, 279
Winkler Sugar Cookies, 279

CORN
Corn on the Grill, 151
Corn Soufflé, 219
Fresh Corn Chowder, 82
Mexicali Creamed Corn, 219
Miss Lottie's Corn Pudding, 220
Seafood Dump, 207
Vegetable Brochettes, 151

CORN BREAD
Hatteras Corn Bread, 37
Jalapeño Corn Bread, 36
Spinach Corn Bread, 36
Country Ham, 170

CRAB
Angler's Crab Imperial, 208
Baked Crabmeat with Sherry, 210
Crab and Mushroom Bisque, 68
Crab Cakes, 211
Crab Cakes with Basil Tartar Sauce, 209
Crab Pasta Salad, 90
Crabmeat Spread, 28
Crabmeat-Vegetable Pie, 211
Crunchy Crab Puffs, 29
Deviled Crab, 210
Devilish Crab, 212
Hot Crab Canapés, 27
San Francisco Crab Louis, 89
Seafood Casserole Miami, 206
Special Crabmeat Appetizer, 28
Vegetable Seafood Salad, 88

CRANBERRIES
Cranberry Apple Salad, 109
Cranberry Muffins, 42
Cranberry Waldorf Salad Ring, 109
Crown Roast Pork with Cranberry
Stuffing and Dijon Mustard Sauce, 168
Cream of Lettuce Soup, 77
Cream of Spinach Soup, 83
Creamy Baked Chicken Breasts, 182
Creamy Basil Dressing, 92
Crème Anglaise, 269
Crème Brûlée with Fresh Raspberry
Sauce, 274
Crème Fraiche, 188
Crescent Chicken Squares, 177
Crown Roast Pork with Cranberry Stuffing
and Dijon Mustard Sauce, 168
Crunchy Crab Puffs, 29
Cucumber Yogurt Sauce, 142
Cucumber-Dill Sauce, 199

CUCUMBERS
Chilled Cucumber Soup with Fresh Dill, 75
Chilled Shrimp and Cucumber Soup, 68
Japanese Cucumber Salad, 99

CURRY
Chicken Bombay, 183
Chutney Cheesecake, 20
Curried Chicken and Artichoke Salad, 105
Curried Chicken Salad, 106
Curried Rice with Pineapple, 229
Curried Zucchini Soup, 73
Curry Dip, 32
Sesame Chicken Rolls, 14
Shrimp Curry, 205

Danish Cheese Melt, 133
Danish Raspberry Shortcake, 263
Date Twists, 50
DATES
  Black-Eyed Susans, 16
  Date Twists, 50
DESSERTS 239-294
  BARS
    Brown Sugar Cookies, 285
    Chocolate Chess Squares, 281
    Congo Squares, 285
    Frosted Brownies, 284
    Harvest Bars, 280
    Mincemeat Squares, 281
    Summit Lemon Squares, 278
    Windy City Brownies, 283
  CAKES
    Almond Brandy Sour Cream Pound
      Cake, 249
    Apple Dapple Cake, 247
    Blueberry Pound Cake, 250
    Bûche de Noël, 294
    Caramel Cake, 244
    Chocolate Bourbon Cake with
      Raisins, 241
    Chocolate Pound Cake, 250
    Chocolate Torte Caramela, 243
    Chocolate Upside Down Cake, 242
    Coffee Almond Torte, 245
    Eggnog Pound Cake, 249
    Four Seasons Cake, 246
    Fourteen Carat Cake, 239
    Ginger Roll Chantilly with Brandied
      Walnut Sauce, 253
    Million Dollar Pound Cake, 247
    Mom's Chocolate Cake, 240
    Orange Blossom Pound Cake, 248
    Pecan Roll with Caramel Nut Sauce, 254
    Showhouse Lemon Cake, 242
  CHEESECAKES
    Amaretto-Amaretti Chocolate
      Cheesecake, 261
    Cheesecake Squares, 282
    Fudge Almond Cheesecake, 259
    New York City Chocolate
      Cheesecake, 257
    Praline Cheesecake, 259
    Pumpkin Cheesecake, 260
    Rum Raisin Cheesecake with Myers's
      Rum Sauce, 262
    White Chocolate Cheesecake, 258
  CONFECTIONS
    Britton Brittle, 290
    Chocolate Truffles, 289
    Christmas Candy House, 293
    Incredible Toffee, 290
  COOKIES
    Double Chocolate Crinkles, 282
    Lemon Hearts, 278
    Molasses Sugar Cookies, 284
    The World's Best Cookie, 279
    Winkler Sugar Cookies, 279
  ICE CREAM AND SORBET
    Chocolate Mint Delights, 280
    Cinnamon Ice Cream, 287
    Coffee Ice Cream Pie, 267
    Fresh Fruit Sorbet, 288
    Frozen Lemon Pie, 267

    Just Peachy Ice Cream, 286
    Lemon Velvet Ice Cream, 286
    Lotus Ice Cream, 286
    Raspberry Buttermilk Sherbet, 288
    Sin, 287
  MISCELLANEOUS
    Blueberry Gingerbread, 271
    Bread Pudding with Whiskey Sauce, 272
    Chilled Fruit Pudding with Caramel
      Crumb Topping, 273
    Chocolate Orange Mousse, 255
    Crème Brûlée with Fresh Raspberry
      Sauce, 274
    Danish Raspberry Shortcake, 263
    English Upside Down Gingerbread
      Pudding, 270
    Frozen Pineapple Yogurt with
      Raspberries, 289
    Fruit Pizza, 263
    Gingerbread, 271
    Individual Chocolate Soufflés, 275
    Mocha Mousse, 255
    Peach and Blackberry Cobbler, 272
    Peaches and Cream, 276
    Raspberries 'n Cream, 275
    Strawberries Romanoff, 276
    Summertime Marinated Fruit, 277
    Swedish Pancake, 277
    Tipsy Trifle, 269
  PIES AND PIE CRUSTS
    Almond Tart, 265
    Basic Food Processor Pastry, 264
    Chocolate Mousse Pie, 256
    Fresh Blueberry Tart, 265
    Frozen Lemon Pie, 267
    Fruit Jewels, 266
    Granny's Pumpkin Pie, 268
    Mile High Strawberry Pie, 266
    Southern Fudge Pecan Pie, 268
Deviled Crab, 210
Devilish Crab, 212
Dijon Hollandaise, 193
Dijon Mustard Sauce, 168
Dill Butter Sauce, 187
Dill Dip, 32
Dilly Bread, 47
Divine Italian Pie, 127
Dixie Pasta, 120
Dot's Waffles, 35
Double Chocolate Crinkles, 282
Drew's Honey Mustard Dressing, 113
DUCK
  Grilled Wild Duck Breasts, 150
  Kingdom Come Duck, 191

Easy Gazpacho, 80
Easy Onion Soup for Two, 81
Egg and Mushroom Casserole, 129
Eggnog Pound Cake, 249
EGGPLANT
  Eggplant Supper Soup, 62
  Eggplant with Cheese, 220
EGGS
  Brunch Casserole, 129
  Egg and Mushroom Casserole, 129
  Fabulous Ham and Cheese Soufflé, 128
  Golden Cheese Strata, 176

English Upside Down Gingerbread
  Pudding, 270

Fabulous Ham and Cheese Soufflé, 128
Fennel Bread Sticks, 50
Feta Tarts, 18
Fettucine with Zucchini and Mushrooms, 121
FISH
  BASS
    Striped Bass (Rock Bass), 197
  FLOUNDER
    Cheesy Broiled Flounder, 197
    Flounder Filets, 149
  Grilled Seafood with Coriander Oil, 145
  GROUPER
    Baked Grouper Provençal, 195
    Baked Grouper with Pesto Tomatoes
      and Mushrooms, 194
    Grilled Grouper Filets, 147
    Grouper St. Charles, 195
  RED SNAPPER
    Baked Whole Red Snapper, 196
  SALMON
    Baked Salmon with Sour Cream
      Sauce, 198
    Grilled Salmon Steaks, 147
    Grilled Salmon with Garlic and Lime, 147
    Grilled Salmon with Honey, Ginger
      and Dark Soy Marinade, 148
    Marinated Salmon Steak, 198
    Poached Salmon with Basil Sauce, 200
    Salmon Loaf with Cucumber-Dill
      Sauce, 199
    Smoked Salmon Filet, 154
    Smoked Salmon Timbales with
      Coulis de Tomatoes, 201
    Smoked Whole Salmon, 153
  Seafood Brochettes, 149
  SWORDFISH
    Oriental Grilled Swordfish Steaks, 144
    Savory Swordfish, 143
    Teriyaki Swordfish, 145
  TROUT
    Grilled Rainbow Trout with Pesto
      Mayonnaise, 148
    Spinach Stuffed Trout, 194
    Trout Moutardé, 193
Flavored Butters for Vegetables, 214
FLOUNDER
  Cheesy Broiled Flounder, 197
  Flounder Filets, 149
Four Seasons Cake, 246
Fourteen Carat Cake, 239
French Bread, 52
French Breakfast Muffins, 42
French Epicurean Peas, 223
Fresh Blueberry Tart, 265
Fresh Carrots Vinaigrette, 218
Fresh Corn Chowder, 82
Fresh Fruit Sorbet, 288
Fresh Green Bean and Zucchini Sauté, 216
Fresh Loaf Bread, 49
Fresh Mushroom Pie, 222
Fresh Raspberry Sauce, 274
Fresh Strawberry Soup, 82
Fresh Tomato Pie, 235
Fresh Vegetable Mold, 11

Frosted Brownies, 284
FROSTINGS AND ICINGS
    Caramel Icing, 241
    Chocolate Icing, 240
    Frostings 1 and 2, 284
    Vanilla Cream Cheese Frosting, 239
Frozen Lemon Pie, 267
Frozen Pineapple Yogurt with Raspberries, 289
Frozen Toasted Almond, 58
FRUIT
    Baked Apricots, 238
    Champagne-Marinated Fruit, 238
    Chicken Veronique, 184
    Chilled Fruit Pudding with Caramel
        Crumb Topping, 273
    Fresh Fruit Sorbet, 288
    Fruit Jewels, 266
    Fruit Pizza, 263
    Grapefruit Sauce, 157
    Holiday Roast Turkey Breast with
        Fruit Stuffing, 188
    Summertime Marinated Fruit, 277
    Tipsy Trifle, 269
Fruit Punch, 55
Fudge Almond Cheesecake, 259

GAME
    Baked Goose with Potato Stuffing, 192
    Grilled Wild Duck Breasts, 150
    Kingdom Come Duck, 191
    Roast Goose with Apricot Stuffing, 192
Garden Chicken Pie, 178
Garlic Cheese Grits, 130
German Cole Slaw, 102
Ginger Roll Chantilly with Brandied
    Walnut Sauce, 253
Gingerbread, 271
Gingerbread Topping, 292
Glazed Broccoli with Almonds, 217
Golden Cheese Strata, 176
GOOSE
    Baked Goose with Potato Stuffing, 192
    Roast Goose with Apricot Stuffing, 192
Granny's Pumpkin Pie, 268
Grapefruit Sauce, 157
Green Bean and Carrot Sauté, 216
GREEN BEANS
    Fresh Green Bean and Zucchini Sauté, 216
    Green Bean and Carrot Saute, 216
    Green Beans and Zucchini Bundles, 216
Green Split Pea Soup, 77
GRILLING 131-154
    APPETIZERS
        Angels on Horseback, 143
        Danish Cheese Melt, 133
        Party Lamb Pitas, 142
        Pork Satés, 140
    Art of Grilling, 131
    BEEF
        Barbecued Beef Brisket, 134
        Grilled Beef Brochettes, 137
        Grilled Bleu Cheese Burgers, 133
        Grilled Flank Steak with Wine Sauce, 135
        Grilled London Broil, 136
        Herbert Smith's Grilled Beef
            Tenderloin, 134
        Lemon Grilled Chuck Steak, 135

London Broil with Honey Ginger
    Marinade, 136
Zesty Grilled Flank Steak, 134
CHICKEN
    Grilled Ginger Chicken Breasts, 139
    Lemon Barbecued Chicken, 138
    Marinated Chicken Sandwiches with
        Hot Mustard Sauce, 137
    Memphis Outdoor Barbecued
        Chicken, 138
    Sesame Chicken Kebobs, 139
FISH
    Flounder Filets, 149
    Grilled Grouper Filets, 147
    Grilled Rainbow Trout with Pesto
        Mayonnaise, 148
    Grilled Salmon Steaks, 147
    Grilled Salmon with Garlic and Lime, 147
    Grilled Salmon with Honey, Ginger
        and Dark Soy Marinade, 148
    Grilled Seafood with Coriander Oil, 145
    Oriental Grilled Swordfish Steaks, 144
    Savory Swordfish, 143
    Seafood Brochettes, 149
    Smoked Salmon Filet, 154
    Smoked Whole Salmon, 153
    Teriyaki Swordfish, 145
LAMB
    Lamb Chops Teriyaki, 141
MARINADES AND SAUCES
    Marinade for Swordfish Steaks, 143
MISCELLANEOUS
    Grilled Cornish Hens with Hot Pepper
        Jelly, 140
    Grilled Pineapple, 154
    Grilled Wild Duck Breasts, 150
PORK
    Pork Loin Lahaina, 141
    Tom's Grilled Pork Chops, 140
SAUCES AND MARINADES
    Admiral Parson's Barbecue Sauce, 153
    Marinade for Beef, 152
    Mustard-Garlic Marinade, 152
SHELLFISH
    Grilled Sea Scallops with Cilantro
        Sauce, 150
    Lemon Shrimp Brochettes, 146
    Sesamed Shrimp Kebob Kelly, 145
    Shrimp Kebobs, 146
VEGETABLES
    Corn on the Grill, 151
    Grilled Potatoes, 151
    Grilled Whole Baby Squash, 152
    Vegetable Brochettes, 151
GRITS
    Garlic Cheese Grits, 130
    Sausage and Cheese Grits, 130
GROUPER
    Baked Grouper Provençal, 195
    Baked Grouper with Pesto Tomatoes
        and Mushrooms, 194
    Grilled Grouper Filets, 147
Grouper St. Charles, 195

HAM
    Best Baked Ham Ever, 171

Bob Neuman's Ham, 172
Broccoli and Ham Soup, 67
Chef's Choice Royale, 177
Country Ham, 170
Dixie Pasta, 120
Fabulous Ham and Cheese
    Soufflé, 128
Ham 'n Cheese Croissants, 84
Pasta Salad with Broccoli and Ham, 94
Roasted Bell Pepper Salad or Sandwich
    with Prosciutto and Provolone, 86
Skiers' Delight Pasta, 120
Spinach and Ham Roll-Ups, 172
Harvest Bars, 280
Hatteras Corn Bread, 37
Health Soup, 80
Herbert Smith's Grilled Beef
    Tenderloin, 134
HERBS
    Basil Tartar Sauce, 209
    Carrots Tarragon, 218
    Cheese and Herbs Appetizer, 18
    Chicken Parmesan with Herbed Tomato
        Sauce, 183
    Chilled Cucumber Soup with Fresh
        Dill, 75
    Cold Poached Tarragon Chicken with
        Horseradish Cream, 180
    Cucumber-Dill Sauce, 199
    Dill Butter Sauce, 187
    Dill Dip, 32
    Dilly Bread, 47
    Fennel Bread Sticks, 50
    Flavored Butters for Vegetables, 214
    Grilled Sea Scallops with Cilantro
        Sauce, 150
    Grilled Seafood with Coriander Oil, 145
    Herb Pizza, 22
    Herbed Cheese Spread, 20
    Herbed Tomatoes, 88
    Herbed Wild Rice, 229
    Lemon Sage Pork Chops, 166
    Pasta with Cream and Fresh Herbs, 119
    Poached Salmon with Basil Sauce, 200
    Pork Roast and Herbs, 170
    Roast Lamb with Herbed Mustard, 163
    Roasted Herbed Walnuts, 13
    Rosemary Potatoes, 225
    Tomato Herb Pasta with Carrot
        Sauce, 125
    Wild Turkey Sandwich with Tarragon
        Dressing, 84
HERITAGE OF HOSPITALITY
    Angel Biscuits, 43
    Angler's Crab Imperial, 208
    Bran Muffins, 38
    Caramel Cake, 244
    Country Ham, 170
    Grilled Flank Steak with Wine
        Sauce, 135
    Grilled Wild Duck Breasts, 150
    Irena Kirshman's Minestrone, 76
    Julia Ross' Moravian Sugar Cake, 54
    Lovefeast Coffee, 59
    Sausage and Cheese Grits, 130
    Scallops Seviche, 27
    Seafood Casserole Miami, 206
    Special Salad Dressing, 114
    St. Timothy's Coffee Cake, 251

Striped Bass (Rock Bass), 197
Summit Lemon Squares, 278
Vermicelli with Clam Sauce, 118
Holiday Roast Turkey Breast with Fruit
    Stuffing, 188
Honey Celery Seed Dressing, 112
Honey-Baked Chicken, 173
Horseradish Whipped Cream, 180
Hot and Sweet Holiday Mustard, 110
Hot Chicken Salad, 106
Hot Crab Canapés, 27
Hot Mustard Sauce, 137
Hot Percolator Punch, 56

ICE CREAM
    Frozen Toasted Almond, 58
ICE CREAM AND SORBET
    Chocolate Mint Delights, 280
    Cinnamon Ice Cream, 287
    Coffee Ice Cream Pie, 267
    Fresh Fruit Sorbet, 288
    Just Peachy Ice Cream, 286
    Lemon Velvet Ice Cream, 286
    Lotus Ice Cream, 286
    Raspberry Buttermilk Sherbet, 288
    Sin, 287
Incredible Toffee, 290
Individual Barbecued Beef Loaves, 161
Individual Chocolate Soufflés, 275
Irena Kirshman's Minestrone, 76
Italian Sausage Soup, 64
Italian Tomato Sauce, 166
Italian Zucchini Pie, 231

Jalapeño Corn Bread, 36
Japanese Chicken Salad, 104
Japanese Cucumber Salad, 99
Jim Kroncke's Famous Spaghetti
    Sauce, 124
Julia Ross' Moravian Sugar Cake, 54
Just Peachy Ice Cream, 286

Kingdom Come Duck, 191

LAMB
    Lamb Chops Teriyaki, 141
    Navarin Printanier, 164
    Party Lamb Pitas, 142
    Roast Lamb with Barbecue Sauce, 163
    Roast Lamb with Herbed Mustard, 163
    Ryan's Rack, 162
Lasagna with Fresh Spinach, 115
Légumes Fricassés, 221
LEMON
    Frozen Lemon Pie, 267
    Lemon Barbecued Chicken, 138
    Lemon Grilled Chuck Steak, 135
    Lemon Hearts, 278
    Lemon Sage Pork Chops, 166
    Lemon Shrimp Brochettes, 146
    Lemon Velvet Ice Cream, 286

Lemon Vinaigrette, 228
Lotus Ice Cream, 286
Showhouse Lemon Cake, 242
Summit Lemon Squares, 278
Lettuceless Salad, 98
Light Tomato Sauce, 123
Linguini with Salmon Sauce, 119
London Broil with Honey Ginger
    Marinade, 136
Lotus Ice Cream, 286
Lovefeast Coffee, 59

MARINADES, MARINATED
    Champagne-Marinated Fruit, 238
    Charleston Marinated Shrimp, 25
    Grilled Beef Brochettes, 137
    Grilled Ginger Chicken Breasts, 139
    Grilled London Broil, 136
    Grilled Salmon with Garlic and
        Lime, 147
    Grilled Salmon with Honey, Ginger and
        Dark Soy Marinade, 148
    Lemon Grilled Chuck Steak, 135
    Lemon Shrimp Brochettes, 146
    London Broil with Honey Ginger
        Marinade, 136
    Marinade for Beef, 152
    Marinade for Swordfish Steaks, 143
    Marinated Beef Brisket, 160
    Marinated Chicken Sandwiches with
        Hot Mustard Sauce, 137
    Marinated Pork Roast, 169
    Marinated Roast Tenderloin, 157
    Marinated Salmon Steak, 198
    Marinated Shrimp, 25
    Marinated Vegetable Salad, 99
    Mustard-Garlic Marinade, 152
    Oriental Grilled Swordfish Steaks, 144
    Pork Loin Lahaina, 141
    Pork Satés, 140
    Sesame Chicken Kebobs, 139
    Shrimp Kebobs, 146
    Teriyaki Swordfish, 145
    Tom's Grilled Pork Chops, 140
    Zesty Grilled Flank Steak, 134
Marinated Broccoli and Cauliflower, 12
Mary's Dubonnet Fizz, 57
MEAT 155-161
    BEEF
        Barbecued Beef Brisket, 134
        Beef Strips Oriental, 160
        Beef Tenderloin with Vegetables, 158
        Cheesy Chili Casserole, 161
        Chinese Casserole, 167
        Civet "Beef and Wine", 158
        Grilled Beef Brochettes, 137
        Grilled Bleu Cheese Burgers, 133
        Grilled Flank Steak with Wine
            Sauce, 135
        Grilled London Broil, 136
        Herbert Smith's Grilled Beef
            Tenderloin, 134
        Individual Barbecued Beef
            Loaves, 161
        Lemon Grilled Chuck Steak, 135
        London Broil with Honey Ginger
            Marinade, 136
        Marinated Beef Brisket, 160

Marinated Roast Tenderloin, 157
        Perfect Tenderloin, 157
        Rib Roast Perfection, 159
        Sauerkraut Stew, 159
        Taco Casserole, 162
        Zesty Grilled Flank Steak, 134
    Brunswick Stew, 72
    HAM
        Best Baked Ham Ever, 171
        Bob Neuman's Ham, 172
        Country Ham, 170
        Spinach and Ham Roll-Ups, 172
    LAMB
        Lamb Chops Teriyaki, 141
        Navarin Printanier, 164
        Party Lamb Pitas, 142
        Roast Lamb with Barbecue
            Sauce, 163
        Roast Lamb with Herbed
            Mustard, 163
        Ryan's Rack, 162
    PORK
        Baked Italian Pork Chops with
            Tomato Sauce, 166
        Crown Roast Pork with Cranberry
            Stuffing and Dijon Mustard
            Sauce, 168
        Lemon Sage Pork Chops, 166
        Marinated Pork Roast, 169
        Pork Chops Capri, 167
        Pork Loin Lahaina, 141
        Pork Roast and Herbs, 170
        Pork Satés, 140
        Stir-Fried Pork, 169
        Tom's Grilled Pork Chops, 140
    SAUSAGE
        Sausage and Peperoni Pizza, 165
    VEAL
        Veal Chops with Morels, 156
        Veal Cushions Capocelli, 155
        Veal Roast with Sour Cream Gravy, 156
        Veal Scallopine with Tomatoes
            and Olives, 155
Melt-in-Your-Mouth Chicken Pie, 178
Memphis Outdoor Barbecued Chicken, 138
MEXICAN
    Mexicali Creamed Corn, 219
    Mexican Meatball Soup, 61
    Mexichili, 61
    Taco Casserole, 162
    Taco Dip, 22
    Tavern Nachos, 23
    Tex-Mex Dip, 23
Mile High Strawberry Pie, 266
Million Dollar Pound Cake, 247
Mincemeat Squares, 281
Mint Tulips, 55
Minted Ice Tea, 60
Miss Lottie's Corn Pudding, 220
Mocha Hot Fudge Sauce, 292
Mocha Mousse, 255
Molasses Sugar Cookies, 284
Mom's Chicken Soup, 70
Mom's Chocolate Cake, 240
More than Mushroom Casserole, 221
Morning Glorious Muffins, 41
MOUSSE
    Chocolate Mousse Pie, 256
    Chocolate Orange Mousse, 255

Mocha Mousse, 255
Salmon Mousse, 30
MUFFINS
Apple Muffins, 39
Applesauce Muffins, 37
Blueberry Muffins, 40
Bran Muffins, 38
Buttermilk Corn-Cheese Muffins, 38
Cranberry Muffins, 42
French Breakfast Muffins, 42
Morning Glorious Muffins, 41
Orange Raisin Muffins, 41
Squash Muffins, 39
Zucchini Raisin Muffins, 40
Mulled Cider, 56
MUSHROOMS
Baked Grouper with Pesto Tomatoes
and Mushrooms, 194
Cognac Mushrooms, 9
Egg and Mushroom Casserole, 129
Fettucine with Zucchini and
Mushrooms, 121
Fresh Mushroom Pie, 222
More than Mushroom Casserole, 221
Mushroom Appetizers, 12
Mushroom Bleu Cheese Spread, 19
Mushroom Puffs, 13
Sour Cream and Mushroom Soup, 78
Veal Chops with Morels, 156
Watercress, Mushroom and Endive
Salad, 85
Mustard Horseradish Sauce, 111
Mustard Sauce, 17
Mustard-Garlic Marinade, 152

Navarin Printanier, 164
New England Clam Chowder, 67
New Potato Salad, 103
New York City Chocolate Cheesecake, 257
NUTS
Almond Tart, 265
Apricot Nut Bread, 45
Black Walnut Coffee Cake, 252
Brandied Walnut Sauce, 253
Cashew Chicken, 190
Coffee Almond Torte, 245
Fudge Almond Cheesecake, 259
Glazed Broccoli with Almonds, 217
Pecan Roll with Caramel Nut Sauce, 254
Praline Cheesecake, 259
Roasted Herbed Walnuts, 13
Shrimp and Walnuts, 203
Southern Fudge Pecan Pie, 268
Vidalia Onions Stuffed with Nuts, 223
Wild Rice and Almond Casserole, 226

Ocean Spray Shrimp, 205
OKRA
Shrimp and Okra Soup, 69
ONIONS
Easy Onion Soup for Two, 81
Sautéed Chicken Livers with Apples
and Onions, 190
Spanish Onion Pie, 222
Vidalia Onions Stuffed with Nuts, 223
ORANGE
Chocolate Orange Mousse, 255

Orange Blossom Pound Cake, 248
Orange Raisin Muffins, 41
ORIENTAL
Beef Strips Oriental, 160
Cashew Chicken, 190
Chinese Casserole, 167
Lamb Chops Teriyaki, 141
Oriental Chicken on Golden Cheese
Strata, 176
Oriental Grilled Swordfish Steaks, 144
Sesame Broccoli, 219
Squash-Zucchini Stir Fry, 231
Stir-Fried Pork, 169
Tea Smoked Shrimp, 26
Teriyaki Swordfish, 145
Oyster Cracker Snacks, 10
OYSTERS
Angels on Horseback, 143
Oysters Orleans, 24
Scalloped Oysters, 201
Seafood Gumbo, 208
Smoked Oyster Spread, 24

PANCAKES
Blackberry Pancakes, 34
Pancake Winx, 33
Potato Pancakes, 225
Swedish Pancake, 277
Wheat Germ Pancakes, 34
Wholewheat Oatmeal Hot Cakes, 35
Pappa's Punch, 57
Party Lamb Pitas, 142
PASTA
HOT
Angel Hair Pasta with Three Caviars, 121
Ann's Canneloni, 126
Baked Pasta with Chicken and
Roasted Red Peppers, 122
Divine Italian Pie, 127
Dixie Pasta, 120
Fettucine with Zucchini and
Mushrooms, 121
Lasagna with Fresh Spinach, 115
Linguini with Salmon Sauce, 119
Pasta Primavera with Shrimp, 116
Pasta with Clam Sauce for Two, 118
Pasta with Cream and Fresh Herbs, 119
Pasta with Uncooked Sauce, 124
Quick Vegetable Lasagna, 115
Sausage and Vegetable Pasta, 123
Shrimp Alfredo, 116
Shrimp and Bay Scallops Marinara, 117
Skiers' Delight Pasta, 120
Spicy Shrimp and Sesame Noodles, 117
Tomato Herb Pasta with Carrot
Sauce, 125
Vermicelli with Clam Sauce, 118
SALADS
Crab Pasta Salad, 90
Pasta Salad with Broccoli and Ham, 94
Pat's Pasta Salad, 95
Seafood Pasta Primavera Salad with
Creamy Basil Dressing, 92
Seafood Pasta Salad, 93
Shrimp and Pasta Salad with
Basil-Lemon Dressing, 91
Spring Pasta Salad with Pesto, 96

Tasty Pasta Salad, 93
PASTA, EGGS, CHEESE 115-130
Pat's Pasta Salad, 95
Paté Hater's Delight, 21
Patricia Inn Fudge Sauce, 291
PEACHES
Just Peachy Ice Cream, 286
Peach and Blackberry Cobbler, 272
Peach Margarita, 58
Peaches and Cream, 276
Spiced Peach Salad, 108
PEAS
French Epicurean Peas, 223
Green Split Pea Soup, 77
Peasant Soup, 65
Pecan Roll with Caramel Nut Sauce, 254
Pennsylvania Dutch Chicken Sauté, 185
Perfect Tenderloin, 157
PESTO
Baked Grouper with Pesto Tomatoes
and Mushrooms, 194
Grilled Rainbow Trout with Pesto
Mayonnaise, 148
Pasta Salad with Broccoli and Ham, 94
Pesto Sauce, 94
Spring Pasta Salad with Pesto, 96
Pesto Mayonnaise, 148
"Petite Marmite" Dressing, 87
PHYLLO
Cheese Roll Ups with Mustard Sauce, 17
Garden Chicken Pie, 178
SECCA Santa Spanakopeta, 128
PIES AND PIE CRUSTS
Almond Tart, 265
Basic Food Processor Pastry, 264
Chocolate Mousse Pie, 256
Coffee Ice Cream Pie, 267
Crabmeat-Vegetable Pie, 211
Divine Italian Pie, 127
Fresh Blueberry Tart, 265
Fresh Mushroom Pie, 222
Fresh Tomato Pie, 235
Frozen Lemon Pie, 267
Fruit Jewels, 266
Garden Chicken Pie, 178
Granny's Pumpkin Pie, 268
Italian Zucchini Pie, 231
Melt-in-Your-Mouth Chicken Pie, 178
Mile High Strawberry Pie, 266
Savory Chicken Pie, 179
Southern Fudge Pecan Pie, 268
Spanish Onion Pie, 222
PINEAPPLE
Curried Rice with Pineapple, 229
Grilled Pineapple, 154
Sauerkraut with Champagne and
Pineapple, 233
Pita Bread, 44
PIZZA
Herb Pizza, 22
Sausage and Peperoni Pizza, 165
Poached Salmon with Basil Sauce, 200
Polynesian Luncheon Salad, 105
Poppy Seed Bread, 46
Poppyseed Dressing, 111
PORK
Baked Italian Pork Chops with Tomato
Sauce, 166
Crown Roast Pork with Cranberry

Stuffing and
Dijon Mustard Sauce, 168
Lemon Sage Pork Chops, 166
Marinated Pork Roast, 169
Pork Chops Capri, 167
Pork Loin Lahaina, 141
Pork Roast and Herbs, 170
Pork Sates, 140
Soupa De Guadalajara, 66
Stir-Fried Pork, 169
Tom's Grilled Pork Chops, 140

POTATOES
Baked Goose with Potato Stuffing, 192
Company Potatoes, 224
Grilled Potatoes, 151
New Potato Salad, 103
Potato and Sour Cream Casserole, 224
Potato Pancakes, 225
Rosemary Potatoes, 225
Three-Potato Soup, 79

POULTRY (See specific types) 173-192
Praline Cheesecake, 259
Praline Sauce, 292

PUMPKIN
Granny's Pumpkin Pie, 268
Pumpkin Cheesecake, 260
Pumpkin Soup, 78

Quick Vegetable Lasagna, 115

RAISINS
Chocolate Bourbon Cake with Raisins, 241
Orange Raisin Muffins, 41
Rum Raisin Cheesecake with Myers's
Rum Sauce, 262
Zucchini Raisin Muffins, 40

RASPBERRIES
Crème Brûlée with Fresh Raspberry
Sauce, 274
Danish Raspberry Shortcake, 263
Frozen Pineapple Yogurt with
Raspberries, 289
Raspberries 'n Cream, 275
Raspberry Buttermilk Sherbet, 288
Raspberry-Tomato Aspic with
Horseradish Sauce, 108
Remoulade Sauce, 110

RESTAURANTS, SPECIALTY
Baked Grouper with Pesto Tomatoes
and Mushrooms, 194
Bragg Bread, 53
Buffalo Hot Wings, 15
Chicken Alouette, 187
Chicken Cacciatore a la Capocelli, 173
Civet "Beef and Wine", 158
Coffee Almond Torte, 245
Cream of Spinach Soup, 83
Gingerbread, 271
Grapefruit Sauce, 157
Grilled Salmon with Honey, Ginger and
Dark Soy Marinade, 148
Grilled Sea Scallops with Cilantro
Sauce, 150
Grilled Seafood with Coriander Oil, 145
Grouper St. Charles, 195
Honey Celery Seed Dressing, 112
Légumes Fricassés, 221

Oriental Grilled Swordfish Steaks, 144
Oysters Orleans, 24
Rum Raisin Cheesecake with Myers's
Rum Sauce, 262
Ryan's Rack, 162
Salem College Iced Tea, 60
Sauerkraut Stew, 159
Sesamed Shrimp Kebob Kelly, 145
Spicy Shrimp and Sesame Noodles, 117
Strawberry Nut Bread, 46
Tavern Nachos, 23
Trout Moutardé, 193
Veal Cushions Capocelli, 155
Wild Turkey Sandwich with Tarragon
Dressing, 84
Winkler Sugar Cookies, 279
Rib Roast Perfection, 159

RICE
Armenian Rice, 227
Brown Rice and Vegetable Casserole, 237
Chicken and Wild Rice Casserole, 175
Curried Rice with Pineapple, 229
Herbed Wild Rice, 229
Rice Primavera, 227
Shrimp Pilau, 204
Summer Wild Rice, 228
Wild Rice and Almond Casserole, 226
Wild Rice and Shrimp Casserole, 207
Wild Rice Mélange, 226
Rich Tea Scones, 33
Roast Goose with Apricot Stuffing, 192
Roast Lamb with Barbecue Sauce, 163
Roast Lamb with Herbed Mustard, 163
Roasted Bell Pepper Salad or Sandwich
with Prosciutto and Provolone, 86
Roasted Herbed Walnuts, 19
Rosa's Cheese Souffle Sandwiches, 30
Rosemary Potatoes, 225
Rum Raisin Cheesecake with Myers's Rum
Sauce, 262
Rum Sauce, 262
Ryan's Rack, 162

Sakowitz Remoulade Sauce, 31
SALAD DRESSINGS
"Petite Marmite" Dressing, 87
Basil Vinaigrette, 86
Basil-Lemon Dressing, 91
Bleu Cheese Dressing, 114
Creamy Basil Dressing, 92
Drew's Honey Mustard Dressing, 113
Honey Celery Seed Dressing, 112
Lemon Vinaigrette, 228
Poppyseed Dressing, 111
Special Salad Dressing, 114
Tomato Dressing, 113
Vinaigrette Aux Fines Herbes, 112
Yogurt Dressing, 113

SALADS
ENTREE
Cobb Salad, 104
Crab Pasta Salad, 90
Curried Chicken and Artichoke
Salad, 105
Curried Chicken Salad, 106
Hot Chicken Salad, 106
Japanese Chicken Salad, 104

Pasta Salad with Broccoli and Ham, 94
Pat's Pasta Salad, 95
Polynesian Luncheon Salad, 105
Roasted Bell Pepper Salad or
Sandwich with Prosciutto and
Provolone, 86
Salad Nicoise, 90
San Francisco Crab Louis, 89
Seafood Pasta Primavera Salad with
Creamy Basil Dressing, 92
Seafood Pasta Salad, 93
Shrimp and Pasta Salad with
Basil-Lemon Dressing, 91
Shrimp Salad New Orleans, 89
Spring Pasta Salad with Pesto, 96
Vegetable Seafood Salad, 88

FRUIT
Cranberry Apple Salad, 109
Cranberry Waldorf Salad Ring, 109
Spiced Peach Salad, 108

GREEN
Apple and Bacon Spinach Salad, 100
Baked Goat Cheese Salad, 85
Belgian Endive Salad with "Petite
Marmite" Dressing, 87
Caesar Salad, 102
Spinach and Avocado or Fruit Salad, 101
Spinach and Strawberry Salad, 100
Watercress Salad, 86
Watercress, Mushroom and Endive
Salad, 85

VEGETABLE
Broccoli and Cauliflower Salad, 97
Broccoli Salad, 97
Cole Slaw Salad, 103
German Cole Slaw, 102
Herbed Tomatoes, 88
Japanese Cucumber Salad, 99
Lettuceless Salad, 98
Marinated Tijuana Tomatoes, 87
Marinated Vegetable Salad, 99
New Potato Salad, 103
Raspberry-Tomato Aspic with
Horseradish Sauce, 108
Sweet 'n Sour Slaw, 101
Tasty Pasta Salad, 93
Tomato Aspic, 107
Vegetable Aspic, 107
Salem College Iced Tea, 60

SALMON
Baked Salmon with Sour Cream Sauce, 198
Grilled Salmon Steaks, 147
Grilled Salmon with Garlic and Lime, 147
Grilled Salmon with Honey, Ginger and
Dark Soy Marinade, 148
Linguini with Salmon Sauce, 119
Marinated Salmon Steak, 198
Poached Salmon with Basil Sauce, 200
Salmon Loaf with Cucumber-Dill
Sauce, 199
Salmon Mousse, 30
Smoked Salmon Timbales with Coulis
de Tomatoes, 201
Smoked Whole Salmon, 153
San Francisco Crab Louis, 89

SANDWICHES
Ham 'n Cheese Croissants, 84
Marinated Chicken Sandwiches with
Hot Mustard Sauce, 137

Roasted Bell Pepper Salad or Sandwich
with Prosciutto and Provolone, 86
Wild Turkey Sandwich with Tarragon
Dressing, 84
Sangria, 57
SAUCES
Admiral Parson's Barbecue Sauce, 153
Barbecue Sauce, 161
Basil Tartar Sauce, 209
Besciamellia Sauce, 126
Best Baked Mustard Sauce, 171
Brandied Walnut Sauce, 253
California Salsa, 31
Caramel Nut Sauce, 254
Carrot Sauce, 125
Cilantro Sauce, 150
Crème Anglaise, 269
Crème Fraiche, 188
Cucumber Yogurt Sauce, 142
Cucumber-Dill Sauce, 199
Dijon Hollandaise, 193
Dijon Mustard Sauce, 168
Dill Butter Sauce, 187
Fresh Raspberry Sauce, 274
Gingerbread Topping, 292
Grapefruit Sauce, 157
Horseradish Whipped Cream, 180
Hot and Sweet Holiday Mustard, 110
Hot Mustard Sauce, 137
Italian Tomato Sauce, 166
Jim Kroncke's Famous Spaghetti
Sauce, 124
Light Tomato Sauce, 123
Mocha Hot Fudge Sauce, 292
Mustard Horseradish Sauce, 111
Mustard Sauce, 17
Patricia Inn Fudge Sauce, 291
Pesto Mayonnaise, 148
Pesto Sauce, 94
Praline Sauce, 292
Raspberry-Tomato Aspic with
Horseradish Sauce, 108
Remoulade Sauce, 110
Rum Sauce, 262
Sauce Provençal, 195
Sesame Dip, 15
Sour Cream Sauce, 198
Strawberry Topping, 291
Tangy Sauce, 202
Whiskey Sauce, 272
Sauerkraut Stew, 159
Sauerkraut with Champagne and
Pineapple, 233
SAUSAGE
Chinese Casserole, 167
Divine Italian Nuts, 127
Green Split Pea Soup, 77
Italian Sausage Soup, 64
Sauerkraut Stew, 159
Sausage and Cheese Grits, 130
Sausage and Peperoni Pizza, 165
Sausage and Vegetable Pasta, 123
Seafood Dump, 207
Sautéed Chicken Livers with Apples and
Onions, 190
Savory Chicken Pie, 179
Savory Swordfish, 143
Scalloped Oysters, 201
Scalloped Tomatoes and Artichoke

Hearts, 234
Scalloped Tomatoes and Artichoke
SCALLOPS
Baked Scallops, 212
Grilled Sea Scallops with Cilantro
Sauce, 150
Scallops Seviche, 27
Seafood Brochettes, 149
Seafood Gumbo, 208
Seafood Pasta Primavera Salad with
Creamy Basil Dressing, 92
Seafood Pasta Salad, 93
Shrimp and Bay Scallops Marinara, 117
Scioto Dip, 32
**SEAFOOD (See also specific types)
193-212**
Seafood Brochettes, 149
Seafood Casserole Miami, 206
Seafood Dump, 207
Seafood Gumbo, 208
Seafood Pasta Primavera Salad with
Creamy Basil Dressing, 92
Seafood Pasta Salad, 93
SECCA Santa Gazpacho, 79
SECCA Santa Spanakopeta, 128
Selfridge's Tea Room Tomato Juice, 56
Sesame Broccoli, 219
Sesame Chicken Kebobs, 139
Sesame Chicken Rolls, 14
Sesame Dip, 15
Sesamed Shrimp Kebob Kelly, 145
Showhouse Lemon Cake, 242
Shredded Zucchini, 232
SHRIMP
Barbecued Shrimp, 204
Batter-Fried Shrimp with Tangy
Sauce, 202
Charleston Marinated Shrimp, 25
Chilled Shrimp and Cucumber Soup, 68
Lemon Shrimp Brochettes, 146
Marinated Shrimp, 25
Ocean Spray Shrimp, 205
Pasta Primavera with Shrimp, 116
Seafood Brochettes, 149
Seafood Casserole Miami, 206
Seafood Gumbo, 208
Seafood Pasta Primavera Salad with
Creamy Basil Dressing, 92
Seafood Pasta Salad, 93
Sesamed Shrimp Kebob Kelly, 145
Shrimp Alfredo, 116
Shrimp and Bay Scallops Marinara, 117
Shrimp and Okra Soup, 69
Shrimp and Pasta Salad with
Basil-Lemon Dressing, 91
Shrimp and Walnuts, 203
Shrimp Creole, 203
Shrimp Curry, 205
Shrimp Dip, 26
Shrimp Kebobs, 146
Shrimp Pilau, 204
Shrimp Salad New Orleans, 89
Spicy Shrimp and Sesame Noodles, 117
Tea Smoked Shrimp, 26
Vegetable Seafood Salad, 88
Wild Rice and Shrimp Casserole, 207
Sin, 287
Skiers' Delight Pasta, 120
Smoked Oyster Spread, 24

Smoked Salmon Filet, 154
Smoked Salmon Timbales with Coulis
de Tomatoes, 201
Smoked Whole Salmon, 153
SOUP
COLD
Avocado Zucchini Soup, 74
Chilled Cucumber Soup with Fresh
Dill, 75
Chilled Shrimp and Cucumber
Soup, 68
Easy Gazpacho, 80
Fresh Strawberry Soup, 82
Health Soup, 80
SECCA Santa Gazpacho, 79
Vichysquash, 73
HOT
Acorn Squash Bisque, 73
Broccoli and Ham Soup, 67
Brunswick Stew, 72
Cabbage Soup, 81
Cheddar Chowder, 75
Chicken Apple Curry Soup, 71
Chicken Vegetable Soup, 70
Clam Bisque, 69
Crab and Mushroom Bisque, 68
Cream of Lettuce Soup, 77
Cream of Spinach Soup, 83
Curried Zucchini Soup, 73
Easy Onion Soup for Two, 81
Eggplant Supper Soup, 62
Fresh Corn Chowder, 82
Green Split Pea Soup, 77
Irena Kirshman's Minestrone, 76
Italian Sausage Soup, 64
Mexican Meatball Soup, 61
Mexichili, 61
Mom's Chicken Soup, 70
New England Clam Chowder, 67
Peasant Soup, 65
Pumpkin Soup, 78
Shrimp and Okra Soup, 69
Soupa De Guadalajara, 66
Sour Cream and Mushroom Soup, 78
Sweet and Sour Beef Stew, 63
Three-Potato Soup, 79
Turkey Vegetable Soup, 71
Zucchini Soup, 74
Soupa De Guadalajara, 66
SOUPS AND SALADS 61-114
Sour Cream and Mushroom Soup, 78
Sour Cream Chicken Breasts, 184
Sour Cream Sauce, 198
Southern Fudge Pecan Pie, 268
Southern Plantation Eggnog, 59
Spanish Onion Pie, 222
Special Crabmeat Appetizer, 28
Special Salad Dressing, 114
Spiced Carrots, 218
Spiced Peach Salad, 108
Spicy Oven Fried Chicken, 174
Spicy Shrimp and Sesame Noodles, 117
SPINACH
Apple and Bacon Spinach Salad, 100
Cream of Spinach Soup, 83
Irena Kirshman's Minestrone, 76
Lasagna with Fresh Spinach, 115
Sakowitz Remoulade Sauce, 31
Scioto Dip, 32

SECCA Santa Spanakopeta, 128
Spinach and Artichoke Casserole, 233
Spinach and Avocado or Fruit
   Salad, 101
Spinach and Ham Roll-Ups, 172
Spinach and Strawberry Salad, 100
Spinach Corn Bread, 36
Spinach Stuffed Trout, 194
Spinach Wrapped Chicken with
   Sesame Dip, 15
Spring Pasta Salad with Pesto, 96
SQUASH
   Acorn Squash Bisque, 73
   Butternut Squash and Apple Bake, 230
   Butternut Squash Souffle, 230
   Grilled Whole Baby Squash, 152
   Squash Muffins, 39
   Squash-Zucchini Stir Fry, 231
   Steamed Spaghetti Squash with Fresh
      Tomatoes, 234
   Vichysquash, 73
St. Timothy's Coffee Cake, 251
Steamed Spaghetti Squash with Fresh
   Tomatoes, 234
Stir-Fried Pork, 169
STRAWBERRIES
   Fresh Strawberry Soup, 82
   Mile High Strawberry Pie, 266
   Spinach and Strawberry Salad, 100
   Strawberries Romanoff, 276
   Strawberry Margarita Sorbet, 58
   Strawberry Nut Bread, 46
   Strawberry Topping, 291
Striped Bass (Rock Bass), 197
Summer Wild Rice, 228
Summertime Marinated Fruit, 277
Summit Lemon Squares, 278
Swedish Pancake, 277
Sweet 'n Sour Slaw, 101
Sweet and Sour Beef Stew, 63
Sweet and Sour Chicken Drummettes, 14
SWORDFISH
   Marinade for Swordfish Steaks, 143
   Oriental Grilled Swordfish Steaks, 144
   Savory Swordfish, 143
   Teriyaki Swordfish, 145

Taco Casserole, 162
Taco Dip, 22
Tangy Baked Tomatoes, 236
Tangy Sauce, 202
Tasty Pasta Salad, 93
Tavern Nachos, 23
Tea Smoked Shrimp, 26
Teriyaki Swordfish, 145
Tex-Mex Dip, 23
The World's Best Cookie, 279
Three-Potato Soup, 79
Tipsy Trifle, 269
Tom's Grilled Pork Chops, 140

Tomato Aspic, 107
Tomato Dressing, 113
TOMATOES
   Avocado and Tomato Dip, 24
   Baked Grouper with Pesto Tomatoes
      and Mushrooms, 194
   Broccoli Stuffed Tomatoes, 235
   California Salsa, 31
   Cherry Tomatoes Stuffed with Pesto, 11
   Chicken Parmesan with Herbed Tomato
      Sauce, 183
   Fresh Tomato Pie, 235
   Herbed Tomatoes, 88
   Light Tomato Sauce, 123
   Marinated Tijuana Tomatoes, 87
   Scalloped Tomatoes and Artichoke
      Hearts, 234
   Shrimp and Bay Scallops Marinara, 117
   Smoked Salmon Timbales with Coulis
      de Tomatoes, 201
   Steamed Spaghetti Squash with Fresh
      Tomatoes, 234
   Tangy Baked Tomatoes, 236
   Tomato Cheese Spread, 21
   Tomato Herb Pasta with Carrot
      Sauce, 125
   Tomatoes Provencal, 236
   Veal Scallopine with Tomatoes and
      Olives, 155
TROUT
   Grilled Rainbow Trout with Pesto
      Mayonnaise, 148
   Spinach Stuffed Trout, 194
   Trout Moutardé, 193
TUNA
   Salad Nicoise, 90
   Turkey Tonnato, 191
TURKEY
   Chef's Choice Royale, 177
   Holiday Roast Turkey Breast with Fruit
      Stuffing, 188
   Turkey Tonnato, 191
   Turkey Vegetable Soup, 71
   Wild Turkey Sandwich with Tarragon
      Dressing, 84

Vanilla Cream Cheese Frosting, 239
VEAL
   Peasant Soup, 65
   Veal Chops with Morels, 156
   Veal Cushions Capocelli, 155
   Veal Roast with Sour Cream Gravy, 156
   Veal Scallopine with Tomatoes and
      Olives, 155
Vegetable Aspic, 107
Vegetable Brochettes, 151
Vegetable Seafood Salad, 88
Vegetable-Cheese Casserole, 237
VEGETABLES 213-238
   Beef Tenderloin with Vegetables, 158

Brown Rice and Vegetable
   Casserole, 237
Chicken Breasts with Vegetables, 186
Chicken Vegetable Soup, 70
Crabmeat-Vegetable Pie, 211
Flavored Butters for Vegetables, 214
Légumes Fricassés, 221
Navarin Printanier, 164
Quick Vegetable Lasagna, 115
Sausage and Vegetable Pasta, 123
Turkey Vegetable Soup, 71
Vegetable Brochettes, 151
Vegetable Seafood Salad, 88
Vegetable-Cheese Casserole, 237
Vermicelli with Clam Sauce, 118
Vichysquash, 73
Vidalia Onions Stuffed with Nuts, 223
Vinaigrette Aux Fines Herbes, 112

Watercress Salad, 86
Watercress, Mushroom and Endive
   Salad, 85
Wheat Germ Pancakes, 34
Whiskey Sauce, 272
White Chocolate Cheesecake, 258
Whole Wheat Bread, 47
Whole Wheat Seed Bread, 48
Whole Wheat Oatmeal Hot Cakes, 35
Wild Rice and Almond Casserole, 226
Wild Rice and Shrimp Casserole, 207
Wild Rice Melange, 226
Wild Turkey Sandwich with Tarragon
   Dressing, 84
Windy City Brownies, 283
Winkler Sugar Cookies, 279

Yogurt Dressing, 113
Yogurt Parmesan Chicken, 184

Zesty Grilled Flank Steak, 134
ZUCCHINI
   Avocado Zucchini Soup, 74
   Baked Zucchini, 232
   Curried Zucchini Soup, 73
   Fettucine with Zucchini and
      Mushrooms, 121
   Fresh Green Bean and Zucchini
      Sauté, 216
   Green Beans and Zucchini Bundles, 216
   Italian Zucchini Pie, 231
   Shredded Zucchini, 232
   Squash-Zucchini Stir Fry, 231
   Vegetable Brochettes, 151
   Zucchini Bread, 45
   Zucchini Raisin Muffins, 40
   Zucchini Soup, 74

Stirring Performances
The Junior League of Winston-Salem, Inc.
P. O. Box 10176
Winston-Salem, North Carolina 27108
(919) 773-0675

Please send _____ copies of *Stirring Performances* . . . . @ 16.95 each_____
Add postage and handling . . . . @ 2.00 each_____
Add gift wrap* . . . . @ 1.00 each_____
North Carolina residents add 5% sales tax . . . . @   .85 each_____

☐ Check or money order enclosed. Make checks payable to *Stirring Performances.*
Please charge to: ☐ Mastercard   ☐ Visa
Card Number ☐☐☐☐ ☐☐☐☐ ☐☐☐☐ ☐☐☐☐
Expiration date: _____ Signature of card holder: _____

From: Ship To:
Name: _____   Name: _____
Address: _____   Address: _____
City: _____ State: _____ Zip: _____   City: _____ State: _____ Zip: _____

*If gift, enclosure card to read _____

- -

Stirring Performances
The Junior League of Winston-Salem, Inc.
P. O. Box 10176
Winston-Salem, North Carolina 27108
(919) 773-0675

Please send _____ copies of *Stirring Performances* . . . . @ 16.95 each_____
Add postage and handling . . . . @ 2.00 each_____
Add gift wrap* . . . . @ 1.00 each_____
North Carolina residents add 5% sales tax . . . . @   .85 each_____

☐ Check or money order enclosed. Make checks payable to *Stirring Performances.*
Please charge to: ☐ Mastercard   ☐ Visa
Card Number ☐☐☐☐ ☐☐☐☐ ☐☐☐☐ ☐☐☐☐
Expiration date: _____ Signature of card holder: _____

From: Ship To:
Name: _____   Name: _____
Address: _____   Address: _____
City: _____ State: _____ Zip: _____   City: _____ State: _____ Zip: _____

*If gift, enclosure card to read _____

I would like to see *Stirring Performances* in the following stores in my area:

Store Name:_____

Address:_____

City:_____ State:_____ Zip:_____

Store Name:_____

Address:_____

City:_____ State:_____ Zip:_____

- -

I would like to see *Stirring Performances* in the following stores in my area:

Store Name:_____

Address:_____

City:_____ State:_____ Zip:_____

Store Name:_____

Address:_____

City:_____ State:_____ Zip:_____